Field guide to common

TREES &

SHRUBS
of East Africa

Najma Dharani

This book is dedicated to my mother-in-law. I am truly blessed by your compassion and wisdom. Thank you for always being there for me whenever I have needed you.

Acknowledgments

I wish to express my gratitude to all those organizations and individuals who helped in the preparation of this guide, and in particular the following: the management and staff of the East African Herbarium Library in Nairobi, the Horticultural Society of Kenya, the National Museum of Kenya Library, the United Nations Library in Nairobi, and the East African Natural History Society. My thanks for their kindness in allowing me the use of their facilities. Many thanks, too, to Anne Birnie for sharing her experience and knowledge. This book has been very much a family affair. Special thanks to my loving husband and best friend, Firoz, for his encouragement and support, and to my wonderful sons, Farhaan and Rizwan, who joined me on most of my trips through the region. Their patience during hours and hours of endless driving through the heat of the East African day is much appreciated.

Struik Publishers
(A division of New Holland Publishing (South Africa) (Pty) Ltd)
Cornelis Struik House, 80 McKenzie Street
Cape Town, South Africa
www.struik.co.za

New Holland Publishing is a member of the Johnnic Publishing Group

First published in 2002

10 9 8 7 6 5 4 3 2

Publishing manager: Pippa Parker
Managing editor: Helen de Villiers
Editor: Piera Abbott
Designer: Dominic Robson
Cartographer: James Whitelaw

Reproduction by Hirt & Carter Cape (Pty) Ltd, Cape Town
Printed and bound by Times Offset (M) Sdn Bhd

ISBN 1 86872 640 1

CONTENTS

Trees

Shrubs

Palms

Mangroves

INTRODUCTION

East Africa, a region embracing Kenya, Uganda and Tanzania, is one of the richest areas on the African continent in terms of its flora and fauna. This natural wealth is, to a very large extent, the product of the region's enormous diversity of habitat and climate. Broadly speaking, rainfall is both generous and reliable at the higher altitudes, the air is cool and the vegetation lush. By contrast the lowland areas tend to be hot and dry; the climate is both hot and humid along the coast and in the basins near the big lakes. Climatic and ecological variety create ideal environments for a great many different species of plants (and, of course, animals and birds).

This *Field Guide to Common Trees and Shrubs of East Africa* is not a botanical textbook, but a selective field guide to the more common trees and shrubs, indigenous, naturalized and exotic, that you will see in the region. It is designed to help the plant enthusiast identify prominent species that can be observed, studied and enjoyed in gardens and parks, along roadsides and in easily accessible parts of the countryside.

In East Africa, indeed throughout sub-Saharan Africa, trees fulfil important social and economic functions. In rural areas, the forests serve as the principal sources of energy, providing fuelwood and charcoal, and they go a long way toward meeting the needs of farmers and herders. They also yield materials for building and for many other domestic purposes.

Trees have profound significance in religious belief and ceremony, and their various components are central to traditional medicine. Indeed the forests are precious, fragile (and irreplaceable) repositories of ingredients basic to the treatment of a surprising number of human ailments. The wider world has only recently (belatedly) begun to appreciate their value, and their potential, in this respect. Indigenous trees and shrubs are part of East Africa's legacy. Not only are they natural resources and things of beauty to be admired, but also symbols of life. Today much of the forested land has been cleared for agriculture, and to fuel industry. There is an urgent need to cherish what remains, and to try to return at least some of the land to its original, pristine condition.

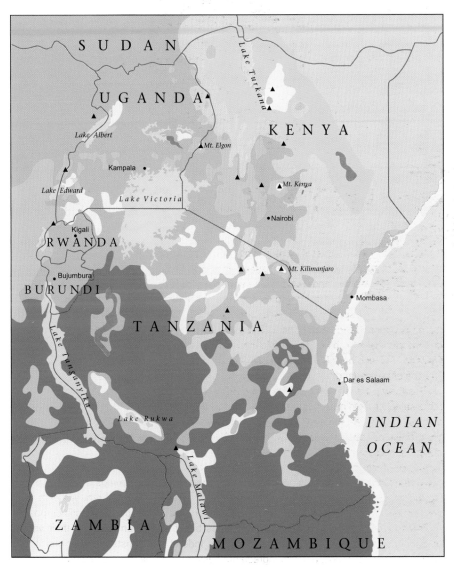

Vegetation zones of East Africa

Desert

Grassland

Forest

Semi-desert

Wooden grassland

Swamp

Bushland

Woodland

How the book is arranged

This book is divided into four parts, or chapters, namely Trees, Shrubs, Palms and Mangroves. The divisions are somewhat arbitrary, since palms and mangroves are trees, and many shrubs grow to tree-like proportions (indeed, depending on climatic, soil and other conditions, a species may well be a tree in one area and a shrub in another). But to the non-technical but reasonably well-informed layperson (and it is for the layperson that the book has been written and designed) these are fairly definite, visually delineated groupings: a shrub is smaller than a tree; palms belong to an obviously distinctive family; mangroves are confined to a particular habitat and are exclusive in form and habit.

The species accounts within each part are arranged in alphabetical order (scientific names from A to Z) and are consistent in style, each specifying the English and the more prominent African common names where these are known, the family to which the plant belongs, and whether it is indigenous to the region or exotic. This is followed by a summary of the main characteristics of the plant's major components (bark, leaves, flowers, fruit and so on), and ends with a description of its various uses. Each entry is illustrated with one or more photographs or illustrations.

Although the book is intended primarily for the layperson, the use of technical terms is unavoidable. Botany is a science that has its own vocabulary, even its own language. The glossaries and diagrams on pages 308–317 will enable non-expert readers to find their way around. Other helpful features include the vegetation map on page 5; the family descriptions (pages 8–24) and the Index (pages 318–320).

Castanospermum australe (above)
Spathodea campanulata (previous page)

Trees and traditional medicine

Medicinal plants are an important part of the daily lives, and the cultural heritage, of many East African peoples. The use of plants in the treatment of various diseases, as a specific antidote against magic, and for religious ceremonies, has been an integral element of African society for centuries. The East African herbalist, often referred to as Bwana Mganga ('Medicine Man') is an important and highly respected figure within the society. Knowledge of medicinal plants is normally passed on orally from one generation to the next. Unfortunately, a great deal of valuable information can be lost or distorted if a medicine man dies without revealing such knowledge.

Acacia nubica. A bark decoction is used as an emetic in the treatment of malaria and rheumatism; ash from the burnt plant is used as protection against anthrax.

In preparing these chapters, it became clear that there is a lack of detailed documentation on the significance and application of curative plants in East Africa. Such documentation is an urgent priority in view of the fragility of oral-tradition knowledge and the rapid pace of urbanization (and the consequent erosion of tribal culture) in this part of Africa.

This book contains information about medicinal plants and their uses, but it should not be regarded as a guide to self-treatment. The notes on traditional medicine at the end of each entry are quite brief and do not provide information on diagnosis or dosage. Rather, they are intended to show the versatility and usefulness of the plants. Keep in mind that many of the plants described are highly toxic and may cause severe allergic reactions or serious poisoning.

Neither the author nor the publishers can be held responsible for the consequences arising from incorrect identification or inappropriate use of a plant. Do not attempt self-diagnosis or self-treatment; always consult a medical professional or qualified practitioner.

Key words (also see Glossary, page 308)

cymose: an inflorescence where the first flower is the terminal bud of the main stem; later flowers develop as terminal buds of lateral stems.

dicotyledonous: plants with two embryonic seed leaves and leaves with net-like veins.

dioecious: male and female reproductive organs (flowers) on separate plants.

drupe: a fleshy, permanently enclosed (indehiscent) fruit whose seed or seeds are enclosed by a hard, stony coating (for example, peaches).

-merous: part of a set (a five-merous corolla has five petals, for example).

monocotyledonous: plants with only one embryonic seed leaf, parallel-veined leaves, fibrous root system and flower consisting of parts in threes or multiples of three.

monoecious: male and female reproductive organs in separate flowers on the same plant.

racemose: an inflorescence where flowers occur along the main stem, the older ones at the base.

xerophytic: adapted to arid conditions.

zygomorphic: having only one plane, which can be dissected so that the two halves are mirror images of each other.

Family descriptions

ANACARDIACEAE

Mango family

A family of dicotyledonous trees and shrubs (see Key words, page 7), often with resinous bark. Its members are mostly tropical but some are found in temperate regions. In some species the resin is an important source of tannin, and in others it is used for gum, mastic, turpentine and varnish. The leaves are simple or compound, usually alternate, the flowers small and regular with three to five sepals, three to five petals, three to ten stamens (occasionally many) and the fruit commonly a drupe (see Key words, page 7). Genera that are represented in East Africa include *Anacardium, Mangifera, Rhus, Schinus.*

APOCYNACEAE

Oleander family

This dicotyledonous (see Key words, page 7) family includes many spectacular tropical trees, shrubs and lianes (lianas), often poisonous or producing important medicinal drugs. Most species also produce a milky white latex that may contain rubber. The leaves are almost invariably simple and entire, often arranged in opposite pairs; leaves are glossy; the flowers regular; calyx of five free or almost free sepals; the tubular corolla is five-lobed and there are five stamens, their anthers free or slightly touching. Members of this family in East Africa include *Acokanthera, Adenium, Carrissa, Nerium, Plumeria, Thevetia, Tabernaemontana.*

ARALIACEAE

Ivy family

This dicotyledonous (see Key words, page 7) family contains chiefly tropical trees and shrubs. The leaves are usually alternate, crowded near branch ends, simple or compound. The East African representatives are mostly trees with large

Cussonia holstii

compound leaves massed at the ends of branches and soft, generally useless wood; flowers are small, massed into heads or umbels, bisexual, regular, normally with five sepals, usually five petals and five stamens, and drupe fruit. Members in East Africa include *Cussonia, Schefflera, Polyscias.*

ARAUCARIACEAE

Monkey-puzzle family

A dicotyledonous (see Key words, page 7) family of tall, prominent conifers with layered branches. Although they bear some resemblance to and are often called pines, Araucarias are in an entirely distinct family. The whorls of branches bear branchlets covered with spirals of small, overlapping leaves that vary in shape with age and on different parts of the tree as well as in different species. Male and female cones grow on different trees or on separate branches of the same tree. The woody female cones are large and distinctive, resembling green pineapples; mature cones disintegrate on the ground to release large seeds, often winged, which develop beneath each cone. The male pollen-producing cones are either solitary, narrow and upright, or form clusters of loose-hanging branchlets resembling fat catkins. Genera of this family in East Africa include *Araucaria*.

ASCLEPIADACEAE

Calotropis and Milk-weed families

A large, dicotyledonous (see Key words, page 7), tropical and warm-temperate family of herbs, twiners, lianes (lianas) or stem succulents and, rarely, shrubs. Closely related to Apocynaceae, having similar toxic properties, although not to such a marked degree. Leaves are opposite or whorled, usually entire but occasionally lobed or dentate margins; flowers five-merous, usually with corona present inside the corolla, anthers with pollen in sticky pollinia. Members of the family in East Africa include *Calotropis*.

BALANITACEAE

Desert date family

A small, tropical dicotyledonous (see Key words, page 7) family of trees or shrubs consisting, in East Africa, of the single genus *Balanites*. Usually with strong spines. Leaves alternate, two-foliate, four or five sepals, four or five petals, eight to ten stamens; the fruit a drupe (see Key words, page 7), one-seeded.

BIGNONIACEAE

Jacaranda family

A tropical family of dicotyledonous (see Key words, page 7) woody plants, generally trees and shrubs with showy flowers. It also includes a number of vigorous climbers. The leaves are generally compound and paired, but occasionally alternately arranged on the stems; flowers regular, usually tubular, flaring out into gaping mouths; the calyx consists of five joined sepals, the corolla of five joined petals, with four stamens; fruit a capsule or berry. Members of this family in East Africa include *Jacaranda, Kigelia, Markhamia, Spathodea, Tecoma, Tecomaria, Podranea.*

Jacaranda mimosifolia

BOMBACACEAE

Baobab family

A small dicotyledonous (see Key words, page 7) family of tropical flowering trees. Leaves alternate, digitate with deciduous stipules; the flowers are asymmetric with five sepals, five petals, five or many stamens; fruit a capsule or nut, many-seeded. Members of the family in East Africa include *Adansonia, Ceiba, Chorisia*.

BORAGINACEAE

Cordia family

A large dicotyledonous (see Key words, page 7) family consisting mainly of herbs, mostly from the Mediterranean region, but includes a largely tropical group of trees and shrubs. Leaves simple, alternate, roughly hairy; flowers bisexual, usually regular with five sepals, five petals (which form a tube or funnel shape), five stamens; fruit a small drupe. Members of this family in East Africa include *Cordia, Ehretia*.

BURSERACEAE

Myrrh family

A tropical family of dicotyledonous (see Key words, page 7) trees or shrubs, often with aromatic resinous bark. Outer bark often translucent and papery, peeling in flakes or scrolls, exposing the green or bluish under-bark. Leaves alternate, pinnate, trifoliate or occasionally unifoliate; flowers small, regular, solitary or in inflorescence, calyx four- or five-lobed, petals four or five, stamens twice as many as the petals; fruit drupe (see Key words, page 7) or capsule. Members of this family in East Africa include *Commiphora*.

CACTACEAE

Opuntia family

This family for the most part contains Cacti, which are xerophytic (see Key words, page 7) plants, particularly from the arid regions of tropical America. Most Cacti are characterized by swollen stems that hold water, or succulent stems. Normally the plants have tufts of spines or bristly hairs and virtually no leaves. The flowers of Cactaceae are often very showy, brilliantly coloured, usually solitary, stalkless. Petals and stamens are usually numerous; the fruit is a berry. Members of the family include *Cereus, Opuntia, Quiabentia*.

Cereus peruvianus

CANELLACEAE

Warburgia family

A small family of tropical trees, glabrous and aromatic; most have medicinal properties. It contains only about 16 species. Leaves alternate, without stipules, simple and gland-dotted; flowers small, regular, cymose, stamens united into a tube; fruit a berry. The only genus is *Warburgia*; widely distributed in the East African highlands.

CAPPARACEAE

Caper family

Small dicotyledonous (see Key words, page 7) trees or shrubs and more rarely herbaceous plants. Their leaves are alternate, simple or palmate; flowers are bisexual, four sepals, four petals, four to numerous conspicuous stamens; fruit a capsule or berry. Members of the family in East Africa include *Maerua, Crateva*.

CARICACEAE

Papaya family

A small family of trees and shrubs, usually with only one trunk, most species found within tropical and subtropical America, a few in tropical Africa. Milky sap in stems; leaves simple, alternate, deeply lobed, large blade with long leaf stalk, clustered in a spiral at the end of the stem; flowers dioecious, sepals five-lobed, united, five petals, more or less free in female flowers, united in male flowers, male flowers with corolla tube, female flowers with free lobes; fruit a fleshy berry with numerous seeds. Members of this family in East Africa include the genus *Carica*.

CASUARINACEAE

Casuarina family

A small but distinctive tropical family of trees and shrubs, with one genus but 65 species; branchlets deciduous, with narrow grooves; leaves reduced to whorls of small triangular scales, united at the base; flowers unisexual, male flowers consisting of a single stamen, arranged in spikes, female flowers arranged in compact heads, cone-like, woody; fruit small, cone-like, releasing hundreds of very small winged seeds. The genus *Casuarina* is very common along the East African coastline.

CELASTRACEAE

Miraa family

These dicotyledonous (see Key words, page 7) trees, shrubs and climbers have simple, opposite or alternate, often leathery leaves, and small, regular and usually bisexual flowers in cymose inflorescences, four to five sepals, four to five petals, free, three to five stamens; fruit various, sometimes a capsule. Members in East Africa include *Maytenus*.

COMBRETACEAE

Terminalia family

A family of trees, shrubs, sometimes climbing, mostly confined to the tropics of both hemispheres. Leaves simple, opposite, rarely alternate or whorled, entire and exstipulate (without stipules). Flowers usually bisexual in elongate or almost spherical spikes or racemes, or in panicles; axillary and/or terminal; regular, four- to five-merous. Stamens are as many, or twice as many, as the sepals; calyx tube cup-shaped or bell-shaped, dividing into lobes; ovary below all the other floral parts; flat, four- or five-winged fruit, indehiscent. East African genera include *Terminalia*.

Terminalia brownii

COMPOSITAE

Sunflower and Daisy families

This is one of the largest dicotyledonous (see Key words, page 7) families of flowering plants on earth. It occurs from the tropics to the Arctic and includes more than one-tenth of all the world's flowers; altogether, it embraces 25 000 species in 1 100 genera, mostly of herbs and shrubs but few real trees. Leaves alternate or opposite, exstipulate (without stipules). Flowers in head or capitulum, consisting of a few or many sessile flowers (ray and disc florets), grouped on a common disc to resemble a single flower. Outer florets are flattened, forming rays; the involucral (or ring) of bracts at the base of the inflorescence resembles a calyx and the rays the petals. True calyx absent or reduced to scales, or turned into bristles or hairs (the pappus); corolla five-lobed, tubular or split down one side and flattened (lingulate); five stamens, united to form a tube around the style; fruit a dry achene. Members of this family in East Africa include *Brachylaena, Tarchonanthus*.

CONVOLVULACEAE

Morning glory family

This is a family of dicotyledonous (see Key words, page 7) plants, shrubs and trees that includes many tropical and subtropical climbers. Their leaves are alternate, without stipules, entire and usually stalked. Flowers axillary or terminal, regular and usually bisexual; five calyxes; corolla usually funnel-shaped, slightly five-lobed. Fruit usually a dry capsule. Members of this family in East Africa include *Ipomoea*.

CUPRESSACEAE

Cypress family

A family of evergreen conifers, either trees or shrubs. The leaves on adult plants are scale-like and oppressed; on juvenile plants needle-like and spreading. Cones are terminal, often on short branchlets. The genus *Cupressus* consists of about 20 species native to the temperate regions of southern Europe, southern USA, China and the Himalayas. None are indigenous to East Africa, but various exotic species have become important plantation trees in the highlands. Members of this family in East Africa include *Juniperus, Cupressus*.

Brachylaena huillensis

CYCADACEAE

Cycad family

An ancient group of woody plants that flourished over 200 million years ago. The survivors are widely scattered throughout the world, mostly in dry areas. They are extremely slow growing, and some of them become hundreds of years old. Male and female plants grow separately; both generally produce cone-like structures between the leaves. All cycads have massive unbranched stems (in older plants); leaves pinnate with linear leaflets becoming spiny towards the base of the petiole. Members of this family in East Africa include *Encephalartos*.

Aleurites moluccana

EBENACEAE

Ebony family

A family of mostly tropical and subtropical trees and shrubs. Leaves alternate, without stipules; inflorescence usually cymose (see Key words, page 7) or raceme; flowers unisexual, three- to eight-merous, corolla with tube, stamens three to many; fruit usually a berry. Members of this family in East Africa include *Diospyros, Euclea*.

EUPHORBIACEAE

Euphorbia family

A very large and variable family of trees, shrubs and herbaceous plants, mainly tropical, varying from tiny desert succulents to tall forest trees such as the Crotons of the East African highlands. The leaves usually have stipules; the flowers are unisexual, monoecious or dioecious (see Key words, page 7), calyx three to six lobes or sepals, petals absent, three to many stamens; fruit a three-lobed capsule. Members of this family in East Africa include *Croton, Euphorbia, Aleurites, Ricinus*.

FLACOURTIACEAE

Kei apple family

A large tropical and subtropical dicotyledonous (see Key words, page 7) family of trees and shrubs, including some timber trees and a few ornamentals. Several species bear woody spines; leaves simple, alternate, stipulate; flowers in axillary groups, either cymose or raceme (see Key words, page 7) or sometimes solitary, three to seven sepals, three to eight petals, free or absent, five to many stamens; fruit a berry or a capsule. Members of this family in East Africa include *Dovyalis, Rawsonia*.

GRAMINEAE

Grass family

This is a large, monocotyledonous (see Key words, page 7) family, consisting of mostly annual or perennial herbs or shrubs, sometimes tree-like, very tall, attaining heights of up to 30 m (bamboos, for example); leaves simple or alternate, sessile, narrow, ribbon-shaped; inflorescence variable, compound spikes or racemes; flowers sessile, bracteate, incomplete, bisexual or unisexual and zygomorphic (see Key words, page 7); fruit achene or caryopsis. This family is very important as it includes species that are worldwide sources of human and animal food, such as wheat, corn, oats, rice, sugar cane, bamboo. Members of this family in the East African highlands include *Bambusa, Arundinaria.*

GUTTIFERAE

Hypericum family

This is a large family of trees and shrubs, chiefly tropical, containing oil glands that sometimes show up as dots on the simple, entire and opposite leaves; flowers usually regular and bisexual, four to five sepals, four to five petals, free; stamens numerous; fruit a capsule or berry. Members of this family in East Africa include *Hypericum.*

LAURACEAE

Avocado family

A large tropical family consisting of dicotyledonous (see Key words, page 7) trees and shrubs, centred in the rain forests of Southeast Asia and South America. Leaves evergreen, occasionally deciduous, alternate, rarely opposite, simple and entire; flowers unisexual or bisexual, regular, usually six perianth segments in two whorls; stamens in three or four whorls; fruit a one-seeded drupe (see Key words, page 7). Members of this family in East Africa include *Persea.*

Persea americana

LEGUMINOSAE

Pod-bearing family

An enormous group of flowering trees, shrubs, climbers, small annuals and herbaceous perennials, with some 17 000 species in a variety of habitats and a cosmopolitan distribution. The family is of major economic importance as a source of food, fodder, timber and other products. Two botanical features are common throughout. First, the fruit is always a one-chambered pod, called a legume. Second, the tap roots bear nodules containing nitrogen-fixing bacteria, commonly classified *Rhizobium radicicola*, which are able to take up nitrogen from the air and incorporate it into the living cells so that, eventually, the plant can use it. This ability to fix atmospheric nitrogen means that legumes can grow in relatively poor soil. This large family is divided into three subfamilies, namely *Papilionoideae, Caesalpiniodeae, Mimosoideae.*

CAESALPINIOIDEAE

Cassia subfamily

A subfamily of Leguminosae that consists of tropical flowering trees, shrubs and a number of climbers. Leaves usually pinnate, bipinnate or, rarely, simple; inflorescence usually spike, panicle or raceme; flowers rather irregular, five petals, ten or less stamens; fruit a pod or legume. Members of the subfamily in East Africa include the genera *Acrocarpus, Bauhinia, Caesalpinia, Cassia, Delonix, Peltophorum, Schizolobium, Tamarindus.*

MIMOSOIDEAE

Acacia subfamily

An important subfamily of Leguminosae, comprising tropical and subtropical trees, shrubs and lianes (lianas), often with prickles or spines. The best known of the many indigenous genera is the Thorn tree genus *Acacia.* Acacias are a very familiar and characteristic part of the East African landscape. Some are found in very dry conditions, others where there is a high water table. Leaves are twice compound or bipinnate. Flowers small, regular, in spikes, racemes or heads, three- to five-, sometimes six-merous; sepals usually united; petals free or united, four to many stamens. Fruit a pod or legume. Members of the subfamily in East Africa include *Acacia, Albizia, Dichrostachys, Newtonia.*

PAPILIONOIDEAE

Pea subfamily

An important subfamily of Leguminosae comprising tropical and temperate herbs, shrubs and trees. The seeds and pods of many herbaceous species are worldwide sources of human and animal food, such as peas, beans, groundnuts and lucerne. Leaves are commonly compound (trifoliate or pinnate). Flowers in racemes or panicles; calyx tubular, fine-toothed or two-lipped, corolla zygomorphic (see Key words, page 7). The typical pea flower has five petals, often brightly coloured, butterfly-shaped, with the big upper standard petal flanked by two pairs of petals of different shapes (the 'wings' and the 'keel'). Stamens ten; fruit a pod or legume. Members of the subfamily in East Africa include *Castanospermum, Dalbergia, Erythrina, Millettia, Sesbania, Tipuana, Crotalaria.*

Acacia nubica

15

LILIACEAE

Lily family

This is one of the largest families of flowering plants, and is found throughout the world. It consists mainly of perennial herbs. The tree-sized Aloes and Dracaenas have been moved back into the Lily family from their former classification among the *Aloeaceae* and *Agavaceae*. Leaves alternate, opposite or whorled, exstipulate, sessile, succulent, with spiny margins in Aloes; narrow and rather leathery in Dracaenas. Flowers are raceme or cymose (see Key words, page 7), rarely solitary. Flowers have a long tube and six small lobes in two whorls. Fruit a fleshy berry, capsule papery or slightly woody. Members of this family in East Africa include *Aloe, Dracaena*.

LOGANIACEAE

Anthocleista family

A family of trees, shrubs and climbers found in both temperate and tropical regions. Some trees provide valuable timber. Leaves opposite or in threes/fours; flowers cymose, four- to five-merous; fruit a capsule or berry. Members of this family in East Africa include *Anthocleista*.

LYTHRACEAE

Pride of India family

A small, tropical family comprising the most ornamental of all flowering trees, shrubs and many herbs, centred in Southeast Asia. Leaves opposite or whorled, stipulate, simple, entire. Flowers in racemes, cymenes or panicles, individually regular, bisex-ual, four to eight divisions (sepals, petals and stamens); petals are usually crumpled in the bud, unfolding to produce showy flowers. Fruit a many-seeded dry capsule. Members of this family in East Africa include *Lagerstroemia*.

MAGNOLIACEAE

Magnolia family

This family comprises dicotyledonous (see Key words, page 7) trees and shrubs from temperate and tropical parts of North America, Southeast Asia and Japan. Leaves alternate, simple, entire, evergreen; flowers big and spectacular, usually solitary, and either terminal or axillary, regular, unisexual or bisexual, scented, three petal-like sepals (petaloids), six to fifteen free petals, many stamens, free; fruit an aggregate of berries or follicles. Members of this family in East Africa include *Michelia*.

MALVACEAE

Hibiscus family

A large, cosmopolitan family of tropical and temperate dicotyledonous (see Key words, page 7) shrubs, herbs, less often trees, usually with stellate hairs; leaves alternate, palmately lobed, stipulate; flowers solitary or compound in cymose form, epicalyx present, often tubular at the base, regular with five sepals, five petals, many stamens; fruit a capsule or composed of follicles. Members of this family in East Africa include *Hibiscus*.

Hibiscus rosa-sinensis

Ficus benjamina

MELIACEAE

Mahogany family

A family of trees and shrubs that includes several important timber trees, most important of which is hardwood mahogany from the rain forests of Africa and South America. Leaves alternate, usually compound (except in *Turraea*), stipules absent; flowers regular, unisexual or bisexual, monoecious or dioecious (see Key words, page 7), normally in panicles, four- to five-merous, petals usually free, eight to ten stamens, united in a tube; fruit a capsule or drupe (see Key words, page 7). Members of this family found in East Africa include *Azadirachta, Melia, Toona, Trichilia, Turraea*.

MELIANTHACEAE

Bersama family

This is a small family of dicotyledonous (see Key words, page 7) trees and shrubs. Leaves alternate, compound, imparipinnate, stipulate; flowers bisexual, slightly irregular, in racemes, five petals, four to six stamens; fruit a capsule. Members of this family in East Africa include *Bersama*.

MORACEAE

Fig and Mulberry families

A family consisting mainly of trees and shrubs, widely distributed in tropical and subtropical regions. All the trees produce a white latex when cut. Leaves alternate, usually simple, stipulate; plants monoecious or dioecious (see Key words, page 7); flowers in catkins or hypanthodium, small, inconspicuous, incomplete, usually unisexual, often many together on a fleshy receptacle; fruit usually multiple (fig, mulberry). Members of this family in East Africa include *Artocarpus, Morus, Ficus*.

MORINGACEAE

Moringa family

A very small family of deciduous trees and shrubs, found from the Mediterranean region eastwards to India, with several species from North Africa, south to Madagascar. Leaves alternate, one- to three-imparipinnate, leaflets mainly opposite, entire; flowers regular or slightly irregular, five-merous; fruit a three-valved capsule, seeds three-winged. Members of this family in East Africa include *Moringa*.

MUSACEAE

Banana family

This family of gigantic, monocotyledonous (see Key words, page 7), herbaceous plants is native to the tropics of Asia, Africa and Australia. They have branching rhizomes from which rise large, sheathed

Musa sapientum

leaves, which are rolled in the bud and have stout midribs and many parallel veins. The leaf blades between the veins are easily torn by wind and rain; flowers are finger-shaped, in racemes, brightly coloured bracts, six petals (five of which are joined); six stamens, free; fruit a berry. Members of this family in East Africa include *Musa, Ensete*.

MYRTACEAE

Eucalyptus family

A large family of dicotyledonous (see Key words, page 7) flowering trees, shrubs, sometimes climbers, for the most part native to the warmer parts of Australia and tropical America. It includes some of the tallest trees in the world. Leaves simple, entire, opposite, rarely alternate, evergreen, special glands produce aromatic oil (gland-dotted); flowers borne in cymes, sometimes solitary, regular, bisexual; four to five sepals; four to five petals, stamens numerous, with long coloured filaments; fruit a berry, capsule or drupe (see Key words, page 7). Members of this family in East Africa include *Eugenia, Psidium, Callistemon, Eucalyptus, Syzygium.*

NYCTAGINACEAE

Bougainvillea and Four o'clock families

Most members of this family are dicotyledonous (see Key words, page 7) trees, shrubs, or herbs native to the tropics, particularly tropical America. They are commonly and alternatively called 'Four o'clock' because flowers of certain genera (*Mirabilis*) open in greatest numbers during the late afternoon. Leaves simple, alternate or opposite, exstipulate; flowers axillary, cymose (see Key words, page 7), with big showy bracts, bisexual or unisexual; five-lobed calyx, no petals, two to many stamens, free; fruit dry, one-seeded anthocarp. Members of this family in East Africa include *Bougainvillea*.

OCHNACEAE

Ochna family

A smallish family of tropical and subtropical trees, shrubs and herbs with simple alternate leaves, usually dentate, and rather distinctive stipules, entire or with a fringed margin. The flowers are usually five in number, with free sepals and petals, bisexual, stamens often numerous; fruit fleshy black drupes (see Key words, page 7). Members of this family in East Africa include *Ochna*.

OLEACEAE

Olive family

A dicotyledonous (see Key words, page 7) family of trees, shrubs or climbers, mainly found in the northern hemisphere. Leaves opposite, exstipulate, simple or compound; flowers in terminal or axillary racemes or cymes (see Key words, page 7); bracteolate, each flower bisexual, regular; calyx tube four- to six-lobed; corolla tube four- to six-lobed, only two stamens; fruit a dry capsule. Members of this family in East Africa include *Schrebera, Fraxinus, Olea*.

PALMAE

Palm family

Palms are an ancient and distinctive family of monocotyledonous (see Key words, page 7) trees and shrubs, most of them originating in tropical America and Asia. The fruit is often a rich food store, and at least three species have worldwide economic importance – the Coconut palm, the Date palm, and the Oil palm from Central Africa. Compared to Asia and America there are very few African indigenous palms. In East Africa there are only six indigenous species, but many exotic species grow as ornamentals. Leaves large, in terminal crown, spirally arranged with a sheathing base; blade palmate or pinnate, with the leaflets or leaf-parts folded. Plants monoecious or dioecious (see Key words, page 7), sometimes dying after flowering; axillary inflorescence, flowers small, sessile, regular, complete, unisexual or bisexual, six sepals and petals in two whorls, six stamens in two whorls, free, sometimes only three; fruit various, can be berry or drupe (see Key words, page 7). Members of this family in East Africa include *Borassus, Brahea, Caryota, Cocos, Raphia, Hyphaene, Roystonea, Archontophoenix, Phoenix, Elaeis, Howea, Thrinax, Chamaedorea, Chrysalidocarpus, Veitchia, Syagrus, Neodyspsis, Licuala, Latania, Washingtonia*.

PANDANACEAE

Screw pine family

A family with only one genus but hundreds of species, including trees with aerial ('stilt') roots at the base of the trunk, found at the water's edge on the tropical shores of the Indian Ocean and Pacific Islands. Stem branched; leaves terminal, long and narrow; flowers unisexual, in a spadix, monoecious; fruit a drupe (see Key words, page 7). Members of this family in East Africa include *Pandanus*.

PHYTOLACCACEAE

Phytolacca family

A small family of dicotyledonous (see Key words, page 7) tree, shrubs, herbs and climbers mainly from tropical America and South Africa. Leaves alternate, entire, without stipules; flowers regular, four to five sepals and petals, four, five or numerous stamens; fruit a berry with several fleshy carpels. The common member of this family in East Africa is *Phytolacca*

PINACEAE

Pine family

Although mainly native to the northern hemisphere, pine trees are found from the Arctic circle to the equator, and are the world's principal source of softwood timber. They are evergreen, resinous trees with needle-like leaves and woody cones, fast-growing, resistant to heat, cold and drought. They also make excellent windbreaks. Members of this family in East Africa include *Pinus*.

PITTOSPORACEAE

Pittosporum family

This is a family of dicotyledonous (see Key words, page 7) trees and shrubs of which eight genera are native to Australia. Leaves simple, alternate, without stipules; flowers small, bell-like, with fine sepals, five petals, five stamens; fruit a capsule or berry. Members of this family in East Africa include *Pittosporum*.

PODOCARPACEAE

Podo family

A small coniferous family, mainly from the southern hemisphere, and the only conifers indigenous to the southern half of Africa. All species are resinous, with linear evergreen leaves, spirally arranged or opposite; cones dioecious (see Key words, page 7), male cones axillary, catkin-like; female cones terminal on short branchlets that develop into fleshy, berry-like fruit containing one seed. Members of this family in East Africa include *Podocarpus*.

PROTEACEAE

Protea and Grevillea families

An interesting family of dicotyledonous (see Key words, page 7) trees and shrubs, mostly from the tropical regions, able to survive long dry seasons. One species, *Grevillea robusta*, is often planted as a windbreak in coffee plantations. Protea, perhaps its most noteworthy genus, is found in the southern and central parts of Africa. Leaves are tough, alternate, simple, entire, exstipulate; flowers grouped in spikes, racemes and heads; individually, the flowers are bisexual, irregular, four petals, four stamens and a long, conspicuous style; fruit a nut, style persistent. Members of this family include *Grevillea, Macadamia, Protea*.

Grevillea robusta

PUNICACEAE

Pomegranate family

The smallest dicotyledonous (see Key words, page 7) family, with just one genus, Punica, and two species, found growing naturally in dense thickets in the Balkans and western Asia but also cultivated and naturalized in the Mediterranean area. Plants are small, shrubby trees, with thorny branches, valuable for their bright red and yellow fruits, including the commercial pomegranates. Leaves are simple, entire; flowers brilliant scarlet with crinkled petals, five to eight sepals, five to eight petals and numerous stamens; fruit a capsule. Members of this family in East Africa include *Punica*.

Punica granatum var. *nana*

RHAMNACEAE

Buffalo-thorn family

A tropical family of small trees, scrambling shrubs and climbers, many of them armed with strong, hooked spines. Leaves always simple, with stipules, alternate or opposite, often serrate; inflorescence cymose; flowers small, regular, four- or five-merous, stamens often hooded by the petals; fruit various, mostly one-seeded drupes. Members of this family in East Africa include *Ziziphus*.

RHIZOPHORACEAE

Mangrove family

A widespread family of trees, shrubs and climbers, of which four genera dominate the mangrove swamps of the tropics and some even extend into warm-temperate regions. The best development of mangrove ecosystems occurs where the upper tidal areas are exposed to a continuous supply of fresh water, as in areas with high rainfall, freshwater seepage and river deltas. Leaves simple, opposite, with or without stipules; flowers regular, axillary, calyx persistent, four- to fifteen-lobed; petals as many as sepals, stamens two to four times as many as petals; fruit a berry or capsule. Members of this family in East Africa include *Rhizophora, Ceriops,* and *Bruguiera*.

Bruguiera gymnorrhiza

ROSACEAE

Rose family

A large and important dicotyledonous (see Key words, page 7) family with over 3 200 species, distributed in the temperate regions but very common in the northern Himalayas. The family is of major economic importance as it contains many fruit-bearing species, including plums, apples, pears and loquats, as well as soft fruits such as blackberries and strawberries. Varieties of these fruits, often adapted to local conditions, are grown in the East African highlands. The family is named after the popular rose, of which there are now more than 5 000 named cultivated varieties. Plants in the family are perennial and include trees, shrubs and herbs, with simple or compound leaves, stipulate, alternate; flowers are solitary or grouped in racemes or cymes (see Key words, page 7), regular, bisexual; four to five sepals, sometimes with epicalyx, five or no petals, one or numerous stamens; fruit variable, a drupe, pome, achene or follicle. Members of this family in East Africa include *Cotoneaster, Eriobotrya, Hagenia, Prunus, Malus.*

RUBIACEAE

Coffee family

This is one of the largest families of dicotyledonous (see Key words, page 7) trees, shrubs, climbers and herbs, most of them tropical but with some temperate species. Leaves are entire, opposite, or occasionally whorled, with inter-petiolar stipules; flowers bisexual, regular; corolla usually tubular, four or five sepals, four to five or twelve petals; four, five or six stamens; fruit a capsule, berry or drupe (see Key words, page 7). Members of this family include *Coffea, Gardenia, Rothmania.*

RUTACEAE

Citrus family

A large family, widespread in the tropics and warm, temperate climates, of trees and shrubs, best known for the genus *Citrus*, which includes oranges, lemons, limes and grapefruit. Leaves are dotted with translucent oil glands, alternate or opposite, aromatic when crushed; flowers small, regular, four to five sepals, four to five petals, as many or twice as many stamens as petals; fruit a berry or drupe (see Key words, page 7). Members of this family in East Africa include *Calodendrum, Teclea, Citrus, Zanthoxylum, Casimiroa.*

Casimiroa edulis

SAPINDACEAE

Lychee family

A family of tropical and subtropical trees, shrubs and climbers, which includes a number of edible fruit, notably the Chinese lychee, *Litchi chinesis*, which is grown as a minor crop in East Africa. Many species have resins or milky juice in their tissues; leaves alternate, compound, pinnate, without stipules, regular; usually dioecious (see Key words, page 7), four to five sepals, five petals, free, five to twelve stamens, flowers in small groups of racemes (see Key words, page 7) or a panicle; fruit mostly a dry capsule or nut, but berries and drupes (see Key words, page 7) are not uncommon. Members of this family in East Africa include *Dodonaea, Filicium*.

SOLANACEAE

Potato family

A large family of dicotyledonous (see Key words, page 7) shrubs, small trees and herbs found in tropical and temperate regions. Included are several economically important plants such as potatoes, tomatoes and peppers, but the *Solanaceae* species also include plants that produce dangerous alkaloides such as nicotine and astropine. However, it has long been recognized that these plants also have valuable medicinal properties. Leaves simple, alternate, exstipulate; flowers solitary or grouped in cymes (see Key words, page 7), regular and bisexual, five petals, five or fewer stamens; fruit a berry or capsule. Members of this family in East Africa include *Datura, Solanum*.

SONNERATIACEAE

Sonneratia family

This is a small family of tropical trees, which includes the important mangrove genus *Sonneratia*, occurring in shallow sea water and deep mud around the East African coast. Leaves opposite, simple, without stipules, obovate to almost round, apex square, occasionally notched, margin entire, petiole up to 10 mm long; flowers have four to eight petals, strap-like, inconspicuous, four to eight sepals, with many stamens in rows; fruit a berry, conical, rots in the water and so releases seeds. *Sonneratia* is the only genus found in this family.

STERCULIACEAE

Cocoa family

This large and handsome family consists, in the main, of tropical trees and shrubs, usually with some stellate hairs on their leaves. Leaves alternate, stipulate, simple or digitate; compound cymes (see Key words, page 7) of regular flowers, unisexual or bisexual, three to five sepals, five or no petals, five to many stamens, may be free or more or less united; fruit a dry capsule. The family includes the Cocoa tree, which is native to South America; the genus *Cola* has its origins in the rain forests of tropical Africa, although it is now widely cultivated for the stimulant in its seeds (a base of Coca Cola). Members of this family in East Africa include *Brachychiton, Dombeya, Heritiera, Sterculia*.

Heritiera littoralis

STRELITZIACEAE

Strelitzia family

This is a small, rather dramatic tropical family of monocotyledonous (see Key words, page 7) perennial herbs closely related to the Banana family (Musacea). Some have tree-like proportions with unusual flowers and enormous, leathery leaves; flowers conspicuous, splaying out from leathery boat-shaped bracts that hold the flower-heads, bisexual, six perianths, in two whorls, free or united, five or six stamens, free; fruit a berry or capsule, dehiscent or indehiscent. Members of this family in East Africa include *Ravenala, Strelitzia, Musa*.

Ravenala madagascariensis

THEACEAE

Tea family

A family of trees and shrubs found in tropical and warm regions, mainly in America and Asia. Leaves alternate, simple, leathery, mostly evergreen, exstipulate; flowers mostly solitary or a few together, usually axillary, regular, usually five to seven sepals and petals, stamens numerous; fruit a capsule or berry with sepals persistent at base. Members of this family in East Africa include *Camellia*.

TILIACEAE

Jute and Lime tree families

A medium-sized family of trees, shrubs or herbs, often with stellate hairs, found throughout the tropics and subtropics, with only Tilia, the Lime tree, occurring in temperate countries. The largest genus is *Grewia*, which occurs in tropical Africa, Asia and Australia. Leaves alternate, with small, deciduous stipules; flowers usually in axillary cymes (see Key words, page 7), bisexual, regular, five sepals, five petals, many stamens, free; fruit fleshy berries. Members of this family in East Africa include *Grewia*.

ULMACEAE

Elm family

A family of trees and shrubs, mostly from the tropical or temperate northern regions. Leaves simple, alternate, stipulate, the leaf blade often unequal-sided; flowers small, solitary or axillary, four to eight sepals, petals absent; fruit a thinly fleshed drupe (see Key words, page 7) or dry and winged. Members of this family in East Africa include *Chaetacme, Celtis, Trema*.

All trees are basically flowering plants with woody stems. A tree has a single stem or trunk. The purpose of the trunk is to raise the leaves above other competing plants, and, unlike annual plants, trees maintain their ascendancy. The tallest trees on soils that suit them and in conditions they can tolerate are therefore able to dominate all other vegetation, including smaller trees. In time, such trees form woods.

Unlike herbaceous plants, trees turn the sapwood of one year into the heartwood of the next, accumulating several annual rings of wood for mechanical support and increasingly thick bark for protection before they mature sexually and produce flowers.

In their form, habit and other characteristics the native trees of East Africa exhibit considerable diversity. This is due to the wide range of soil types and climatic conditions throughout East Africa. There are two main vegetation zones, namely the forest and woodland zones.

Forest can be divided into lowland and montane forests. In lowland forest the canopy height varies between 30 m and 50 m and in montane forest canopies reach a height of 15 m to 30 m. The average height of the tree layers thus decreases at higher altitudes. The canopy cover of forests is closed as the crowns of the trees are interlaced. The ground layer is subsequently sparse, except where gaps occur in the canopy. A shrub layer is normally present, being denser where canopy is more open. The trees are either evergreen or deciduous depending on water availability, and the leaves are generally dark green.

Woodlands contain a mixture of trees, shrubs and grasses, with trees dominating, as in the case of *Acacia* woodland. Canopy height of woodland trees varies between 10 m and 15 m at lower altitudes, and at higher altitudes it is usually between 5 m and 10 m. Woodland trees are mostly deciduous or semi-deciduous, and they have lighter green foliage than forest trees. Where fires are frequent the bark may be thick, rough and fissured and trees and shrubs stunted with sucker growth.

Wooded grassland is characterized by scattered or grouped trees and is also called savanna woodland. Canopy height varies between 4 m and 10 m.

In addition to indigenous trees, East Africa also has many naturalized, non-indigenous species of trees, such as the Jacaranda from Brazil. These naturalized trees are not only planted for shade or as ornamentals, but also make good fuelwood.

Acacia abyssinica

MIMOSOIDEAE

Flat-top acacia

Indigenous

Local names: Njora rahisi (Swahili); Mugaa (Kikuyu); Munyinya (Rukiga)

A large tree with a flat crown that grows 6–20 m in height; well distributed throughout East Africa, occurring at the edges of highland forest and in wooded grassland from 1 200–2 300 m.

Bark: Dark brown; rough.

Thorns: In pairs at nodes; whitish when elongated; variable length; usually less than 3 cm. Sometimes no thorns.

Leaves: Feathery pinnae; 15–40 pairs; leaflets very small; in 20–30 pairs.

Flowers: White; in round heads; buds reddish pink.

Fruit: Grey or brown pods; straight or slightly curved; 5–12 measuring 1.2 x 2.1 cm; split open to release seeds.

Uses: A very useful tree for fuel (wood, charcoal) and timber (posts, bridge-building). Also used as food (edible gum), and for shade.

Fruit and flowers

Tree

Acacia elatior

River acacia   Indigenous

Local names: Muswiswa (Kamba); Ol-lerai (Maasai); Esanyanait (Turkana)

A tall, riverine tree that grows up to 25 m in height, occasionally to 40 m, with a large trunk and rounded crown. Confined to the arid and semi-arid areas of northern and eastern Uganda and Kenya. Only common along rivers and lakes and in dry riverbeds at altitudes of 180–1 100 m.

Bark: Dark brown-black; longitudinally fissured; young twigs reddish-brown.

Spines: Two types: short, brown, sometimes curved spines alternating with long, straight white spines; up to 9 cm; swollen base.

Leaves: 5–13 pairs of pinnae; leaflets in 13–25 pairs; small, narrow, glabrous.

Flowers: In round heads, white to pale yellow.

Fruit: Brown to purplish brown pods, straight or nearly so; 3–12 cm x 1.2–1.8 cm; dehiscent.

Uses: The wood is used for fuelwood, charcoal and as general timber; branches are used in the construction of Maasai *bomas* (homes); pods and young shoots serve as fodder for domestic and wild animals. The tree is very good for soil conservation (nitrogen fixing) and riverbank stabilization.

Traditional medicine: A decoction from the bark used to treat diarrhoea and coughs.

Flowers

Pods

Trees

Acacia gerrardii

MIMOSOIDEAE

Gerrard's acacia

Indigenous

Local names: Ol-debbei (Maasai); Saie (Luo); Munyinya (Luganda)

This flat-topped or spindly tree grows up to 15 m in height and is widely distributed in wooded grasslands at altitudes of 1 500–2 500 m; sometimes found in riverine, arid and semi-arid areas. In East Africa it occurs in the eastern Kenya highlands and Rift Valley.

Bark: Brown or dark grey; rough and fissured.

Spines: In pairs; straight or hooked; short; up to 1 cm.

Leaves: 5–12 pairs of pinnae; leaflets in 12–18 pairs; narrow; small.

Flowers: In round heads; white or cream.

Fruit: Dark brown; sickle-shaped; long; about 7–16 cm x 0.6–1.2 cm; veins clear; dehiscent.

Uses: Leaves and pods serve as fodder, wood is used for fuel and as general timber, for poles and posts, and to make carvings.

Traditional medicine: The bark is widely used in traditional medicine to treat coughs and sore throats (the inner portion is chewed, the juice producing a burning sensation; this twice-daily routine apparently effects a cure in about a week).

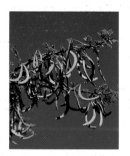

Fruit pods

Flowers

Tree

28

Acacia kirkii

Kirk's acacia

Indigenous

Local names: Ol-lerai (Maasai); Kimwea (Kamba)

A beautiful flat-topped acacia growing 2–15m in height; either single- or many-stemmed. Found in riverine woodland, grasslands and in the lower highlands, especially in areas of seasonal drainage, from 1 500–1 900 m.

Bark: Greenish yellow to yellow-brown. Peeling or flaking to show greenish-yellow underlayer.

Spines: In pairs at the nodes; straight; 0.4–8 cm long.

Leaves: 6–14 pairs of pinnae; leaflets in 7–20 pairs; small and narrow.

Flowers: In heads; cream or white (red in bud).

Fruit: Brown to reddish brown; oblong; straight; 2–10 cm x 0.8–2 cm; small projection on top of the pod between the two seeds.

Uses: Used in the construction of *bomas* (Maasai houses) and for firewood. The Maasai people also make tea from the bark.

Traditional medicine: A decoction of the roots serves as a remedy for stomach ailments.

Flowers

Tree

Fruit pods

Acacia lahai

MIMOSOIDEAE

Red thorn acacia

Indigenous

Local names: Ol-tepessi (Maasai); Mugaa (Kikuyu); Kmatso; (Sebei); Melelek (Arusha)

A tall tree, 3–15 m in height with a flat crown, found in highland mountain forest. It is also an invader of highland grassland, forming dense, cool, moist woodland at altitudes of 1 500–2 500 m. Common throughout East Africa.

Bark: Brown; rough and fissured.

Spines: Straight; in pairs; some small, others up to 7 cm.

Leaves: 6–15 pairs of pinnae; leaflets in 10–28 pairs; narrow.

Flowers: In spikes; white, cream or pale yellow; flower branchlets covered with red glands.

Fruit: Straight or curved; wide pods; 4–7 cm x 1.5–3 cm; they split on the tree.

Uses: The wood is hard and red in colour, very useful as fuel, for fence posts, in bridge-building and as timber in heavy construction work.

Traditional medicine: The bark is used in the treatment of skin eruptions in children, and is also believed to clear toxaemia during pregnancy and in the bowels.

Flowers

Tree

Fruit pods

Acacia mearnsii

Black wattle   **Exotic, native to Australia; naturalized**

Local names: Muwati (Swahili); Muthanduku (Kikuyu); Man'goi (Chagga)

A round or shapeless tree growing to 15 m in height and widely naturalized, commonly planted in the highlands (up to an altitude of 2 500 m). Grows in most soil types.

Bark: Smooth; grey, becoming black and fissured; splits to give resinous gum.

Leaves: Feathery; dull green; leaflets extremely small, less than 4 mm long.

Flowers: Pale yellow; fragrant; in small round heads.

Fruit: Straight or twisted; up to 10 cm long; 3–12 joints between the seeds; dries to dull brown.

Uses: The black wattle is a fast-growing but short-lived tree with hard, strong wood useful for fuel, poles, fencing posts and tool handles. The bark features in the tanning process and in the production of gum.

Fruit

Flowers

Tree

Acacia nilotica

MIMOSOIDEAE

Egyptian thorn, Scented-pod acacia

Indigenous

Local names: Mgunga (Swahili); Ol-kiloriti (Maasai); Ekapelimen (Ateso Karamajong)

An exceedingly variable species, common in Africa's arid and semi-arid regions. It is usually a small tree, seldom exceeding 6 m in height, often branched from the base, with a flat or umbrella-shaped crown. It grows in various soils from the sandy coastal soils to black-cotton soil types.

Bark: Fissured; young shoots red-brown and hairy.
Spines: In pairs at the nodes; straight or nearly so; sharp and whitish; up to 8 cm long.
Leaves: 2–11 pairs of pinnae; leaflets in 7–25 pairs; small and narrow.
Flowers: In round heads; bright golden-yellow; fragrant.
Fruit: Straight or curved; 8–17 cm x 0.9–2.2 cm. Pods have a fruity odour and break up on the ground.
Uses: The leaves and pods provide good fodder. The wood is hard, tough and termite resistant, and is used for fuel, poles, carvings, bee forage, gum and dyes.
Traditional medicine: Bark, leaves and roots have wide application. The bark is peeled off and the inner portion folded into a ball and chewed; the juice is used in the treatment of coughs and sore throats; boiled leaves are sometimes added to tea or coffee as a treatment for chest pains or pneumonia; boiled roots are taken for indigestion and other stomach trouble. Roots also feature in the treatment of gonorrhoea and chest diseases, and a decoction of the roots is taken as a cure for impotence.

Pods

Flowers

Tree

Acacia podalyriifolia

MIMOSOIDEAE

Golden wattle

Exotic, native to Australia; naturalized

Local name: None known

This beautiful ornamental tree reaches 12 m in height and grows in the highlands at altitudes of up to 2 500 m. The species is widely naturalized.

Bark: Dark grey; fissured when older.
Leaves: Young seedlings have feathery, juvenile leaflets that soon fall; mature leaves are silvery white; oval to oblong; finely tipped; up to 5 cm.
Flowers: Golden yellow; in round heads in profuse, terminal clusters.
Fruit: Flat; a little twisted; raised over the seeds; up to 8 cm; split to show a coppery inside.
Uses: A fast-growing but short-lived tree; an ideal decorative specimen for the garden.

Fruit pods

Flowers

Tree

Acacia polyacantha (A. campylacantha)   MIMOSOIDEAE

Falcon's claw acacia   Indigenous

Local names: Mgunga (Swahili); Msukanzi, Mtopotopo (Hehe); Musewa (Kamba)

A fast-growing, robust tree with feathery foliage that reaches up to 18 m in height. Widely distributed at altitudes of 200–1 800 m; commonly found near river banks and in swampy valleys.

Bark: Yellow-brown; fissured or flaking. The trunk and branches are often scattered with hooked prickles.

Spines: Well-developed axillary hooks in pairs. Spaced one each side, often deciduous, 2–8 mm.

Leaves: 13–40 pairs of pinnae; leaflets in 26–64 pairs; long and narrow.

Flowers: Creamy white; in spikes up to 12 cm; two or more together; fragrant; flower with new leaves; hairy flowering stalk.

Fruit: Brown; smooth; up to 6.5–18 cm x 0.9–2.1 cm; straight; flat; dehiscent.

Uses: The wood is resinous and termite resistant. Useful in the manufacture of posts, fencing and farming tools.

Traditional medicine: The leaves are pounded, dried, ground and then applied to sores. Ground roots mixed with water serve the same purpose. The roots are also used in the treatment of snakebite.

Pods

Trees

Flowers

Acacia seyal

White thorn

Indigenous

Local names: Mgunga (Swahili); Mwera (Chagga); Epujaiit (Ateso Tororo)

A small tree with irregularly flattened, spreading crown that grows to 12 m in height. It is sometimes shrubby in form. Widely distributed throughout East Africa at altitudes up to 2 200 m. Found in colonies on flats of black-cotton soil and on stony ground at the base of hills.

Bark: Distinctive; powdery white to pale green or orange-red.

Spines: In diverging pairs; white; stout; up to 8 cm; sometimes smaller or absent altogether.

Leaves: 3–8 pairs of pinnae; 11–12 pairs of leaflets; narrow; elliptic.

Flowers: Bright yellow; numerous; in large, round heads; fragrant.

Fruit: Narrow; curved; brown when dry; slightly constructed between seeds; 7–22 cm x 0.5–0.9 cm; split on the tree.

Uses: The tree produces an edible medium-quality gum. The wood can be used for fuel, poles, fencing posts, and in the tanning process; foliage serves as fodder.

Traditional medicine: The bark is widely used to treat colds and the gum to treat dysentery and stomachache.

Fruit and flowers

Tree

Flowers

Acacia sieberiana

MIMOSOIDEAE

No English name known

Indigenous

Local names: Munga kuu (Swahili); Mwera (Chagga); Muwawa (Luganda)

A tall tree with an umbrella-shaped or rounded crown that grows to 15 m, sometimes to 25 m. It occurs in wooded grassland from near sea level to 1 950 m.

Bark: Grey to yellowish brown; rough and flaky; especially on branches.

Spines: In pairs; whitish; straight; up to 10 cm; often absent over much of the tree.

Leaves: 6–23 pairs of pinnae; leaflets in 14–52 pairs.

Flowers: In round heads; creamy white or pale yellow.

Fruit: Thick and hard; curved; 5–21 cm x 1.3 x 3.5 cm; yellow-brown; smooth and shiny when mature; very slow to split.

Uses: The wood is used for fuel. Pods, leaves and young branches serve as fodder.

Traditional medicine: The bark is used to treat children's fevers; a decoction of the root is prepared as a remedy for stomachache.

Fruit

Flowers

Tree

Acacia tortilis (A. spirocarpa)

MIMOSOIDEAE

Umbrella thorn

Indigenous

Local names: Mgunga (Swahili); Ol-gorete, Ol-tepesi (Maasai), Etirr (Ateso tororo)

A typically spreading acacia with a flat or umbrella-shaped crown; grows up to 18 m. This is a very common tree, widespread over most savannah Africa; found on river terraces, dry courses and hill slopes at altitudes of 600–2 000 m, often in black-cotton soil.

Bark: Grey to black; fissured and rough; young twigs red-brown.

Spines: In pairs at the nodes; of two kinds: straight and long (3–8 cm) and hooked and short (up to 7 mm).

Leaves: 2–10 pairs of pinnae; leaflets in 6–19 pairs.

Flowers: In round heads; white or cream; fragrant.

Fruit: Pale brown; spirally twisted, sometimes curled into rings.

Uses: A hardy acacia of great value; its hard, red wood makes excellent fuel (wood and charcoal) and timber; used for live fencing; serves as fodder (pods and leaves); used for tanning, dyes, as a shade tree and for ornamental purposes. The plant also features in witchcraft among some groups (the thorns are stuck in a goat's pancreas to blind a man who has the 'evil eye').

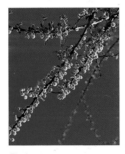

Flowers

Fruit pods

Tree

Acacia xanthophloea

MIMOSOIDEAE

Fever tree, Naivasha thorn

Indigenous

Local names: Mgunga (Swahili); Olerai (Maasai); Murera (Kikuyu)

A tall, handsome tree reaching 25 m or more in height, very common in west-central and east-central Kenya. Often grows with others of its kind, often in black-cotton soils, in areas with high groundwater tables, and on the banks of lakes and rivers, at altitudes of 600–2 000 m. Widely planted in and around Nairobi as an ornamental.

Bark: Easily recognized by its yellow-green bark; hairy or powdery; fissured when older.

Spines: In pairs at the nodes; straight or diverging; whitish; up to 10 cm; many nodes in young trees.

Leaves: 3–6 pairs of pinnae; leaflets in 8–17 pairs; narrow; feathery.

Flowers: In round heads; white or yellowish white.

Fruit: Yellow-brown; straight or slightly curved; up to 3–13 cm x 0.7–1.4 cm; flat; slightly constructed (small projection between the seeds).

Uses: Foliage and pods are used as fodder; wood is used as fuel and as timber for poles and fence posts. The species also serves as bee forage.

Traditional medicine: The bark is used in the treatment of coughs and sore throats (it is rolled into a small ball and chewed).

Fruit

Flowers

Bark

Trees

Acokanthera oppositifolia (A. longiflora) APOCYNACEAE

Poison arrow tree

Indigenous

Local names: Mururu (Kikuyu); Ol-morijoi (Maasai); Mukweu (Kamba)

An attractive small, evergreen tree, growing 4–7 m high, but sometimes a multi-stemmed shrub; found in dry forest margins, riverine forest and woodland at altitudes of 1 450–2 100 m.

Bark: Rough; brown; deeply fissured with age.

Leaves: Shiny above; tough; larger than leaves of *Acokanthera schimperi* (see page 40); elliptic; up to 10 cm in length; opposite; pointed apex.

Flowers: White with a pink tube; longer than *A. schimperi*; in dense, fragrant axillary clusters.

Fruit: Larger than that of *A. schimperi*; up to 5 cm long; plum-shaped and purple when ripe.

Uses: The bark, root and leaves are used in the preparation of arrow poison.

Traditional medicine: A decoction of roots is used in the treatment of syphilis; powdered dried leaves and roots are used to treat headaches and snakebite; weak leaf infusions are taken for abdominal pain. This plant can, however, be toxic and should be approached with caution.

Flowers

Fruit

Tree

Acokanthera schimperi

APOCYNACEAE

Poison arrow tree   **Indigenous**

Local names: Mchungu (Swahili); Msungu (Hehe); Kelyo (Sebei); Murichu (Kikuyu)

A dark evergreen tree, sometimes shrubby with a dense crown, multi-stemmed, up to 5 m in height, occurring in dry forest margins, wooded grassland and rocky bushland at altitudes of 1 200–2 300 m.

Bark: Corky; deeply fissured; dark brown.

Leaves: Shiny, dark glossy green above, paler and dull below; opposite; broadly rounded; apex often pointed.

Flowers: White with pink tube; in dense, fragrant axillary clusters.

Fruit: Oval berries; up to 1.5 cm long; red-purple and black when ripe.

Uses: The ripe fruit is favoured by birds and monkeys. Roots, bark, twigs and leaves are used in the preparation of arrow poison.

Traditional medicine: An infusion of the roots is used in the treatment of syphilis.

Flowers

Fruit

Trees

Acrocarpus fraxinifolius

Indian ash, Australian ash

Exotic, native to India, Southeast Asia

Local name: None known

A very tall (up to 60 m high), fast-growing deciduous tree with bright red young foliage and a clean, smooth, straight trunk.

Bark: Smooth; pale grey; with horizontal markings.

Leaves: Twice-compound; forming a regular, spreading pattern; leaflets opposite; 7 to 10 pairs; tapering apex; thin texture; wavy.

Flowers: On long stalk from terminal branches; heads in dense clusters; each flower has 5 orange-red stamens protruding from a cup of equal green petals. Flowers are short-lived, conspicuous when tree is bare of leaves; they attract many sunbirds.

Fruit: Thin; green to dark brown; up to 12 cm in length; split down both sides on the tree.

Uses: The timber can be used for light construction, but is prone to attack by borer beetle; also used for making beehives.

Flowers

Fruit pods

Tree

Adansonia digitata

BOMBACACEAE

Baobab

Indigenous

Local names: Mbuyu (Swahili); Ol-mesera (Maasai); Maramba (Pare)

A deciduous tree with an enormously wide trunk, growing up to 20 m in height. One of the longest-lived trees in the world, the baobab is commonly found in coastal and inland bush and woodland. It is widely distributed in Kenya and Tanzania at altitudes from sea level to 1 000 m. It has never been recorded in Uganda.

Bark: Smooth; grey and fibrous; branches stout and stiff.

Leaves: Compound digitate (finger-like) with long leaf-stalk; about 10 cm; tapering base and apex; lower leaflets smaller.

Flowers: Solitary; 5 waxy white petals surrounding a ball of fine stamens; hanging stalks; very short-lived and unpleasantly scented; open at night.

Fruit: Large; hard-shelled; covered in greyish, velvety hairs; hang from a stalk.

Uses: The leaves of the baobab are used as a vegetable by local people. Ripe fruit contains numerous dark-brown seeds enclosed in a whitish, edible pulp that contains tartaric acid; pulp can be used for flavouring or soaked in water to make a refreshing drink. A red dye is obtained from the roots. The fibrous bark is used for weaving and making ropes.

Traditional medicine: A refreshing drink, prepared from the whitish fruit pulp, is used to treat fevers and diarrhoea; bark and leaves are said to have anti-inflammatory and diaphoretic properties; boiled bark is used as a cure for pains in the body; the leaves feature in the treatment of fever and as an astringent.

Flowers

Fruit

Tree

Albizia amara (ssp. sericocephala)

Bitter albizia

Indigenous

Local names: Mwowa (Kamba); Ruga (Luo); Muhogolo (Gogo)

A deciduous tree, often rounded in shape, reaching 10 m in height but often smaller; widely distributed in wooded grassland and *Acacia-Commiphora* bushland. The species grows at altitudes of 500–1 050 m above sea level.

Bark: Dark brown; roughly cracked.

Leaves: Compound; bright pale green; leaflets numerous; very small and narrow; feathery in appearance. Branchlets and leaves are covered with distinctive, soft, golden hairs.

Flowers: Numerous; small creamy pink or white heads; up to 2.5 cm across; semi-spherical.

Fruit: Large pods; thin; up to 20 x 3 cm; bulging over the few seeds; thick margin; purplish when young, later becomes brown and papery.

Uses: The wood is hard and used for general timber, poles and tools and as fuel. Leaves serve as fodder and mulch. The tree also yields a good-quality resin, and assists in soil conservation (nitrogen fixation).

Traditional medicine: Bark serves as an emetic to induce vomiting; crushed leaves are used in the treatment of wounds.

Fruit and flowers

Tree

Albizia grandibracteata

MIMOSOIDEAE

Large-leafed albizia

Indigenous

Local names: Owak, Awak (Luo); Mulongo (Luganda)

A very graceful deciduous tree with either a round or flat crown that grows to 15 m in height. Found in lowland and upland rain forest, riverine forest, sometimes in grasslands at altitudes of 1 200–1 800 m. Very common throughout Uganda, around Mt Elgon (on the border between Uganda and Kenya), in the western and Rift Valley areas of Kenya and in Tanzania's lake areas. The species is now widely planted in Nairobi as an ornamental tree.

Bark: Grey; smooth.

Leaves: Leaflets distinctive; sparse; broadly oval but sides unequal; terminal pair curved; large, up to 6 cm long; acute apex in all leaflets.

Flowers: In colourful heads, mostly pink, with dark red anthers.

Fruit: Flat; glossy; reddish brown; up to 12 cm long, with a blunt point. Clusters of pods often conspicuous when the tree is bare.

Uses: The wood is used for fuel and timber; leaves and pods serve as fodder. An attractive ornamental tree.

Traditional medicine: An infusion from the root is used in the treatment of tonsillitis.

Fruit

Tree

Flowers

44

Albizia gummifera

Peacock flower

Indigenous

Local names: Mcani mbao (Swahili); Mboromo (Chagga); Chiruku, Kirongo (Lugishu)

A deciduous forest tree with a flat crown growing to 15 m in height; found mainly in East Africa. This is the most widespread albizia in Kenya, ocurring from dry or wet lowlands to upland forest edges, and also in riverine forest, at altitudes from sea level to 2 400 m.

Bark: Grey and smooth.
Leaves: Shiny, dark green; leaflets up to 12 pairs; 1–2 cm long; almost rectangular; midrib diagonal; one outer corner rounded.
Flowers: White or pale pink clusters; pale staminal tubes topped with tufts of bright red anthers.
Fruit: Glossy pale brown with raised margin; thin, papery; up to 17 x 3 cm; often profuse clusters.
Uses: Pods, leaves and branches serve as fodder. The wood is used for fuel, timber and in boat construction.
Traditional medicine: Bark extracts feature in treatments of fevers such as malaria; crushed pods are used to cure stomachache; crushed roots for skin diseases; powdered bark as a kind of snuff for headaches, and a cold infusion is made to treat inflammation of the eyes.

Tree

Fruit

Flowers

Albizia schimperiana

MIMOSOIDEAE

Long-podded albizia

Indigenous

Local names: Mukurue (Kikuyu); Mfuranje, Mruka (Chagga)

A tree very similar to *Albizia gummifera* (see page 45), but more umbrella-shaped, growing to 24 m in height with a flat or rounded crown. It commonly occurs in riverine forest, dry forest (remnants) and evergreen bushland, at altitudes of 1 400–1 800 m.

Bark: Smooth; pale grey to brownish; transverse ridges; sometimes rough.

Leaves: Compound; leaflets less than 2 cm long; 6–18 pairs; obliquely oblong with rounded rather than angular corners.

Flowers: White or creamy; in loose, conspicuous heads; stamens white; flower stalk hairy.

Fruit: Numerous; persistent; brown; thick margin; up to 30 x 5 cm, but often smaller; contain many large seeds.

Uses: The leaves and pods are used as fodder. The wood is hard and heavy, good for furniture, posts and poles and in the construction of buildings.

Traditional medicine: An infusion of the roots is added to porridge (made from germinated grain) and taken as a pain reliever.

Flowers

Fruit pods

Tree

Aleurites moluccana

Candlenut tree

Exotic, native to Malaysia and
the islands of the South Pacific

Local name: Kabakanjagala (Luganda)

A large, leafy tree with light greyish green foliage, growing to 11 m in height.

Bark: Smooth; grey-brown; finely fissured with wavy vertical lines..

Leaves: Large; spade-shaped; up to 18 cm long; pointed tip; shiny; on long stalks in terminal whorls; covered with powdery, whitish hairs; rust-coloured on the lower surface.

Flowers: Small; white; in thick terminal clusters.

Fruit: Big; rounded; up to 5 cm; contain 2 black seeds.

Uses: The seeds are rich in oil, which is used for candles, soap, paint and varnish.

Fruit

Flowers

Tree

Aloe bainesii

LILIACEAE

Tree aloe

Exotic, native to South Africa

Local name: None known

An unusual, solitary, evergreen tree that grows 10–18 m in height, with a massive trunk, much-branched from a high, rounded crown.

Bark: Greyish brown; roughens with age. Branches either two or three-forked.

Leaves: Long and narrow; dull dark green; deeply channelled and recurved; in terminal rosettes; leaves up to 90 x 6 cm; leaf margin armed with small, firm, whitish teeth.

Flowers: Orange to pinkish, tipped with green; branched inflorescence; about 500 mm long; erect spikes up to 30 cm long.

Fruit: Dry oval capsules containing many seeds.

Uses: An ornamental that can be grown in almost any climate and soil type from cuttings.

Tree

Anacardium occidentale

Cashew nut, Cashew apple   **Exotic, native to Brazil, Caribbean region**

Local names: Mkanju (Swahili); Nkorosho (Mwera); Mutua (Kamba)

A medium-sized, spreading tree that is naturalized at the coast, growing to 10 m in height. The cashew is one of the region's oldest cash crops; widely planted all over the tropics.

Bark: Rough; dark brown.

Leaves: Leathery; dark green; oval; 15 cm long and 8 cm wide; apex rounded, wavy.

Flowers: In terminal clusters; small; star-shaped; creamy white; sometimes marked with red.

Fruit: Hard, kidney-shaped nuts attached to the base of shiny orange-yellow 'cashew-apple' (swollen flower stalk); nuts fall to the ground when ripe.

Uses: The cashew apple is edible; the juice can be drunk fresh or fermented to make a liqueur-type wine. Pulp can be used for jam. Cashew nuts are low in calories and high in edible oil and protein, but the outer covering contains a poisonous oil that burns the skin (must be roasted off before the kernel can be eaten). Cashew shell oil is used in cement for weather-proofing and as a wood preservative against termites; the distilled oil features in the manufacture of varnishes, inks, tiles and in brake linings.

Flowers

Fruit (nuts)

Tree

Anthocleista grandiflora (A. zambesiaca) LOGANIACEAE

Cabbage tree Indigenous

Local name: Mutunguru (Kikuyu); Sagalituet (Kipsigis); Mutete (Meru)

A very tall tree that grows between 10–25 m in height. It is found along the rivers in forest areas, and along swamp edges, at altitudes of 1 250–2 200 m.

Bark: Brownish grey.

Leaves: Narrowly obovate; apex rounded; base narrow; 20–70 cm x 10–25 cm.

Flowers: Cream or white; in erect terminal bunches; up to 45 cm long; older flowers turn brown.

Fruit: Green; ellipsoid; 1.3–2.2 cm long.

Uses: This is a softwood tree; wood is used as fuel.

Flowers

Fruit

Tree

Araucaria bidwillii

Bunya Bunya pine, Monkey puzzle tree

Exotic, native to
Queensland, Australia

Local name: None known

A fast-growing tree reaching up to 45 m in height, conical when young, tall column when fully mature, developing long, drooping branches. The species is grown in East Africa as an ornamental tree. It does well in lower altitudes in areas with good rainfall.

Bark: Rough, bumpy bark with prominent leaf scars; trunk up to 1 m across.

Leaves: Juvenile leaves easily identified: double rows along the branchlets; each leaf is shiny, tough and sharp-tipped; 3–6 cm long; leaves at the end of branchlets are smaller and form tight, thorny spirals.

Cones: Male cones up to 16 x 1 cm, occur near the ends of top branches; female cones erect, large and heavy, up to 30 x 22 cm, weighing up to 4.5 kg.

Seeds: Joined to the cone scales; pear-shaped; up to 6 x 3 cm.

Uses: The seeds are much favoured by monkeys.

Male cones

Tree

Leaves

Araucaria columnaris

ARAUCARIACEAE

Cook's Island pine, Cook's araucaria

Exotic, native to New Caledonia, Polynesia

Local name: None known

A narrow, tall tree growing to 65 m in height with short horizontal branches covered with slender branchlets, giving the impression of a dense green column.

Leaves: In tight rows; mature leaves rigid, curved inwards, up to 5 mm long; juvenile leaves larger and softer.

Cones: Male cones up to 6 cm long; female cones egg-shaped, up to 16 cm long, each scale covered with bristle-like appendages.

Seeds: Up to 3 cm; well-developed membranous wings.

Uses: A very popular ornamental tree for gardens and for roadsides.

Leaves

Tree

Araucaria cunninghamiana

Hoop pine, Moreton Bay pine

Exotic, native to Australia

Local name: None known

A tree that generally reaches 50 m in height, sometimes up to 70 m, with long, upward-growing branches bearing dense clusters of branchlets.

Trunk: Rough; shiny brown in horizontal hoops; peeling in thin layers; trunk can become massive, reaching up to 3 m in diameter.

Leaves: Juvenile leaves triangular, sharp-pointed; up to 2 cm long; mature leaves softer, curved inwards, crowded and overlapping on the branchlets.

Cones: Male cones up to 7 cm long, in pendulous clusters, turning orange-red with pollen; female cones green, up to 8 cm high, covered with stiff recurved points from each scale.

Seeds: Small, with membranous wings.

Uses: An ornamental indoor and outdoor tree in East Africa; in Australia, the softwood timber is used for furniture and plywood.

Female cone

Tree

Artocarpus heterophyllus (A. integrifolius) MORACEAE

Jack fruit Exotic, native to region from India to Malaysia

Local names: Mfenesi, Mfenesi mfuu (Swahili); Yakobo, Kifenensi (Luganda)

An evergreen tree growing to 5 m in height, occasionally to 20 m. Generally found at the coast. Very common in Uganda, where it has become naturalized.

Leaves: Oval; up to 15 cm; glossy.

Flowers and fruit: Borne on the trunk or large branches, where the world's largest known fruit then develops – massive and irregular with spiky, yellow-green rind, up to 20 kg in weight and 1 m in length.

Uses: A good shade tree, which yields gum. The ripe flesh is sweet and edible. Wood used for general timber (doors, furniture, carts, truck-bodies), as fuelwood and for charcoal. Leaves and rind serve as fodder.

Tree

Fruit

Azadirachta indica

Neem tree

Exotic, native to India, Sri Lanka

Local names: Mkilifi, Mwarubaini kamili (Swahili)

A hardy, fast-growing, medium-sized tree growing from 15–20 m in height, with a dense, leafy, oval-shaped canopy; evergreen except in the driest areas; drought-resistant, flourishing in arid and semi-arid regions.

Bark: Pale; grey-brown; rough.

Leaves: Shiny; green; crowded towards the end of branches; compound leaves; 5 to 8 pairs of leaflets; up to 10 cm long; smaller, terminal leaflet; pointed apex; margin coarsely dentate.

Flowers: Small; scented; creamy white; hang down in long sprays.

Fruit: Oval; yellow berries when ripe; up to 2 cm across; long. Fruit yields an aromatic oil.

Uses: A valuable species with multiple uses. The wood is used for general timber, furniture, poles, and as fuel. The oil can serve as a paraffin substitute and is used to make soap; the residue ('neem cake') makes both a good cattle feed and a fertilizer. The leaves contain azadirachtin, which is a powerful insecticide. Dried leaves placed among clothes protects against moths, and in stored grain they repel insects without leaving any smell or aftertaste. Smoke from burning leaves drives off mosquitoes and sand-flies. A solution from the leaves serves as an anti-locust crop spray. Powdered leaves are widely used to make facial creams. Purified neem oil is used in nail polish and other cosmetics. Neem sticks serve as disposable toothbrushes.

Traditional medicine: Aromatic neem oil features in the treatment of skin diseases such as leprosy and eczema. Twigs contain antiseptic ingredients that help maintain healthy teeth and gums. Leaves are also used in the treatment of malaria.

Evergreen leaves

Berries

Flowers

Balanites aegyptiaca

BALANITACEAE

Desert date

Indigenous

Local names: Mjunju (Swahili); Mohoromo (Chagga); Musongole (Luganda)

A slow-growing evergreen tree that reaches 6–10 m in height, its rounded crown a tangled mass of thorny branches. The species is found in dry bushland, wooded grassland and woodland from sea level to 2 000 m, often in sandy or black-cotton soils.

Bark: Smooth; green or dark brown; fissured; young branchlets green and smooth, with thorns of up to 8 cm; soft at first, then woody.

Leaves: Distinctive pairs of grey-green leaflets; oval; up to 5 cm long but often smaller; short stalk; tapering to the base.

Flowers: Yellow-green clusters; fragrant; up to 1.5 cm.

Fruit: Oblong; up to 5 cm; both ends round; yellow when ripe; the hard, pointed seed inside is surrounded by yellow-brown, bitter-sweet flesh.

Uses: The wood is heavy, durable and termite resistant, and is used for furniture, tool handles, poles, carvings and as construction timber. The fruit and leaves are browsed by goats, camels and game, especially giraffe. The gum is used to fix arrow-heads and spear-heads to their shafts.

Traditional medicine: The emulsion of the fruit is lethal to freshwater snails that carry the bilharzia micro-organism, and to water-fleas that carry guninea (worm disease). An infusion of the roots is used in the treatment of malaria, abdominal pains, and as a purgative. Heated gum from the wood is mixed with maize meal porridge and eaten as a remedy for chest complaints. The fruits are used to treat coughs.

Fruit

Old tree

Flowers

Bauhinia variegata *var.* variegata

Camel's foot, Orchid tree

Exotic

Local name: None known

A small, semi-deciduous tree, grows to 6 m in height, sometimes much taller; occurs throughout the tropics at altitudes of up to 2 200 m; most commonly planted in Kenya as an ornamental in parks, avenues and gardens.

Bark: Grey and smooth; furrows with age.

Leaves: Alternate; dull; blue-green; the two rounded lobes are 10–15 cm across ('camel's foot' shape); veins radiate from the leaf base.

Flowers: Pink in short sprays; each flower has 5 deep pink petals, marked with rose or yellow-green; one petal different in shape (orchid-like); 5 arched stamens. *Bauhinia variegata* var. *candida* has stiff pure white flowers, sometimes with yellow markings. All other features are similar to those of *B. variegata* var. *variegata*.

Fruit: Flat brown pods up to 20 cm long; twist open on the tree to release round seeds.

Uses: An ornamental shade species. The tree yields tannin. The wood is used for implements, and as fuel. The shoots are eaten as vegetables.

Pink flowers and fruit

White flowers *(B. v. candida)*

Tree

Bersama abyssinica

MELIANTHACEAE

Bersama

Indigenous

Local names: Mwangwakwao (Swahili); Manguwe (Chagga); Muthandi (Kikuyu)

A tree or shrub that grows 2–18 m in height, found in upland grassland, and in dry and wet montane and riparian forest glades and edges, at altitudes of 1 200–2 400 m.

Bark: Smooth to rough; cracking lengthwise.

Leaves: Compound; in clusters at branch ends (which show conspicuous leaf scars) up to 1 m long: 5–10 pairs of leaflets; opposite; lanceolate; oblong to ovate; base broadly rounded; apex acute; sessile to shortly stalked; the uppermost leaflets are the largest.

Flowers: White to cream; sweet-smelling.

Fruit: Capsule splits into 4–5 lobes, revealing a white interior and bright red seeds with yellow arils.

Uses: The wood is soft, not durable; leaves are poisonous to stock.

Traditional medicine: Leaves are crushed and used as snuff for colds; also chewed as an aphrodisiac; juice from the bark acts as a purgative; extract from young twigs used in the treatment of dysentery and roundworm; a root decoction is taken for epilepsy and for haemorrhoids; it is also useful for cleansing wounds. These plants, however, may be toxic and should be approached with caution.

Flowers

Capsule opening to reveal seed

Tree

Bolusanthus speciosus

Tree wisteria, Elephant's wood

Exotic, native to South Africa

Local name: None known

This handsome, deciduous, very slow-growing ornamental, which reaches 7–10 m in height, has gracefully arching and drooping branches that bear long sprays of purple pea-flowers resembling those of Wisteria in the spring.

Bark: Dark brown; fissured.

Leaves: Compound; 6–8 pairs of leaflets; pale green when young; dark, shiny green later; tapering apex.

Flowers: Purple; pea-like; in sprays 150 mm long.

Fruit: Borne in pendent clusters; bulges over each seed; turns brown to black when ripe.

Uses: *Bolusanthus speciosus* is named in honour of Harry Bolus (1834–1911), a famous South African amateur botanist. It is a beautiful ornamental tree, yielding a wood considered one of the best for furniture. The inside bark is used medicinally in South Africa.

Flowers

Fruit pods

Tree

Brachychiton acerifolium (Sterculia acerifolia) STERCULIACEAE

Australian flame tree   Exotic, native to Australia

Local name: None known

A spectacular, erratically flowering tree, found throughout East Africa as an ornamental; usually grows to about 15 m, sometimes twice that. It is widely planted in the highlands. Its distinctive cone-like shape is recognizable from great distances.

Bark: Grey; smooth; rough when old; bears scars from detached branches.

Leaves: Large; palmately lobed; up to 30 cm across; radiating veins prominent below; shiny green above; resemble paw-paw leaves; stalk long and slender.

Flowers: Bright red; 5 joined petals; bell-shaped; up to 2.5 cm across. Long, loose sprays; flowers appear when the tree is bare of leaves.

Fruit: Smooth black capsules; up to 10 cm long; split down one side while still on the tree.

Uses: The smooth grey bark of the tree produces both a gum and a useful fibre. The wood is used for poles, posts and as fuel.

Fruit capsules

Flowers

Tree

Brachylaena huillensis (B. hutchinsii)

COMPOSITAE

Silver oak

Indigenous

Local names: Muhuhu (Swahili); Ol-magogo (Maasai); Muhugu (Kikuyu)

A tall tree with grey-green foliage and steeply ascending branches that form a narrow crown, dividing close to the ground. The species grows from 10–18 m in height, in exceptional cases up to 30 m, with a bole that can reach a width of up to 60 cm. It occurs in upland semi-deciduous forest and lowland dry forest or thicket, at altitudes of up to 2 000 m, and is often prominent above the forest canopy.

Bark: Grey-brown; vertical cracks.
Leaves: Narrow; spear-shaped; up to 10 cm long; sharply tipped; base long and tapering; margin often wavy; in upright bunches; shoots with cream hairs; mature leaves white and hairy below but shiny above.
Flowers: Very small; white; in axillary clusters; male and female flowers on different trees; flower stalk covered with white hairs.
Fruit: Tiny hairy seeds; look like white fluff once they have fallen on the ground.
Uses: The wood is hard, strong and durable and is used for general timber, wood-carving, poles, posts and as fuel.

Leaves

Fruit

Tree

Callistemom citrinus *var.* splendens   MYRTACEAE

Bottlebrush tree   Exotic, native to Australia, New Zealand

Local name: None known

Also known as *Callistemom lance-olatus*. A purely ornamental small tree, reaching 6 m in height, with drooping foliage; planted in parks and gardens for its decorative effect. This is a remarkably hardy tree, tolerating a wide range of temperatures, altitudes and soils.

Bark: Grey; smooth; rough and furrowed when old.
Leaves: Narrow; tough; grey-green; up to 8 cm long; lemon-scented when crushed; young leaves pink-green.
Flowers: Vivid crimson brush-like cylindrical spikes with no obvious petals; a mass of long red stamens; nectar attracts sunbirds and bees; the shoot continues to grow after the flowers have formed.
Fruit: Small; woody capsules; persisting for many months.
Uses: Mainly ornamental. There are several other species and cultivated varieties of bottlebrush, some with deep red and some with white flowers. A slightly smaller variety is *Callistemom rigidus* (*Calistemom erectus*), which has upright foliage and stiff, erect red flowers.

Flowers and fruit

Flowers

Tree

Calodendrum capense

Cape chestnut

Indigenous

Local names: Murarachi (Kikuyu); Ol-larashi (Maasai); Mpisili (Chagga)

A semi-deciduous tree growing to 20 m, with a sharply spreading crown; bare for several months; widespread in evergreen and riverine forest in the highlands at altitudes of 1 600–2 300 m. Also widely planted as an ornamental.

Bark: Grey; smooth; young branchlets hairy.

Leaves: Opposite; simple; dark green; broadly oval; wavy; up to 14 cm long; midrib and veins very clear underneath.

Flowers: Large; showy; pink; with pink or white dark-dotted staminoides; purple-brown anthers on the long stamens; 5 strap-shaped petals.

Fruit: Round; covered in warty prickles; 3–5 cm across; capsules (chestnut) hang from the tree; split open from below to release shiny black, angled seeds.

Uses: The timber is tough but bends well, and is used in house building, for tool handles and poles, and as fuelwood and bee forage. A very beautiful tree; also planted in gardens.

Fruit

Flowers

Tree

Casimiroa edulis

RUTACEAE

Mexican apple

Exotic, native to Mexico, Central America

Local name: None known

A very fast-growing tropical fruit tree that can grow up to 15 m high. It grows as an ornamental shade tree at high altitudes.

Bark: Brown; rough.

Leaves: Palmately compound; 5–7 leaflets; each roughly 12 cm long.

Flowers: Small; greenish or whitish; in bunches.

Fruit: Apple-shaped fruit up to 10 cm in diameter; pendant on long stalks; yellow-green with thin, waxy, glaucous cover.

Uses: The fruit, which resembles a mango, is soft, juicy, with creamy flesh, very sweet and with a fragrant aroma, though it may have a bitter aftertaste. The seeds are used medicinally in Mexico to induce sleep. The Nairobi Arboretum contains a very good specimen.

Fruit

Tree

Flowers

Castanospermum australe

Moreton Bay chestnut

Exotic, native to Queensland, Australia

Local name: None known

A tall, evergreen species reaching 22 m in height, often with low-hanging branches. Grown as an ornamental tree in Nairobi and the highlands, rarely at the coast.

Bark: Grey; finely fissured.

Leaves: Large; compound; leaflets glossy; wavy; 5 to 7 pairs; slightly oval; apex tapering to a point.

Flowers: Striking orange-red; about 3 cm long; in short sprays; arise from older, woody branches.

Fruit: Thick cylindrical pods; up to 22 cm long; brown; very hard when mature.

Uses: In Australia the tree provides valuable timber for furniture. The substance castanospermime, extracted from the nuts, is of particular interest to scientists (it is currently being tested for its possible effect on the AIDS virus).

Young fruit

Flowers

Tree

Casuarina cunninghamiana

CASUARINACEAE

Australian beef wood, River she oak, Casuarina

Exotic, native to eastern Australia, Pacific islands

Local name: Mvinje (Swahili)

A savannah tree, usually growing 20 m high; pyramidal in shape when young; widely planted in the highlands as a windbreak.

Trunk: Thick at the base; grey to black; fissured with age.
Branchlets: Short; thin; soft; 9–20 cm in length; bearing 7–9 white-tipped leaf scales in each of the whorls.
Flowers: Male flowers very small, greenish, at ends of branches; female flowers in clusters on woody branches.
Fruit: Small, prickly capsules; 1 cm long.
Uses: The hard timber is used as fuel, and for poles and posts. Dry leaves used as mulch; green leaves used as fodder. Roots contain a nitrogen-fixing agent.

Fruit

Tree

Casuarina equisetifolia

Casuarina, Swamp she oak, Whistling pine

Indigenous

Local names: Mvinje, Moinga (Swahili)

A coastal tree growing up to 20 m high, with 'weeping' foliage; sometimes stunted by wind; common in sand or coral near high-water mark and in coastal bushland.

Bark: Grey-black; rough; cracked with age.
Leaves: Minute scales, just visible on the green branchlets in whorls of 6 to 7; up to 30 cm long; hang down in crowded tufts along the woody branches.
Flowers: Male flowers small, visible as pollen-bearing tips on some branchlets; female flowers in tiny heads with red stigmas.
Fruit: Prickly; brown; cone-like; up to 2.5 cm long; in dense clusters; release hundreds of tiny winged seeds when they start to dry.
Uses: The tree grows quickly in dry and infertile areas, and is planted for soil stabilization; the roots have nodules containing nitrogen-fixing bacteria. The timber is used for dhow masts, poles, tool handles and fuel. The bark contains tannin, which yields a reddish dye.

Tree

Male flowers

Fruit

Ceiba pentandra (Bombax ceiba)

BOMBACACEAE

Kapok tree

Exotic, native to South and Central America

Local names: Msufi (Swahili); Kafamba, Kifampa (Luganda)

A distinctive, tall tree growing to 30 m in height, with conspicuous horizontal, layered branches. The trunk is covered with sharp, conical spines when young and it becomes heavily buttressed with age. The tree is commonly planted at the coast.

Bark: Young branches green; old bark grey, smooth.
Leaves: Compound; digitate; 5–10 leaflets radiating from a long stalk; narrow; up to 20 cm long.
Flowers: Small; up to 3 cm across; white to pink colour; in axillary clusters; petals woolly on the outside; pollinated by bats.
Fruit: Large woody capsules; up to 30 cm across; conspicuous on the bare tree; rounded black seeds with long, silky, white fibres (kapok).
Uses: The fruit yields a valuable fibre, as light as cotton, used for life jackets, mattresses, protective clothing and insulation. The wood serves as fuel and as general timber; leaves and branches are used as fodder.

Bark

Flowers

Young fruit

Mature fruit with kapok

Trees

Celtis africana (C. kraussiana)

ULMACEAE

White stinkwood

Indigenous

Local names: Murundu (Kikuyu); Akasinsa (Luganda); Chepkeleliet, Nyasiat (Kipsigis)

A deciduous forest tree, with a spreading crown, that grows up to 12 m in height, but sometimes as high as 35 m. It occurs mainly in high rainfall areas, but also in either dry or moist evergreen forest and in riverine forest, at altitudes of 1 300–2 400 m.

Bark: Smooth; pale grey; marked with horizontal rings; branchlets have rust-coloured hairs.

Leaves: Rough; dull green above; up to 10 cm long; 3–5 clearly visible veins arise from the base; margin dentate; elongated apex; base slightly unequal.

Flowers: Sepals only, no petals; very small; greenish; on thin stalks in clusters beside leaves.

Fruit: Small; rounded; orange; fleshy.

Uses: The wood is strong and tough and is used in construction, to make furniture and tool handles, and as fuel. Leaves serve as fodder for domestic stock.

Leaves and fruit

Tree

Cereus peruvianus

CACTACEAE

Giant cactus

Exotic, native to Brazil

Local name: None known

This is a sturdy, tall-growing plant that often forms a tree in its natural habitat. It may reach 4–6 m in height.

Branches: 5-7 sides; succulent; thick; covered with tan to black spines; up to 4 cm long.

Flowers: Large; whitish; trumpet-shaped; nocturnal.

Uses: Grows as an ornamental cactus, notably in rock gardens. Can be cultivated from both seeds and cuttings.

Tree

Flowers

Chorisia speciosa (Bombax chorisia)

Bombax

Exotic, native to Brazil

Local name: None known

A spectacular deciduous species with a swollen, spiny trunk and rounded crown, growing to 25 m in height. It is planted at altitudes from sea level to 2 000 m. An attractive tree for parks, avenues and golf courses.

Bark: Grey and smooth; covered with spines.

Leaves: Compound; digitate; 5 to 7 leaflets; radiate from a long stalk; each up to 15 cm long but often shorter; tapering apex; midrib prominent below.

Flowers: Large; 5 mauve-pink petals, yellowish white streaked with pink towards the centre; central thick column of joined stamens, protruding style and stigma.

Fruit: Oval; big woody capsules; up to 15 cm long; pale brown; split open on the tree.

Uses: The fruit contains seeds embedded in masses of fine white fibres, which yield cotton-like material useful for stuffing cushions and toys.

Flowers

Fruit

Tree

Cordia africana (C. abyssinica, C. holstii)

BORAGINACEAE

Large-leafed cordia

Indigenous

Local names: Makobokobo (Swahili); Mukebu (Luganda); Mringaringa (Chagga)

A large, deciduous forest tree with rounded crown and often crooked trunk, growing to 15 m in height; widely distributed in wooded grassland, forest and riverine areas at altitudes of 1 200–2 100 m. Very common throughout East Africa, and very attractive in flower.

Bark: Pale brown; rough and fissured with age.
Leaves: Large; oval; up to 16 cm in length; apex tapering and base rounded; dull dark green above, paler below; veins prominent below; young shoots, leaf stalks and underside of leaves covered with soft brown hairs.
Flowers: White; showy; funnel-shaped; sweetly scented and attractive to bees; in dense terminal masses.
Fruit: Yellowish; round; about 1 cm in diameter, held in a hairy cup-shaped calyx. The seeds are enclosed in sweet, sticky flesh.
Uses: The heartwood is reddish brown; light; durable; used in the making of furniture and beehives; also as general timber and fuel. The fruit gum serves as a glue; the fruit is edible.
Traditional medicine: Fresh juice from the bark is applied to the affected area to treat broken bones.

Flowers

Fruit

Tree

Crateva adansonii

No English name known

Indigenous

Local names: Eiyoroit (Turkana); Nagarida, Koleonik (Tugen)

A savannah tree that grows 3–9 m in height, sometimes up to 15 m; found in savannah woodland at altitudes of 600–1 400 m.

Bark: Pale brown.

Leaves: Trifoliate; pale green; tufted at the end of branches; leaflets ovate-lanceolate; up to 10 cm long.

Flowers: Four pale green sepals; 4 petals; all on one side of the flower; white or creamy; stamens numerous; 2–2.5 cm long; pale lilac; green-yellow when mature; round; 2.5–5 cm across.

Fruit: Green at first, becoming yellow when mature; round; 2.5–5 cm across.

Uses: The seeds are edible; the wood is used to make implements and as fuel.

Traditional medicine: A decoction of boiled roots features in the treatment of rheumatism.

Tree

Fruit

Flowers

Flowering branches

Croton macrostachyus

EUPHORBIACEAE

Broad-leafed croton

Indigenous

Local names: Mutundu (Kikuyu); Mfurufuru (Chagga); Musogasoga (Luganda)

A medium-sized deciduous species in East Africa, the crown rounded and open with large spreading branches, occasionally growing to 25 m in height; widely distributed in both moist and dry evergreen upland forest (remnant edges), riverine forest, woodland and wooded grassland. The tree occurs at altitudes of 600–2 250 m.

Bark: Pale grey; smooth; fissured with age.

Leaves: Large; soft; green; heart-shaped; up to 15 x 10 cm; on long stems. Crowded at the edge of branchlets; vein prominent; margin slightly dentate.

Flowers: Creamy yellow; sweetly fragrant; in erect spikes up to 25 m long; short-lived but conspicuous, covering much of the tree.

Fruit: Pea-sized capsules; pale green; on drooping spikes up to 30 cm long; split open on the tree to release 3 shiny green seeds.

Uses: The wood is used for making stools, axe handles, poles and as general timber and fuelwood.

Traditional medicine: The roots serve as a remedy for stomach worms; burnt leaves are used in the treatment of coughs; a root decoction is used in the treatment of malaria, venereal diseases and coughs; leaf juice improves clotting around wounds. Bark peeled from the stem and roots and boiled in water helps protect newborn babies against skin rashes.

Flowers

Fruit

Tree

Croton megalocarpus

EUPHORBIACEAE

Croton

Indigenous

Local names: Mukinduri (Kikuyu); Mbali, Mlalai (Chagga); Nkulumire (Luganda)

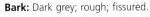

A dominant, spreading upper-storey forest tree, reaching 35 m in height, with distinctive layering of branches and a rather flat crown. It occurs in dry upland evergreen or semi-deciduous forest, moist upland forest, dense woodland and scattered tree grasslands at altitudes of 900–2 100 m.

Bark: Dark grey; rough; fissured.

Leaves: Variable; long; oval; pointed; up to 12 cm long, often shorter; silvery beneath and dull green upper surface.

Flowers: Pale yellow; hanging spikes up to 25 cm long; very short-lived; conspicuous; appear after heavy rain.

Fruit: Greyish woody capsule; about 2.5 cm long with 3 flat seeds.

Uses: The wood makes a good fuel but the smoke tends to irritate the eye. Also used for general timber and poles. Seeds have high oil and protein content, and are an effective purgative. The seeds are also eaten by birds and squirrels. The species grows as an ornamental shade tree and as a live fence. Leaf fall is extensive; leaves are used as a mulch and as green manure.

Traditional medicine: The bark has been used to kill intestinal worms and to relieve whooping cough; a concoction of the roots of *Croton megalocarpus* and *Euclea divinorum* (see page 102), boiled together, features in the treatment of chest pains, pneumonia and internal swellings.

Tree

Flowers

Fruit

Croton sylvaticus (C. oxypetalus)

EUPHORBIACEAE

Forest croton

Indigenous

Local names: Mutundu (Kikuyu, Kamba, Meru); Musogasoga (Luganda)

A forest tree that grows 7–13 m in height, occasionally up to 30 m, with a weak trunk and narrow crown; found in moist evergreen forest, thickets and forest edges at altitudes of 350–1 800 m.

Bark: Thin; grey; smooth; becoming darker and rough; smells of black pepper.

Leaves: Broadly oval; 6–15 cm long with 5–7 spreading veins; tip slightly pointed; base often rounded; stalk up to 10 cm long; old leaves turn orange before falling.

Flowers: Greenish cream; up to 3 mm long (all-male, all-female or mixed flowers); in racemes; 10–30 cm long.

Fruit: Light green when young, turning to orange or red; tri-lobed; oval in shape; hairy.

Uses: The bark is used as general timber, for poles, posts, and as fuel.

Traditional medicine: Sap from leaves is used for healing cuts; bark is used in the treatment of malaria; a decoction from the bark of the roots is taken orally as a remedy for tuberculosis; an infusion of the leaves acts as a purgative.

Flowers

Fruit

Tree

Cupressus cashmeriana

CUPRESSACEAE

Kashmir cypress

Exotic, native to Kashmir

Local name: None known

The most elegant tree in the cypress family: it has a narrow pyramidal shape with ascending branches, and long, pendulous branchlets that are prominently flattened. Grows to 12–15 m. The cones are small and dark brown.

Bark: Straight trunk; dark brown.

Leaves: Blue-green; scale-like; overlap so that no branches are visible.

Fruit: Male cones like fat tips on the ends of fertile branches; female cones small, dark brown, round.

Uses: An ornamental in gardens and along roadsides.

Tree

Cupressus lusitanica

CUPRESSACEAE

Mexican cypress

Exotic, native to Mexico, Guatemala

Local names: Mutarakwa (Kikuyu); Mtarakwa (Chagga); Omobakora (Kisii)

A fast-growing evergreen cypress that reaches 35 m in height, growing best above the altitude of 1 500 m in areas with good soil and fair rainfall. The tree has a straight trunk, and is generally conical but irregular in shape. Branches hang down but are spread wide.

Bark: Red-brown, with vertical grooves; grey with age.
Leaves: Dull blue-green; small; pointed tips; in four ranks.
Cones: Male cones look like fat tips of branchlets, produce clouds of yellow pollen dust. Female cones round, up to 1.5 cm across, ripen in two years, then open to release many small, narrow-winged seeds.
Uses: The timber is used for furniture, construction wood, fuel, poles, posts and pulp-wood. The species also makes a good hedge and shade tree.

Leaves and male cones

Tree

Female cones

Cupressus sempervirens

Italian cypress, Mediterranean cypress   Exotic, native to the Mediterranean

Local name: None known

An evergreen cypress growing to 15 m in height, though some trees can reach tremendous heights of up to 45 m in their native Mediterranean habitat.

Trunk: Straight; stiff, erect branches parallel to the stem.
Leaves: Dull blue-green; tiny; with pointed tips.
Cones: Oval; large; up to 3 m long; contains a few large, winged seeds.
Uses: This tree is planted as an ornamental in gardens with good soil.

Tree

Cupressus torulosa

CUPRESSACEAE

Himalayan cypress, Bhutan cypress

Exotic, native to the
Himalayas, Bhutan

Local name: None known

This is a tall, attractive cypress tree with a massive trunk, regularly pyramidal in shape with pendulous branches reaching to the ground if not pruned. Grows 12–15 m in height. The branchlets are often long and four-sided, flattened into one plane, with the ultimate divisions curved.

Bark: Red-brown; thick; straight trunk.

Leaves: Light green; tiny; with pointed tips.

Cones: About 1 cm in diameter; with 8–10 scales bearing small triangular bosses; often recurved; 6–8 seeds beneath each scale.

Uses: Planted as an ornamental; found in gardens, parks and in the grounds of lodges and resorts.

Tree

Cussonia holstii

Cabbage tree

Indigenous

Local names: Lulukwet (Kipsigis); Muroha (Kikuyu); Malende (Kamba)

A big, rounded tree, growing 6–15 m in height, widely distributed in highland forest, forest margins and evergreen bushland on rocky slopes, at altitudes of 1 500–2 500 m.

Bark: Rough; grey; peeling in oblong scales.

Leaves: Compound; crowded at the end of branches in large, rounded clusters; usually 5–7 leaflets; leaf stalk up to 6 cm in length; leaflets dark shiny green; margin serrated; apex pointed; veins conspicuous above. Each leaflet is about 30 cm long.

Flowers: Greenish yellow; inconspicuous; packed along thick flower spikes up to 30 cm in length; the spikes are crowded and arise from the tip of branchlets.

Fruit: Crowded very closely along the flower spikes; small and fleshy.

Uses: The trunks of these trees are hollow, and feature in the construction of beehives. The wood is soft and often used to make doors.

Traditional medicine: Some local communities use a bark decoction to clean the uterus after childbirth.

Leaves

Flowers

Tree

Cussonia spicata

ARALIACEAE

Cabbage tree, Elephant's toothbrush

Indigenous

Local names: Mwenyiere (Kikuyu); Olurur (Maasai); Sokwet (Kipsigis)

A species that reaches 6–15 m in height and looks rather like a pawpaw tree; occurs in scattered fashion on dry upland forest edges, in riverine forest and in open areas at altitudes of 1 200–2 200 m.

Bark: Grey; rough; thick and corky.

Leaves: Compound; in large clusters at the ends of branches; each up to 70 cm in diameter; leaflets usually 1–3 pairs, plus a larger terminal leaflet; dentate margin; leaflet stalk bears unusual wings.

Flowers: Greenish yellow; in spikes up to 15 cm in length; forming conspicuous heads above the leaves.

Fruit: Small; angular; soft and purple when ripe; packed along the spike.

Uses: The wood is highly perishable, used to make mole traps; roots are succulent and edible – mashed roots once featured in the treatment of malaria.

Traditional medicine: The leaves are used in the treatment of indigestion.

Tree

Flowers

Leaves

Delonix elata

No English name known

Indigenous

Local names: Ol-derkesi (Maasai); Muangi (Kamba); Ekurinchanait (Turkana)

A deciduous tree of the bushland, usually growing 4–6 m in height, sometimes up to 12 m, with a spreading crown and drooping branches. It occurs in hot, dry thorn-bush at altitudes of 100–1 000 m.

Bark: Shiny; smooth; greyish white; sometimes flaky.
Leaves: Compound; bipinnate; with 2–12 pairs of pinnae, each oval-shaped; less than 1 cm long.
Flowers: White; fading to creamy orange with 4 wavy white petals and one smaller, yellow petal; stamens orange-brown; long; protruding. Only one flower in a group opens at a time.
Fruit: Thin, reddish brown pods; tapering at both ends; up to 20 cm long; persisting on the tree.
Uses: The leaves, pods and young branches are used as fodder; the wood for making utensils, poles and posts and as fuel.
Traditional medicine: Twigs are used as toothbrushes, and are believed to cure bleeding gums and other mouth diseases. An infusion of the bark features in the treatment of bilharzia and diarrhoea.

Fruit

Flower

Tree

Delonix regia (Poinciana regia)

CAESALPINIOIDEAE

Flamboyant

Exotic, native to Madagascar

Local names: Mjohoro, Mkakaya (Swahili)

The Flamboyant is one of the most striking exotic trees found in East Africa. It reaches 10 m in height, 15 m under ideal conditions, and has an umbrella-like crown. It grows in most of the world's lowland tropical areas.

Bark: Grey; smooth.

Leaves: Light green; feathery; each compound leaf up to 45 cm long; with leaflets less than 1 cm.

Flowers: Brilliant clusters; scarlet to orange; each flower up to 10 cm across with 5 wavy petals, of which the uppermost petal is cream; heavily spotted.

Fruit: Conspicuous; dark brown; long woody pods up to 75 cm; remaining on the tree for many months.

Uses: This beautiful ornamental tree can be used for fuel, and as bee forage. Beads are fashioned from the seeds.

Flowers

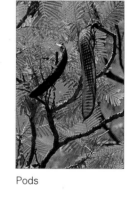

Pods

Trees

Diospyros abyssinica (Maba abyssinica)

EBENACEAE

Giant diospyros

Indigenous

Local names: Mdaa-mwitu (Swahili); Mpojwa (Luganda); Muiruthi (Kikuyu)

A tall forest tree, reaching 9–30 m, with a dark, slender trunk and mushroom-shaped crown. Occurs in coastal and highland forests at altitudes up to 2 200 m.

Bark: Very dark grey; rough; in old trees it scales off in narrow fibrous strips; the bole is long, straight, slender.
Leaves: Glossy dark green above; up to 12 cm long; lance-shaped; apex pointed; wavy margin; midrib prominent below; leaf stalk short and grooved.
Flowers: Small; creamy white (drying black); in axillary clusters.
Fruit: Round; up to 1.5 cm across; red or yellow; black when ripe; held in persistent cup-shaped calyx; sometimes in dense clusters.
Uses: The ripe fruit is much favoured by birds. It produces an excellent tough timber, used in building and furniture making, and for axe handles, knife handles and other hand tools. The wood is also good for fuel.

Fruit

Flowers

Trees

Dombeya goetzenii (D. torrida)

STERCULIACEAE

Forest dombeya

Indigenous

Local names: Mueku, Mukeu (Kikuyu); Ol-subukiai (Maasai); Gabaluwa (Lugishu)

A timber tree that reaches 15 m in height; grows mainly in the wetter highland forests of East Africa above 2 200 m, but does occur at lower altitudes.

Bark: Grey; smooth.

Leaves: Heart-shaped; broadly ovate; apex tapering; base rounded; stalk up to 12 cm long; vein network very clear below; hairy.

Flowers: Pink-red or white; 3–5 cm across; on long axillary stalks.

Fruit: Small capsules; densely hairy.

Uses: The wood is used for fuel, tool handles, bows and in building. Bark fibres are used to make rope.

Traditional medicine: A decoction of the bark is taken for indigestion, especially after a large meal of meat.

Tree

Flowers

Dombeya rotundifolia

STERCULIACEAE

White dombeya

Indigenous

Local names: Mtorobwe (Swahili); Olawuo (Maasai); Mringaringa porini (Chagga)

A small, deciduous tree, usually growing up to 4 m in height, found in dry wooded grassland at altitudes of 1 400–2 200 m.

Bark: Rough; corky; dark brown.

Leaves: Broadly ovate or rounded; rough; dark green above; hairy; 6–18 cm across; 5-veined from the base; serrated margin; leaves crispy and hard when dry.

Flowers: Showy white or pink; in axillary clusters; up to 2 cm across; sweet-scented; buds densely woolly; flowers attract many bees.

Fruit: Small, round, hairy capsules.

Uses: The wood is used to make bows, tool handles, and for fuel and general timber; leaves serve as fodder.

Traditional medicine: Boiled roots feature in the treatment of rheumatism; a juice of pounded roots, soaked in water, helps cure diarrhoea in children.

Tree

Flowers

Dovyalis abyssinica

FLACOURTIACEAE

No English name known

Indigenous

Local names: Muirungi (Kikuyu); Ol-morogi (Maasai); Songla, Sangana (Luo)

A small, spiny evergreen tree that grows to 9 m in height, sometimes shrubby, with rounded crown; common in highland forest areas, along river banks and sometimes in more open woodland; also on dry forest edges and in nearby thicket and scrubland. It occurs at altitudes of 1 800–2 500 m.

Bark: Grey; young bark covered with brown breathing pores or lenticels.

Leaves: Shiny; thin; dark green; oval to oblong; up to 5 cm long; tip blunt; edge unevenly rounded; stalk and veins reddish.

Flowers: Small; 5–8 green sepals; petals absent; female flower solitary; male flowers in clusters with 40–60 stamens.

Fruit: A round berry; about 2 cm across; surrounded by calyx; green and hairy at first, smooth, yellow-orange when ripe; sour to sweet.

Uses: The ripe fruit is edible. The species makes a good live fence; attracts bees.

Traditional medicine: Leaves are pounded and soaked in water to produce an infusion taken for indigestion.

Fruit

Dracaena steudneri

Steudner's dracaena

Indigenous

Local names: Msanaka (Swahili); Muthari (Kikuyu); Kajolyanjovu (Luganda)

A distinctive tree, growing 3–12 m in height, common in forest areas with high rainfall; occurs at altitudes of 1 200–2 000 m. The species prefers moist forest soil.

Bark: Grey-brown; trunk is often swollen at the base, and the few branches rise steeply from the woody stem.
Leaves: Narrowly lanceolate; dark, shiny green; in large terminal rosettes; can reach over 1 m in length; with no defined midrib or veins.
Flowers: Cream or pale yellow-green; 6 narrow petals joined in a tube; 6 stamens; in tight terminal clusters on green branchlets forming a massive flowering head. Flowers open at night, are sweetly scented, and fade the next day.
Fruit: Small; round; green turning orange to red.
Uses: The tree is grown as an ornamental.
Traditional medicine: A decoction of stem bark is used for the treatment of hepatic (liver) disease.

Flowers

Fruit

Tree

Encephalartos hildebrandtii

CYCADACEAE

Cycad

Indigenous

Local names: Mkwanga, Msapo (Swahili)

A non-branched, palm-like tree with a stout stem. It grows up to 6 m in height, is white and woolly when young, often appears as a rosette of dark green, spiny leaves at ground level, and is commonly found in evergreen coastal bushland and dry coastal forest at altitudes below 30 m. However, it can also grow at higher altitudes.

Bark: Thick trunk up to 6 m around; covered in leaf scars.
Leaves: Compound; up to 2.5 m in length; each leaflet linear, leathery; apex spiny; margin toothed and spiny, often near the base, borne in whorls at the top of the stem; leaflets in about 80 pairs, very stiff and tough.
Cones: Female cones dull yellow, cylindrical, up to 60 cm long; in the centre of the rosette of leaves; bear fleshy, orange-red seeds, up to 3 cm long, beneath each scale. Male cones shorter, narrower, borne on separate trees.
Uses: The fleshy seed-covering and the starchy pith of the stem are edible. The hard, nut-like kernel can be boiled, dried and ground into a flour and used to make a kind of bread.

Tree

Cones

Ensete ventricosum (E. edule) MUSACEAE

Wild banana Indigenous

Local names: Sasuriet (Kipsigis, Nandi); Ihindu (Kikuyu); Kitembe (Luganda)

A herbaceous tree, growing up to 6 m high; swollen below. It grows in wet upland valleys and ravines and along streams in the forests of lower mountain slopes, at altitudes of 1 000–2 400 m.

Trunk: False stem formed by old leaf bases.
Leaves: Large; oblong; up to 6 m long and 1 m wide; bright geen with pink-red midrib and short red stalk.
Flowers: In large hanging heads; 2–3 m long; white flowers with one petal protected by large dark red bracts; 5 stamens.
Fruit: Small, yellow clusters of inedible bananas; each about 9 cm long; whole plant dies down after fruiting.
Uses: The petiole yields a strong, fine fibre. The leaves are used for thatching. The tree is a popular ornamental.
Traditional medicine: A decoction of the stem is used to treat liver problems. Leaf or fruit juice, as well as burnt stalk ash, is taken for hepatic diseases.

Tree

Eriobotrya japonica

ROSACEAE

Loquat

Exotic, native to China, Japan

Local names: Murungati (Kikuyu); Mtangawizi (Chagga); Ekeragwati (Kisii)

A dense evergreen tree growing up to 7 m high, widely planted in the highlands at altitudes of 1 500–2 400 m. It is drought resistant when established but prefers moderate to heavy rainfall.

Bark: Grey; rough; young stems hairy; pale green.
Leaves: Stalkless; dark green; shiny above in terminal whorls; up to 35 x 10 cm; tip pointed, widest towards the apex; edge slightly dentate.
Flowers: Creamy white; scented; in woolly terminal clusters; flower bud covered with golden brown hairs.
Fruit: Yellow; pear-shaped; up to 3 cm across. Young fruit and stalk covered with soft creamy yellow hairs.
Uses: The flesh of the ripe fruit is sweet, and can be eaten raw or made into jam, jelly or syrup. The long-lasting leaves are popular for flower arrangements. Wood is used for fuel, carvings, posts and poles.

Fruit

Flowers

Tree

Erythrina abyssinica (E. tomentosa)

Red-hot poker tree, Flame tree, Lucky bean tree

Indigenous

Local names: Mwamba-ngoma (Swahili); Muyirikiti (Luganda); Mriri (Chagga)

A deciduous tree with a short trunk and thick, spreading branches, 6–12 m in height, widely distributed in scattered tree grassland, open woodland, forest edges and rocky bushland at altitudes from sea level to 2 000 m.

Bark: Yellowish brown; thick and corky; fissured; usually with thick spines.

Leaves: Trifoliate; leaflets broadly ovate; round; wider than long; terminal leaflet the largest, with 3 prominent veins rising from the base; branchlets and undersides of leaves densely covered with brownish grey hairs.

Flowers: Brilliant orange-red heads, seen all over the bare tree; slender calyx lobes and coloured petals.

Fruit: Woody; straight or curved; furry brown pods up to 10 cm long; constructed between seeds; bright red seeds with a black patch.

Uses: The round, shiny red seeds are popular as curios and for necklaces. The soft wood is used for carvings, drums, beehives, and as bee forage. The leaves can serve as fodder.

Traditional medicine: The bark is used for treating gonorrhoea; bark is also roasted until black, powdered and applied to burns and general body swellings; the bark of green stems is crushed, tied into a fine piece of cloth, and squeezed to produce a liquid used to cure inflammation of the eyelids. The roots feature in the treatment of malaria, syphilis and snakebite.

Flowers

Tree

Pods and seeds

Erythrina burtii

PAPILIONOIDEAE

Lucky bean tree, erythrina

Indigenous

Local names: Mboosi, Kikunguu (Kamba); Engaroji (Maasai)

A flat-topped deciduous tree that grows 3–15 m in height, commonly found in wooded or scattered-tree grassland and *Acacia-Commiphora* bushland at altitudes of 950–1 800 m.

Bark: Very rough and corky; deeply fissured; dark brown; usually with thick spines. Stems grey; wrinkled; roughened by leaf scars; soon become glabrous and prickly.

Leaves: Trifoliate; broadly oval or rounded; wider than long; round at the base and apex; prickles present on petiole, sometimes on midrib of leaflet.

Flowers: Red or scarlet; in dense masses 6–9 cm long; 5 petals, one bigger than the other four; the 4 small petals overlap each other; veins on petals brownish black and very prominent.

Fruit: Straight or curved pods, with red or orange seeds.

Uses: The wood is used as general timber and for making stools and camel bells. Also serves as fuel.

Fruit

Flowers

Tree

94

Erythrina lysistemom

Lucky bean tree, Flame tree

Exotic, native to South Africa

Local name: None known

This is a very attractive deciduous flowering tree that grows as a garden ornamental in East Africa. It is usually smaller than *E. abyssinica* (see page 93), reaching 5–8 m in height.

Bark: Pale grey-brown; fairly smooth; with scattered, brown, hooked thorns on the trunk.
Leaves: Trifoliate; leaflets are broadly triangular, tapering to the apex.
Flowers: Conspicuous; erect; brilliant red flower spikes; tightly packed tubular; a large tube-like petal encloses the stamens and smaller petals.
Fruit: Tightly constructed pods; black when dry; hang in clusters, which burst open on the tree to release shiny, scarlet and black seeds that resemble lucky beans.
Uses: Wood is used as fuel, for beehives and carvings.
Traditional medicine: The bark features in the treatment of sores, wounds, abscesses and arthritis; powder of burnt bark may be used to dress open wounds; an infusion of the leaves is applied as an ear-drop.

Flowers

Tree

Fruit

Eucalyptus citriodora (E. maculata *var.* citriodora)   MYRTACEAE

Lemon-scented gum, Spotted gum   Exotic, native to Australia

Local names: Mkaratusi (Swahili); Kalitunsi (Luganda)

A very tall tree, which may reach 40 m in height; grows in a wide range of climates. It has leafy, drooping foliage and a rounded crown. Easily identified by the strong lemon scent of the leaves, which perfumes the air, especially after it has rained.

Bark: Mottled, with patches of grey, brown, yellow; older bark smooth and grey-white.

Leaves: Very long and narrow; veins parallel to the edge.

Flowers: Smooth, oval buds on stalks; white flowers; in groups of 4 to 8.

Fruit: Cup-shaped; about 1 cm across; in clusters.

Uses: The timber is hard; used to make poles, posts and in construction work.

Traditional medicine: Leaves produce an essential oil used for the treatment of colds, coughs, flu and asthma.

Bark

Tree

Eucalyptus ficifolia

Red flowering gum

Exotic, native to southwestern Australia

Local name: None known

An ornamental tree with the showiest flowers of all gum trees, a favourite for park and domestic gardens. The species grows up to 10 m in height (although it is often smaller); the crown is more or less rounded. Commonly seen in the wetter highlands.

Bark: Dark; rough and fissured.
Leaves: Alternate; lance-shaped; broad; with a pale yellow midrib.
Flowers: Large; in terminal clusters; colours of the stamen vary from deep crimson or pale pink to white.
Fruit: Big; bell-shaped; 2–4 cm long; in heavy clusters.
Uses: This is a splendid ornamental species.

Pink flowers

Tree

Crimson flowers

White flowers and fruit

Eucalyptus globulus

MYRTACEAE

Tasmanian blue gum

Exotic, native to southwestern Australia

Local names: Mkaratusi (Swahili); Mbanyi (Chagga)

A dense species that reaches 55 m in height; found at the higher altitudes; tolerates frost. The tree is rather narrow, its crown rounded and open, the main stems straight.

Bark: Blue-grey; smooth.

Leaves: Young leaves opposite; oval; blue-grey without stalks; mature leaves deep blue-green; very long and thin; up to 30 cm long; slightly curved; stalked; tip sharp; smell of camphor if crushed.

Flowers: Buds grey-green; wrinkled; 2.5 cm across; flower white, usually single, rarely 2 or 3.

Fruit: Woody half-spheres; rough; 3 cm across; stalkless.

Uses: The timber is very hard; used for light and heavy construction, poles, posts and plywood, and as fuel.

Traditional medicine: Leaves are boiled to produce an essential oil, which is used variously in the treatment of influenza, coughs, colds, hay fever and asthma.

Mature tree

Young tree

Flowers and mature seeds

Young seeds and flowers

Eucalyptus maculata

Spotted gum

Exotic, native to eastern Australia

Local name: None known

A tall tree with a distinctive, spotted stem, growing to 40 m in height, sometimes more; found at altitudes of 1 800 m and higher.

Bark: Jig-saw patterned; cracking into patches of grey, brown or pale yellow; older bark smooth; greyish white.
Leaves: Long; narrow; with numerous thin veins parallel to the margin.
Flowers: Small; white; in groupings of 6 to 8.
Fruit: Bell-shaped; about 1 cm long.
Uses: The wood is used for general timber, poles and posts and as fuel. The species is grown as a shady ornamental in towns.

Flowers and seeds

Tree

Eucalyptus paniculata

MYRTACEAE

Grey iron bark gum

Exotic, native to Australia

Local name: None known

A very tall tree, reaching up to 55 m in height; conical when young; hardy; fairly slow-growing and found at high altitudes.

Bark: Dark brown; distinctive; deeply fissured.
Leaves: Long; narrow.
Flowers: Very small; white; in clusters.
Fruit: Small; up to 7 mm long.
Uses: The timber is very hard and resistant to decay; useful for poles and in heavy construction work.

Flowers and seeds

Tree

Bark

Eucalyptus saligna

Sydney blue gum

Exotic, native to coastal eastern Australia

Local names: Mkaratusi, Mtimbao (Swahili); Mbanyi (Chagga); Muringamu (Kikuyu)

A straight, massive tree growing up to 60 m in height, with a round, open (not dense) crown. It is the dominant Eucalyptus of the highland region, found at altitudes of 200–2 400 m.

Bark: Rough; brown; peeling in strips lower down; upper bark smooth; greenish white.

Leaves: Long and thin; often sickle-shaped; up to 20 cm in length.

Flowers: Small; white; 4–8 flowers in each group; buds pointed green cones.

Fruit: Small capsules; 4–8 together; conical; with protruding valves.

Uses: The wood is used for furniture, veneer/plywood, posts, poles, in construction, and as fuel. The species is very common in towns, where it provides both shade and decoration.

Flowers and seeds

Tree

Euclea divinorum (E. Keniensis)

EBENACEAE

Euclea

Indigenous

Local names: Mdaa (Swahili); Iwaruka, Mkenye (Chagga); Mukinyai (Kikuyu)

A small, many-branched evergreen tree, growing to 10 m in height; can have a rounded crown, but shape varies; widespread in dry forest margins, wooded grassland and evergreen bushland. It occurs at altitudes of up to 2 400 m.

Bark: Grey-brown; becomes darker, then cracks and flakes with age.

Leaves: Opposite; dull green; stiff; long and narrowly oval; up to 8 cm; tip blunt; edge wavy.

Flowers: Very small; creamy white; fragrant flowers in small sprays that persist after fading; short-lived.

Fruit: Round; small; up to 5 cm; green at first, purple-black when ripe.

Uses: The wood is hard and close-grained, widely used in hut construction, for tool handles and as general timber. Twigs serve as toothbrushes.

Traditional medicine: A soup made from bark and roots is used as a purgative by certain groups; infusions of dried and powdered roots have served as remedies for headaches and toothaches; dried and powdered bark infusions are used as an appetizer.

Tree

Flowers

Fruit

Eugenia jambos

Rose apple

Exotic, native to India, Malaysia

Local name: None known

An evergreen ornamental fruit tree, growing up to 8 m in height; spreading.

Bark: Grey; slightly rough.
Leaves: Lance-shaped; up to 20 cm; opposite; dark glossy green above. Young leaves and stems have a pink flush.
Flowers: Creamy white; up to 10 cm across; scented terminal heads; stamens white and very prominent.
Fruit: Round; up to 4 cm across; green, turning yellow tinged with pink when ripe; rose-scented; calyx lobes large and persistent on the fruit.
Uses: The ripe fruit is quite soft and edible; used to make jelly and jam.

Fruit

Tree

Flowers

Euphorbia bussei *var.* Kibwezensis   EUPHORBIACEAE

No English name known   Indigenous

Local name: Kithui (Kamba); Kithuri (Kikuyu)

A succulent tree, reaching a height of up to 6 m or more, mostly found in semi-arid and arid areas of thicket bush, on rocky shores at the coast, at altitudes from sea level to 2 000 m.

Bark: Long, cylindrical bole surrounded by a crown of curved ascending succulent branches; branches grey-green, hairless, 2–5 winged, segmented, up to 14 cm wide; spine shield continuous, spines 0.5–3 cm long.

Leaves: Deciduous; very small.

Flowers: Golden yellow; in clusters; 6–7 mm across.

Fruit: Three-angled; up to 9 x 16 mm; red.

Uses: Wood is used in the building of grain stores.

Flowers

Trees

Euphorbia candelabrum

EUPHORBIACEAE

Tree euphorbia, Candelabra euphorbia

Indigenous

Local names: Mtungutungii, Mtupa (Swahili); Ol-bobongo (Maasai); Epopong (Ateso)

An attractive savannah tree that grows to 15 m or more in height, with a short, thick trunk up to 90 cm in diameter. A crown of massive ascending branches is its characteristic feature. The tree is widely distributed on steep rocky slopes and rocky outcrops in bushland, thickets and wooded grassland from the coast to an altitude of 1 800 m.

Stems: Four-winged; dark green; wavy when young; constricted at irregular intervals, bearing small paired spines; all branches succulent; spines may be absent in older trees.

Flowers: Yellow-green; in small groups of 3–6 above the pairs of spines; fleshy; with 5 glands.

Fruit: Green; 2–3-lobed; pea-sized.

Uses: Flowers attract bees but the honey cannot be eaten as it irritates and burns the mouth. The soft branches produce a very sticky white latex, which is extremely poisonous – a single drop in the eye can cause blindness, and will blister the skin of a cow.

Traditional medicine: A decoction of the stem is administered to women after childbirth to clear out the afterbirth (this is done with extreme caution).

Tree

Flowers

Euphorbia robecchii

EUPHORBIACEAE

No English name known

Indigenous

Local names: Dagerai, Shatetai (Maasai); Eopong (Turkana)

A familiar tree, growing 5–10 m in height, commonly found in dry bushland as well as in *Acacia-Commiphora* bushland, at altitudes from sea level to 1 800 m.

Bark: Grey; with succulent branches; cylindrical; 1.5–2.5 cm wide and spineless when mature; 3–4-angled; with recurved spines of up to 1 cm when young.
Leaves: Deciduous; very small.
Flowers: Yellow-green, in short cymes.
Fruit: Purple-grey, 3-angled; up to 15 mm across.

Trees

Ficus benjamina

Weeping fig, Java fig

Exotic, native to India, Malaysia, Indonesia

Local name: None known

A huge, evergreen, shady tree that reaches 10–20 m in height, with drooping foliage; hardy and fast-growing, with an extensive and strong root system; powerful enough to crack walls and tarmac.

Bark: Grey, with horizontal markings.
Leaves: Shiny, dark green; narrowly oval; up to 8 cm long; tapering tip.
Fruit: Orange to red; hard berries; often in pairs, axillary; about 1 cm across.
Uses: The Weeping fig is increasing in popularity as both an indoor and outdoor plant.

Tree

Fruit

Ficus elastica

MORACEAE

Indian rubber plant

Exotic, native to Southeast Asia

Local names: None known

A dense evergreen tree growing up to 30 m in height, occurring from the coast to the highlands. It is popular as a pot plant both indoors and outdoors. Its common name (Rubber plant) refers to a rubber-like latex contained in its stems and foliage.

Trunk: Greyish brown, multi-stemmed.
Leaves: Large, shiny, dark-green, up to 30 cm long; ovate-elongate in shape, with pointed tips. The young leaves appear wrapped in a bright red bract.
Uses: The species is at its best as an ornamental and shade tree; should be planted well away from walls because of its strong root system.

Young leaves

Tree

Ficus lutea (F. quibeba, F. vogelii)

Fig tree

Indigenous

Local names: Mumbu (Kikuyu), Mkuyu (Digo)

A spreading evergreen tree reaching 16 m in height; occasionally epiphytic; may have aerial roots; often grows in wetter forests (edges), riverine forest or woodland, occasionally on rocks, at altitudes between sea level and 2 000 m. This is a huge, shady tree with a powerful root system.

Bark: Grey-brown.

Leaves: Elliptic; about 20 cm long; apex pointed, base round; leaf stalk long, up to 12 cm. The leaves arise in dense spirals from rather stout branchlets, which end in small pointed buds.

Fruit: Figs in leaf axils or just below the leaf; sessile; fig green to yellow or orange when ripe; softly hairy; young fruit bear a brown cap, which falls off as the fruit matures.

Uses: The ripe figs are much favoured by birds, monkeys and baboons; leaves are used as fodder.

Tree

Fruit

Branches with fruit

Ficus natalensis

MORACEAE

Bark cloth fig

Indigenous

Local names: Mugumo (Kikuyu); Mutuba (Luganda); Mugaire (Lusoga)

A big, leafy, deciduous tree growing to 30 m in height, scattered throughout riverine and ground-water forest, at altitudes of 900–1 800 m above sea level. The species is very similar to *Ficus thonningii* (see page 113). The commonest fig tree in Uganda, it occurs over most of Africa but is less common in Kenya than in the rest of the region.

Bark: Grey, smooth.

Leaves: Variable; generally oval; up to 12 cm; apex rounded; petiole 1.5 cm long.

Fruit: Figs in leaf axils; 8–18 mm across on stalks 2–10 mm in length; leafy bracts at the base of the fruit, which fall off early.

Uses: Bark cloth is made from this tree. The fabric was once used for ceremonial wear and for wall hangings, and is still used for burial shrouds in central Uganda.

Traditional medicine: The bark is crushed and boiled in water. The extract is then drunk as a remedy for influenza. Fresh bark is chewed and the juice swallowed to induce lactation.

Leaves and fruit

Tree

Ficus sur (F. capensis)

Cape fig

Indigenous

Local names: Mukuyu (Kikuyu), Ol-ngaboli (Maasai), Kabalira (Luganda)

A spreading deciduous tree growing to 25 m in height. The crown is rounded, the trunk often buttressed. Widespread in riverine forest and well-watered grassland, less frequent in forest away from water; occurs from sea level to an altitude of 2 100 m.

Bark: Grey to pale grey; smooth; coarsens with age.
Leaves: Broadly oval; large, up to 20 x 13 cm; upper surface smooth; margin dentate, entire or wavy; veins prominent below; grooved stalk, up to 6 cm long.
Fruit: In heavy clusters on branches; figs rounded; usually up to 3 cm, occasionally 5 cm across; orange to red when ripe; covered with short hairs.
Uses: Ripe figs are edible, although often full of insects.
Traditional medicine: An infusion from the pounded bark is used as a cure for stomachache and diarrhoea; the milky sap from a cut branch serves as a remedy for toothache; a decoction of the roots is taken for coughing. The species also features in the traditional ceremonies of certain tribes.

Fruit

Tree

Ficus sycomorus (F. gnaphalocarpa, F. mucoso)   MORACEAE

Sycamore fig   Indigenous

Local names: Mukuyu (Kikuyu); Ol-gnagboli (Maasai); Mukunyu (Luganda)

A large, deciduous, spreading tree, occasionally buttressed, growing up to 21 m. Widespread near rivers, in the drier woodland and in bushland, at altitudes from sea level to 1 850 m.

Bark: Distinctive; yellow to creamy brown; smooth; cracks with age.

Leaves: Oval to almost circular; up to 12 cm long; upper surface rough; margin wavy, roughly dentate; base heart-shaped; hairy stalk up to 3 cm long.

Fruit: In leaf axils or in dense clusters of figs on main trunk or branches; each rounded; up to 4 cm across, yellow-red when ripe; edible.

Uses: The wood is used for doors, carvings, in house construction and as fuel. The inner part of the root yields a fibre used for weaving. Fruits are eaten by birds, monkeys, baboons and hyraxes.

Traditional medicine: A bark decoction is taken as a remedy for abdominal pains and stomach disorders.

Fruit

Tree

112

Ficus thonningii (F. eriocarpa)

MORACEAE

Wild fig, Strangler fig

Indigenous

Local names: Ol-endeti, Oretiti (Maasai); Mkuu (Chagga); Mugumo (Kikuyu)

A large, evergreen species, reaching up to 25 m in height; sometimes epiphytic, often buttressed or multi-stemmed from the growth of aerial roots. The tree has a wide spread, and occurs in both wet and dry upland forest, open grassland and in riverine areas at altitudes of 1 000–2 500 m above sea level.

Bark: Grey; smooth; often many aerial roots present.

Leaves: Variable; generally oval; up to 12 cm, but often smaller; rounded apex, base rounded or tapering; young leaves pale and hairy below.

Fruit: In axillary clusters on terminal branches, prominent on the bare trees; round; small, up to 1.5 cm across; stalk absent or very short; smooth or bumpy; yellow or purple-red when ripe; attract birds, small mammals and monkeys.

Uses: Leaves used for fodder, mulch and green manure; bark fibre used for string; branches for fire-sticks. The tree is regarded as the sacred home of ancestral spirits among several tribal groups, including the Kikuyu, and serves as an important ceremonial meeting place.

Traditional medicine: Both the root and bark are either boiled or pounded, soaked in water and the infusion taken to induce lactation. The bark is also used in the treatment of influenza.

Tree

Fruit

Filicium decipiens

Fern-leaf tree, Thika palm

Indigenous

Local name: Kamiti (Kikuyu)

A well-shaped evergreen tree that grows to 8 m in height, occasionally to 25 m; occurs in riverine forest and swampy sites in forests; also widely planted in the highland areas; grows at altitudes of 100–1 500 m above sea level.

Bark: Grey; smooth; becomes dark brown, fissured.

Leaves: Compound; up to 30 cm in length, with conspicuously winged stalks; leaflets 6–10 pairs, each long and narrow, up to 14 x 2 cm; apex round; leaflet stalks absent.

Flowers: White; very small; in branched axillary panicles; 12 cm long.

Fruit: Purple-black when ripe; small; round berries.

Uses: An ornamental shade-tree. Ripe fruit eaten by birds. The wood is used as fuel.

Berries

Flowers

Tree

Fraxinus pennsylvanica

OLEACEAE

Mexican ash, Green ash

Exotic, native to North America

Local name: None known

A spreading, shapely, deciduous tree that grows up to 15 m, widely planted at high altitudes (of 1 500–2 800 m above sea level).

Bark: Grey; becomes darker and cracks with age.

Leaves: Compound; opposite; up to 30 cm long; rather crowded at the ends of branches; leaflets 2–3 pairs plus a terminal leaflet; unequal-sided; up to 18 cm long; spear-shaped, tapering apex, toothed margin towards the apex.

Flowers: Without petals; male stamens purple-brown; female flowers separate, very small, lime-green; both in terminal sprays.

Fruit: Single-winged; up to 5 cm on thin stalk, hang for a long time in dry, light-brown clusters on the tree.

Uses: The wood is used as general timber, for making posts, and as fuel. Leaves are used as cattle fodder. The tree provides good shade and is an excellent windbreak.

Flower

Tree

Fruit

Grevillea robusta

PROTEACEAE

Silky oak, Grevillea

Exotic, native to eastern Australia

Local names: Mgrivea (Swahili); Meresi (Chagga); Mukima (Kikuyu)

A semi-deciduous, naturalized tree reaching 20 m or more in height, very fast-growing, widely planted at altitudes of 1 200 m above sea level. It does best in areas with deep soil and good rainfall, but tolerates poorer soils.

Bark: Dark grey; rough; furrowed vertically.

Leaves: Distinctive; deeply divided; fern-like; up to 3 cm long; leathery olive-green above, silky silvery grey below; fallen leaves grey, stiff, slow to decompose.

Flowers: Numerous; in one-sided golden orange spikes up to 12 cm in length; showy.

Fruit: Dark capsules, about 1 cm long, with slender beaks; young capsule grey-green in colour; splits to release two winged seeds.

Uses: The timber is tough and durable, used for quality furniture, veneer/plywood, fuel, posts, fencing and wooden toys. Leaves serve as fodder.

Flowers and seeds

Flowering branch

Trees

Hagenia abyssinica (Brayera anthelmintica)   ROSACEAE

Hagenia   Indigenous

Local names: Muthithiku (Kikuyu); Mlanga (Chagga); Kisichetwa (Lugishu)

A beautiful tree of the upland and high mountain forest regions, growing to 20 m in height. The species is confined to Africa, occurring at altitudes of 2 400–3 600 m, occasionally in lower areas. The crown is leafy and rounded.

Bark: Reddish brown, flakes irregularly; branchlets covered in silky brown hairs and ringed with leaf scars.
Leaves: Compound; up to 40 cm long; in large terminal tufts; leaflets bright green, with silvery hair below, red and sticky when young; 5 or 6 pairs and a terminal leaflet; leaf edge dentate and fringed with hairs; stalk winged, hairy.
Flowers: In large, attractive masses; up to 60 cm in length; female heads pink-red, male heads more feathery, orange-white.
Fruit: Small; dry; one-sided.
Uses: The hard, dark-red wood is used in carpentry, for flooring, for carving, and as fuel.
Traditional medicine: Dried female flower-heads serve as a powerful remedy for intestinal worms (especially tapeworms); an infusion of the bark cures diarrhoea and stomachache. This is a strong medicine and is taken in small quantities. It is also used to induce abortion.

Flowers

Tree

Leaf tuft

Harpephyllum caffrum

ANACARDIACEAE

Wild plum

Exotic, native to South Africa

Local name: None known

A large, evergreen, high-branching, single-stemmed tree that grows 10–15 m in height, sometimes up to 25 m. It has a round, dense canopy.

Bark: Light brown; smooth in young tree; becomes darker and rougher, fissured in older trees.

Leaves: Compound; clusters in a spiral towards the end of thick, unbranched twigs; leaflets in 4–10 pairs; sickle-shaped; stalkless; with a single leaflet at the tip. Leaflets leathery, shiny, dark green above, paler below.

Flowers: Small; white; star-shaped; in long sprays in the centre of leaf whirlpools.

Fruit: Plum-like; smooth, fleshy berries; oblong; hang in bunches from the centre of the whirlpool; green turning to apple-red when ripe.

Uses: The wood is used for furniture. Fruit is edible; the sour pulp makes a good jelly.

Traditional medicine: A bark extract was used as an emetic and blood purifier, and for skin problems such as acne and eczema. Certain South African tribes applied powdered burnt bark to broken skin to treat sprains and fractures.

Tree

Berries

Ipomoea arborescens

Morning glory tree

Exotic, native to Central America

Local name: None known

A small deciduous tree with arching branches, 3–4 m in height, often multi-stemmed. Morning glory thrives in hot, dry areas at most altitudes.

Bark: Pale grey.
Leaves: Heart-shaped; tapering to the apex and unfolding from the centre; soft texture; veins clear; wavy margin; stalk up to 5 cm long.
Flowers: White; funnel-shaped; up to 10 cm across; the flowers often cover the tree for several weeks before the leaves develop. The flowers start from the short, rounded calyx as pink-tipped buds, and close at night.
Fruit: Dry oval capsules; up to 2 cm long; dark brown; split on the tree into 4 parts; seeds black.
Uses: An attractive ornamental plant when in flower.

Flowers

Seeds

Tree

Jacaranda mimosifolia

BIGNONIACEAE

Jacaranda, Brazilian rosewood

Exotic, native to Brazil

Local names: Mucakaranda (Kikuyu); Omosaria (Kisii)

A deciduous tree, spectacular in full-flower bloom, reaching up to 20 m in height, grows in most soils except waterlogged ones. The Jacaranda occurs widely throughout East Africa at altitudes of up to 2 200 m above sea level. It fares best in the highlands but can also grow in some of the drier areas.

Leaves: Fern-like and feathery; bipinnate; crowded in terminal whorls; numerous leaflets, very small; with pointed apex; leaflets bright green when young, becoming darker with age.

Flowers: Striking mauve-blue clusters; bell-shaped; tree mostly in flower when not in leaf.

Fruit: Flattened; rounded (circular), woody capsules with wavy edges; up to 7 cm in diameter; green when young, brown to black when mature; split on the tree to release numerous seeds with transparent wings.

Uses: This species is used for fuel, as general timber, to make carvings, as fencing, and it is frequently planted as an ornamental.

Seed capsules

Flowers

Tree

Juniperus procera

African pencil cedar

Indigenous

Local names: Mutarakwa (Kikuyu); Ntorokya (Lugishu); Nso, Mtarakwa (Chagga)

A large, evergreen, valuable timber tree, growing up to 40 m in height; has a straight trunk, pyramidal shape when young, spreading later. Occurs in highland forest, rocky hills and mountains at altitudes of 1 500–3 000 m.

Bark: Grey-brown; thin; fissured; peels with age.

Leaves: Young leaves prickly, needle-like; up to 1 cm long; mature leaves scale-like, blue-green, triangular, closely overlapping on the branchlets.

Cones: Male cones small and yellow with pollen; female cones purple-blue, fleshy, berry-like.

Uses: Timber used in house-building and to make poles, posts, furniture, pencils and beehives, and as fuel.

Traditional medicine: Young twigs and buds are ground, soaked in water, and the infusion is taken as a remedy for intestinal worms.

Female berries

Juvenile foliage

Tree

Bark

Kigelia africana (K. aethiopum)

BIGNONIACEAE

Sausage tree

Indigenous

Local names: Mwegea (Swahili); Ol-darboi (Maasai); Mussa (Luganda)

A tree with a rounded crown, grows to a height of 9 m in open woodland, 18 m in riverine areas. Widespread throughout East Africa; found in wet savannah and along rivers in dry areas, from the coast to the highlands, at altitudes from sea level to 1 850 m.

Bark: Grey-brown; smooth; becomes fissured and flakes with age.

Leaves: Compound; wavy; occur in threes; crowded at the ends of branches; 3–5 pairs plus a terminal leaflet, each broadly elliptic; up to 10 cm in length; apex round or tapering, often with a sharp tip.

Flowers: On long rope-like stalks; 2–3 m; each containing up to 12 dark maroon flowers; unpleasantly scented; with trumpet-shaped petals, folded and wavy.

Fruit: Large, grey-green 'sausages'; heavy; about 30–70 cm long; hanging stalks remain on the tree.

Uses: The unripe fruits are poisonous; ripe fruits, although inedible, are baked and sliced to help fermentation of local beer.

Traditional medicine: A decoction from the bark serves as a remedy for headaches and dysentery; a leaf decoction is taken for malaria. The dried fruit is powdered and used as a dressing for ulcers, sores, and syphilis, and is also applied locally for rheumatism. Beer made from the fruit appears to be an excellent cure for childhood measles (the patient is washed with it; no soap is used). The fruit is also reported to be purgative. A decoction of fruit and bark may also be taken for juvenile stomach ailments. The fruit is also known to induce abortion.

Fruit

Flowers

Tree

Macadamia tetraphylla

PROTEACEAE

Macadamia nut

Exotic, native to northern Australia

Local name: Mukandania (Kikuyu)

A low-branched evergreen tree that reaches 15 m in height; it grows in the coffee-producing areas of the highlands and yields a valuable nut.

Bark: Grey; smooth.

Leaves: In clusters of 4; dull to olive-green; wavy; margin with sharp-pointed spines; texture tough; midrib prominent below; young leaves and shoots often entirely pinkish red.

Flowers: Slender; whitish or lilac-coloured; in axillary drooping spikes; up to 25 cm in length.

Fruit: Hard, round nut; up to 3 cm across; the husk dries black and contains the exceptionally hard, shiny brown nutshell. The kernels are white, with a very high oil content.

Uses: A tree with high commercial value and a good cash crop. The white kernels are delicately flavoured and delicious when roasted. The oil features in the cosmetics and animal-feed industries; the shell is used for charcoal. Older trees provide a useful all-purpose timber.

Tree

Young fruit

Flowers

Mature fruit

Maerua triphylla ssp. johannis

CAPPARACEAE

Small bead-bean, Maerua

Indigenous

Local names: Ol-amalogi (Maasai); Mutumburu (Kikuyu); Kipegero (Hehe)

An erect or scandent small tree or shrub, growing 4–6 m in height, with a round crown; evergreen, widely found in evergreen or deciduous bushlands, wooded grassland, thickets and the margins of the drier forests, and along rivers and lakes. It occurs at altitudes from sea level to 2 300 m.

Bark: Brownish grey.

Leaves: Dull; grey-green; simple or 1–3-foliate; narrowly oval; 2–10 cm long; apex rounded, often notched.

Flowers: Small; whitish; several flowers in a head; greenish white stamens prominent; 4 green sepals joined in a tube below the petal.

Fruit: Smooth; pale creamy brown and furry; constricted between the seeds; cylindrical; 5–10 cm long.

Uses: Fruit is edible if boiled for a long time. Flowers attract many bees and butterflies. Leaves are browsed by domestic stock and wild game (including elephant).

Traditional medicine: An infusion from the roots has served as a remedy for snakebite; the roots are used to cure headache and, when mixed with lemon juice, as an aphrodisiac.

Flowers

Tree

Fruit

Mangifera indica

Mango   Exotic, native to northern India, Burma

Local names: Mwembe (Swahili); Muyembe (Luganda); Maembe (Luo)

A densely leafed evergreen tree with sturdy trunk and rounded crown; grows 10–15 m in height; one of the most important fruit trees of the tropics, planted from sea level to 2 000 m.

Bark: Dark brown; cracks with age.

Leaves: Dark green; alternate; crowded at the end of branches; up to 30 cm long. Younger leaves soft, copper-coloured and wavy; mature leaves leathery, lance-shaped; midrib prominent below.

Flowers: Numerous; small; cream to pinkish brown; pyramidal heads; pollinated by flies and other insects.

Fruit: Large and heavy; up to 15 cm in length; variable shapes, round to oval; ripen from green to yellow, red or orangey pink. Each fruit has a large seed surrounded by golden, juicy flesh; very rich in vitamins A and C.

Uses: The flesh of the fruit is eaten when ripe; also used to make fresh juice and jam. The wood provides a good fuel; also used in small-boat (canoe) construction. Leaves serve as fodder, mulch and green leaf manure.

Flowers

Tree

Fruit

Markhamia lutea

BIGNONIACEAE

Markhamia   **Indigenous**

Local names: Muu, Muho (Kikuyu); Msambia (Haya); Nsambya (Luganda)

An upright, evergreen tree with a narrow, irregular crown, usually 10–15 m in height, found in tree bushland, grassland and highland areas at altitudes of 1 000–2 000 m. The species can tolerate acid, heavy clay soil, but not waterlogging.

Bark: Reddish brown; finely cracked.

Leaves: Compound; often in bunches; thin and wavy; each leaflet up to 10 cm long; 7–11 leaflets; wider towards the apex and narrowing towards the base; veins are prominent.

Flowers: Bright yellow; terminal clusters; trumpet-shaped; with 5 frilly orange-red stripes in the throat; buds furry; splitting on one side.

Fruit: Very long, thin capsules; brown; twisted; linear; 40–80 cm long; hang in spiral clusters; split on the tree to release many flat-winged seeds.

Uses: Leaves used as mulch. Timber is hard, tough, and termite-resistant; used for fuel, furniture, poles, posts, tool handles, general timber and in boat-building.

Traditional medicine: The leaves are used in the treatment of snakebite; powdered bark forms part of a medicinal compound taken for syphilis; bark is also chewed to alleviate toothache.

Tree

Flowers

Fruit

Melia azedarach

Persian lilac, Bead tree

Exotic, native to western Asia, Himalayas

Local names: Mwarubaini nusu (Swahili); Lira (Luganda); Dwele (Luo)

A popular deciduous tree, reaching up to 10 m in height; grows in most soils, both acidic and saline, at altitudes from sea level to 2 000 m.

Bark: Grey; smooth; rough and brown with age; branchlets have bumpy lenticels.

Leaves: Compound; leaflets pale green at first, then become a dark shiny green later; hang in terminal bunches; leaflets slightly dentate, pointed.

Flowers: Small; scented; pale lilac at first, later turning white; in profuse rounded clusters; each tiny flower with a dark purple staminal tube.

Fruit: Fleshy yellow berries; 1.5 m in diameter; clusters of berries are prominent and persist on the bare tree.

Uses: Berries are extremely poisonous to humans, livestock and poultry. The timber is used for making furniture, poles, tool handles, posts and as fuel. Seeds are hard, and can be strung as beads.

Traditional medicine: Leaves and bark used to treat malaria; oil from seeds to treat skin rashes and itching.

Berries

Flowers

Tree

Michelia champaca

MAGNOLIACEAE

Fragrant champaca, Orange champak   Exotic, Himalaya region, India, Java

Local name: None known

A small, evergreen tree with rounded crown, usually growing to 10 m in height, but occasionally to 30 m.

Bark: Grey; smooth.

Leaves: Large; oval; glossy above; paler and duller below; up to 25 cm in length; tapering to pointed apex; midrib prominent below; side veins regular, tapering off before the margin; margin wavy.

Flowers: Orange-yellow, turning brown; sweet-scented; up to 7 cm across with 15–20 waxy, pointed sepals and petals in whorls; stamens short.

Fruit: Tightly packed groups of capsules, each 1 cm long; green in colour, covered in white wart-like dots; crowded in terminal clusters up to 15 cm in length. Fruit turns from green to brown to black, splitting on the tree to release 2–5 tightly packed pink, angular seeds.

Uses: Seeds produce a scented oil when crushed. Champaca oil, which features in the production of some of the finest French perfumes, is distilled from the flowers. Wood is used for poles and general timber.

Tree with fruit

Flowers and young fruit

Millettia dura

Millettia   Indigenous

Local names: Muhatia (Kikuyu); Omulongo (Haya); Mutete (Rukiga)

A small deciduous flowering tree, growing to 12 m in height in secondary scrub and moist forest edges. It is found at altitudes of 1 500–2 000 m above sea level. Hardy and drought resistant; grows moderately fast in forest soil.

Bark: Grey; smooth; with fine vertical scales.

Leaves: Compound; dull green; 5–12 pairs; up to 5 cm long; often unequal-sided; pointed tip; young leaflets and leaf stalks covered with short, rust-coloured hairs.

Flowers: Lilac or purplish; in dense clusters; up to 20 cm in length; often on the bare tree.

Fruit: Thick, flat pods; up to 25 x 2 cm; bluntly pointed; hang singly or in small clusters; split open explosively.

Uses: The wood, which is tough and durable, is used for poles and to make handles for implements. Leaves serve as fodder, mulch and green-leaf manure.

Fruit pods

Flowers

Trees

Moringa oleifera

MORINGACEAE

Drumstick tree, Horseradish tree

Exotic, native to India, Arabia

Local names: Mlonge, Mzunze (Swahili); Mlonge (Lugu)

A feathery-looking, deciduous tree growing up to 10 m, but usually shorter; commonly planted in well-drained soil at the coast and at low altitudes (usually sea level to 500 m).

Bark: Grey; thick and corky; peeling in patches.

Leaves: Pale green; thrice compound; 30–60 cm long; leaflets oval; tip rounded; 1–2 cm long.

Flowers: Cream, fading to yellow; in long sprays; sweet-scented; attract insects.

Fruit: Long, hanging, stick-like capsules; up to 45 cm in length; bluntly triangular in cross-section; split when dry to release dark-brown three-winged seeds from the pith.

Uses: The leaves and young green fruit are popular as vegetables and for use in curries; oil from the seeds, known as 'ben oil', is used in salads, for skin poultices, and for making soap. The seeds have some commercial application (they are exported from Sri Lanka for use in the French cosmetic and textile industries). The powder ground from the seeds serves as a water purifier and also in the treatment of scurvy.

Flowers

Tree

Fruit

Moringa stenopetala

Moringa   Indigenous

Local names: Lorsanjo (Samburu); Mau, Mawali (Somali)

A very graceful tree, growing up to 12 m in height, with bright green, feathery foliage, often found in riverine and lakeside areas, also in dry areas (often on rocky ground), at altitudes of 450–1 200 m above sea level.

Bark: Smooth; white to pale grey.

Leaves: Compound; 2–3 pinnate; leaflets ovate; base rounded; apex acute; in 5 pairs.

Flowers: White or yellowish; scented; numerous.

Fruit: Typically long, three-angled fruit capsule; reddish with grey bloom.

Uses: Powder ground from the seed of this plant is used as a water purifier. The roots serve as a powerful medicine for stomach ailments.

Traditional medicine: A leaf infusion is taken for leprosy and fever.

Fruit

Tree

Leaves

Morus alba

MORACEAE

Mulberry

Exotic, native to China

Local names: Mforsadi, Mfurusadi (Swahili); Nkenene (Luganda)

A small deciduous tree, growing 6–8 m in height, sometimes taller; loosely rounded in shape. The species prefers a moist climate.

Bark: Pale brown; smooth.

Leaves: Heart-shaped; 3 veins from the base; about 10 cm long; coarsely dentate; pointed apex; long stalk.

Flowers: Dioecious; small; greenish; in drooping spikes.

Fruit: Compound; up to 5 cm long; pink to dark maroon; sweet and juicy.

Uses: The juicy, sweet fruit is used to make jams and chutneys. Silkworms feed on the leaves. Wood is used for fuel; leaves as fodder. The tree serves as a good live fence or hedgerow.

Fruit

Tree

Leaves

132

Musa paradisiaca

MUSACEAE

Plantain, Starch banana

Exotic, native to Indonesia

Local names: Matooke (Swahili); Gonja, Mbidde (Luganda); Isubi (Rukiga)

A tree-like perennial herb, usually growing 2–6 m in height, with a basal corm below ground and milky sap in all parts. Plantain or starch bananas are grown throughout the global equatorial belt from the Atlantic to the Indian oceans, and form a mainstay of the Ugandan economy.

Flower and fruit

Stem: The lower leaf stalks and sheaths are folded around each other to make a 'false stem' from which the upper leaf blades push out and spread into the light.

Leaves: Arise in a spiral, about 30 together, each made up of a sheath; leaf stalk 30–90 cm long; a leaf blade emerges as a roll that slowly unfolds. Lateral veins are at right angles to the midrib; wind may tear the blade into strips along the veins. Old leaves hang down and the blades die.

Flowers: Single; large flowering head curves downwards; the head arises from the tip of the corm, taking 9–10 months to develop, emerging between the leaves. Its thick stalk bears many flower clusters in spirals. Each cluster of 12–20 flowers in two rows is covered by a large red-brown or purple bract with a waxy blue bloom on the outside. All flowers are rich in nectar; have a female pistil and male stamens, but only the first 5–15 clusters produce fruit.

Fruit: The 5-sided berry fruit develops without fertilization, taking 3 months to ripen; contains no seeds.

Uses: It is normally eaten cooked or made into a flour. Porridge and cakes are made from the flour. Leaves are used for thatching, the leaf stalk (petiole) yields a strong, fine fibre.

Trees

Musa sapientum

MUSACEAE

Sweet banana

Exotic, native to Indonesia

Local names: Ndizi (Swahili); Isubi, Kayinja, Musa (Luganda); Isubi (Rukiga)

A tree-like perennial herb, usually growing 2–6 m in height, with a basal corm below ground and milky sap in all parts. A crop of the tropical lowlands, it is the most important fruit in the world trade.

Stem: The lower leaf stalks and sheaths are folded around each other to make a 'false stem' from which the upper leaf blades push out and spread into the light.

Leaves: Arise in a spiral; about 30 together, each made up of a sheath; leaf stalk 30–90 cm long; a leaf blade emerges as a roll that slowly unfolds. Lateral veins are at right angles to the midrib; wind may tear the blade into strips along the veins. Old leaves hang down and the blades die.

Flowers: Single; large flowering head curves downwards; the head arises from the tip of the corm, taking 9–10 months to develop, emerging between the leaves. Its thick stalk bears many flower clusters in spirals. Each cluster of 12–20 flowers in 2 rows is covered by a large red-brown or purple bract with a waxy blue bloom on the outside. All flowers are rich in nectar; have a female pistil and male stamens, but only the first 5–15 clusters produce fruit

Fruit: The 5-sided berry fruit develops without fertilization, taking 3 months to ripen; contains no seeds.

Uses: It is normally eaten raw, but is sometimes fried; also used to make jam and syrup.

Trees

Tree

Fruit

Myrianthus holstii

MORACEAE

Giant yellow mulberry

Indigenous

Local names: Mutuya (Kikuyu); Mfutsa (Hehe); Mugunga (Luganda)

A large evergreen tree of the rain forest, growing up to 15 m or more in height. The species occurs in lowland and mountain forests, preferring moist valleys and river banks.

Bark: Light grey-brown; smooth; watery.

Leaves: Large; palmate; with 5–7 leaflets; each elliptic and obovate; margin dentate; upper surface smooth and dark green; lower side grey-green; hairy with conspicuous veins; stalked.

Flowers: Male and female flowers on separate trees; male greenish; female small, round, with yellow heads on the stalk.

Fruit: Roundish (pineapple shape); green, turning yellow when ripe; 4 cm across.

Uses: The fruit is edible, sweet-and-sour in taste. The timber is soft, used to make charcoal and as general fuel; leaves serve as mulch.

Traditional medicine: Roots are used in the treatments of sore throats.

Fruit

Tree

Newtonia buchananii

MIMOSOIDEAE

Newtonia

Indigenous

Local names: Mukui (Kikuyu); Mkufi (Chagga); Mpewere (Luganda)

A large spreading tree, rather flat-topped and layered, growing 15–40 m in height. The species occurs in lowland and upland rain forest at altitudes of 600–2 200 m.

Bark: Smooth; light grey; older trees have strongly fluted buttresses.

Leaves: Feathery; compound; numerous; very small; young leaflets light green in contrast to the mature dark-green leaflets. Branchlets have rust-brown hairs.

Flowers: Clusters of erect, creamy spikes; up to 18 cm; fading to brown.

Fruit: Brown pods; 15–30 cm long; straight, flat and thin, splitting open on one side only to release distinctive red, winged seeds up to 7 cm in length.

Uses: The timber is durable in water; used for canoes (the small local fishing boats), for furniture and in building. Pods, seeds and leaves serve as fodder and mulch.

Traditional medicine: A decoction of boiled roots, drunk twice a day, removes intestinal worms.

Flowers

Fruit

Tree

Ochna holstii (O. prunifolia)

Forest ochna

Indigenous

Local names: Mungirima (Kikuyu); Mutandi (Kamba); Mundugiti (Kipsigis)

A deciduous forest species, growing up to 20 m tall in the high podocarpus forest, but usually seen as an understorey shrub or spindly tree reaching 3–7 m in height. Found in woodland areas at altitudes from 1 400–2 300 m.

Bark: Grey-brown; rough; branchlets dotted with pale breathing pores.

Leaves: Alternate; shiny green; lanceolate; 10–14 cm long; apex pointed; tapering base; margin dentate.

Flowers: Yellow; 2–3 cm across; stalked; in clusters arising from short side twigs.

Fruit: Soft; up to 1 cm long; in groups of up to 9 drupelets; black when ripe.

Uses: The wood is hard and tough, used for general timber and as fuel.

Flowers

Tree

Olea europaea subsp.africana

OLEACEAE

Wild olive, Brown olive

Indigenous

Local names: Mutamaiyu (Kikuyu); Mlamuru (Chagga); Muthata (Kamba)

Also known as *O. africana* or *O. chrysophylla*. A handsome tree growing 10–15 m in height, but can also be a stunted shrub with a much-branched, rounded crown and grey-green foliage; widely distributed in dry forest and forest margins at altitudes of 750–3 000 m above sea level.

Bark: Bark brown and rough; trunk crooked and gnarled with characteristic pockets. Young white branchlets bear large breathing pores.

Leaves: Opposite; narrowly oval; stiff; sharply pointed; dull-green above; underside almost white; with prominent midrib; up to 8 cm long.

Flowers: Small; with four white petals; two stamens; in branched heads; up to 5 cm across.

Fruit: Oval; fleshy; up to 1 cm long; purple; bitter-sweet when ripe.

Uses: Ripe fruit attracts flocks of birds, such as olive pigeons. The wood is golden brown with dark figuring and is very hard. It is used to produce quality furniture and woodcarvings, and for poles, posts, panelling, flooring, walking sticks and as general timber. It also makes excellent firewood and charcoal, and serves as bee forage, as a windbreak, and as an ornamental.

Traditional medicine: An infusion of the bark is taken as a remedy for tapeworm; a bark decoction is added to the bath to alleviate itchy rashes.

Fruit

Flowers

Tree

Pandanus kirkii

PANDANACEAE

Screw pine, Walking palm

Indigenous

Local names: Mkadi (Swahili)

An unusual tree, growing 4–8 m in height, which has 'stilt' roots rising from the lower trunk that anchor the tree in the sand. Each stilt is up to 2 m high. The species is commonly found on beaches, just above the high water mark.

Bark: Grey-white trunk.
Leaves: Dark; strap-like; up to 90 x 5 cm; in stiff terminal whorls; margin and midrib very spiny.
Flowers: Male flowers white, very small, scented, in hanging spikes up to 10 cm long; female spikes smaller and greenish.
Fruit: Yellow to red when ripe; massive; resembling a hard pineapple; about 20 cm long.
Uses: The dried leaves make woven baskets and mats. They are also widely used for thatching.

Fruit

Roots

Tree

Pandanus utilis

PANDANACEAE

Stilt palm

Exotic, native to Madagascar

Local name: None known

An unusual, decoratively branching tree (and not a palm, despite its common name) that reaches 6–12 m in height, with a thick grey trunk. It grows well at the coast, more slowly at higher altitudes (up to 1 800 m above sea level).

Bark: Greyish white; branched from the flower end.
Leaves: Upright; leathery; in stiff whorls at the end of branches; dark green; strap-like; up to 1 m long; spiny tip.
Fruit: Conspicuous, resembling a hard pineapple.
Uses: An ornamental plant; also provides material for woven mats and baskets.

Fruit

Tree

Parkinsonia aculeata

Jerusalem thorn

Exotic, native to the tropical Americas

Local names: Okwato (Luo); Muk-bee (Orma)

A spiny, small tree or shrub, usually growing 5–10 m in height, with feathery foliage, a low crown and drooping branches. The species is almost naturalized in East Africa, occurring at altitudes from sea level to 1 400 m. It is widely planted in poor or sandy soils in arid and semi-arid regions.

Bark: Greenish yellow; smooth; branches have spines.
Leaves: Groups of thin leaf stalks, each stalk flattened and winged; up to 30 cm long but less than 5 mm wide; leaflets tiny, oblong, in widely spaced pairs; often completely absent during drought, when the tree is almost bare.
Flowers: Bright yellow, with orange stamens; on spikes up to 10 cm long; scented; leaf stalk, flower stalk and calyx covered with rusty brown hairs.
Fruit: Bunches of woody pods; 10 cm long; pale brown when mature; narrow; constricted between seeds.
Uses: The species is widely cultivated as a hedge in near-desert areas. Leaves and pods are browsed by wild game and domestic stock. The leaves are also used as mulch and green leaf-manure; the wood as fuel.

Flowers

Fruit pods

Tree

Peltophorum africanum

CAESALPINOIDEAE

African false wattle

Exotic, native to Southern and Central Africa

Local name: None known

An attractive flowering tree with a rounded spreading crown, occurring in wooded grassland and growing 10 m or higher at altitudes up to 1 800 m.

Bark: Brown; rough; with wide vertical fissures.
Leaves: Feathery; twice compound; with small, numerous oval leaflets.
Flowers: Bright yellow; fragrant; in conspicuous erect spray about 10 cm in length; leaf stalk, flower stalk and calyx covered with rusty brown hairs.
Fruit: Flat pods; up to 10 cm in length; tapering at both ends; in dense clusters.
Uses: The wood is used for fuel, poles and posts.

Tree

Mature fruit pods

Flowers

Persea americana

Avocado

Exotic, native to the tropical Americas

Local names: Mparachichi, Mwembe mafuta (Swahili); Mukorobea (Kikuyu)

A densely leafy, evergreen tree that grows 10 m or higher, widely planted at altitudes up to 2 200 m above sea level.

Bark: Grey to dark brown; rough and fissured with age.
Leaves: Large; alternate; up to 20 cm long; midrib and veins prominent; glossy dark-green above; young leaves pinkish, turning bright green.
Flowers: In large terminal heads; small; abundant; pale yellow; only one in 5 000 flowers produces fruit.
Fruit: Large; round to pear-shaped; central seed surrounded by a thick layer of yellow-green flesh.
Uses: The fruit is edible, rich in fat, protein and vitamins. Its oil is used in cosmetics; dry leaves serve as fodder. The green leaves, bark and stones from the fruit are all toxic to browsing stock.

Fruit

Flowers

Phytolacca dioica

PHYTOLACCACEAE

Phytolacca

Exotic, native to South America (Brazil to Argentina)

Local name: None known

A semi-deciduous tree with a spreading crown, can grow up to 10 m high but generally smaller. The trunk is swollen at the base (a unique feature), which may grow to 4 m in diameter, spreading over ground.

Bark: Grey; rough when old.

Leaves: Simple; alternate; terminal whorls; each one smooth, oval, somewhat recurved; up to 15 cm in length. Young leaves have light-green leaf stalks and midribs tinged with red.

Flowers: Small; creamy white; with many stamens; arise from 5 green sepals; hang in terminal catkins up to 15 cm in length.

Fruit: Juicy; yellow; berry-like; with 10 lobes; hang in clusters; irregularly produced after flowers.

Uses: Planted as an ornamental tree in East Africa.

Fruit

Flowers

Tree

144

Pinus patula

Mexican weeping pine

Exotic, native to Mexico

Local name: Msindano (Kikuyu)

An evergreen pine tree that grows to 35 m in height, with light green, 'weeping' foliage and a long straight trunk. The branches are more or less horizontal, turning up at the tips. The species can grow in most soils, at altitudes of 1 700–3 000 m.

Bark: Grey to dark brown; fairly smooth; papery red-brown on young branches.
Leaves: Long slender 'needles'; soft but hard-tipped; 15–22 cm long; in bundles of 3.
Cones: Female: small, hard, red sphere, up to 1 cm long, maturing in 2 years to form shiny, clustered brown cones. Male: on the same tree, short terminal catkins, yellow to orange-brown, producing clouds of pollen.
Uses: The timber is light brown, soft and brittle, and is used for boxwood, wood pulp, posts (treated with wood preservatives) and also as fuel. This is an attractive tree, good for ornamental and shade purposes.

Female cones

Male catkins

Tree

Pittosporum rhombifolium

PITTOSPORACEAE

Queensland pittosporum,
Diamond leaf pittosporum

Exotic, native to
Queensland, Australia

Local name: None known

A large evergreen tree growing
up to 10 m or higher; planted as
a street ornamental.

Bark: Greyish brown.

Leaves: Glossy green; oblique ovate; tapering tip and
base; leaf petiole 1 cm long; margin irregularly dentate.

Flowers: Very floriferous, with terminal clusters of
white or cream flowers; each up to 1 cm across.

Fruit: Bright orange berries; in terminal clusters.

Uses: The fruit is edible; the wood is used as fuel, and
for poles and posts.

Tree

Flowers

Berries

Podocarpus falcatus (P. gracilior)

Podo, East African yellowwood

Indigenous

Local names: Ol-pirripirri (Maasai); Muthengera (Kikuyu); Mvavavi (Chagga)

An evergreen forest tree with a straight bole, growing to 25 m or higher, occurring in upland rain forest range at altitudes of 1 500–2 400 m, often associated with the genus *Juniperus*. It is a conifer, not a pine.

Trunk: Grey to dark brown; flakes in irregular rectangles.

Leaves: Narrow; shiny dark green; 2–5 cm long; gradually tapering to apex; juvenile leaves are larger and paler, giving an attractive bright green flush.

Cones: 1–3 male catkins; axillary; yellow-brown; about 2 cm long.

Fruit: Hard; rounded; up to·2 cm long; very slow to develop; green with a dull purple bloom, sometimes turning yellowish; outer shell thin; inner flesh eaten by monkeys and birds.

Uses: A good timber tree, used for fuel and for making furniture, boxes, poles, plywood, panelling.

Traditional medicine: The Maasai (a Kenyan people) used an infusion from the bark to treat stomachache.

Male catkins

Fruit

Tree

Polyscias fulva (P. kikuyuensis, P. ferruginea) ARALIACEAE

Parasol tree   Indigenous

Local names: Mutati (Kikuyu); Mborori, Yaroro (Chagga); Setala (Luganda)

A tall, prominent, deciduous forest tree, growing up to 25 m in height, with a straight, slender bole rising to about 9 m before the development of whorls of branches, like spokes of an umbrella, supporting a flat-topped crown. The species is widely distributed in wetter highland forests, often occurring in tea-growing districts, at altitudes of 1 500–2 500 m.

Bark: Grey; smooth; leaf scars prominent on the bole, branches and stems.
Leaves: Compound; pinnate; up to 1 m or more in length; leaflets opposite, usually 8 to 14 pairs plus a terminal leaflet; dark green above; about 14 cm long; apex tapering; base rounded; soft golden hairs below.
Flowers: Creamy yellow; honey-scented; very small; in loose heads; up to 60 cm long; main stalk covered in red-brown hairs.
Fruit: Small; oval-shaped; often ribbed; closely clustered.
Uses: Soft, white, odourless wood for boxes, beehives and plywood. Poor fuelwood. Leaves yield good mulch and green-leaf manure.

Tree

Protea gaguedi (P. abyssinica)

PROTEACEAE

Sugar bush

Indigenous

Local names: Emungomani (Maasai); Etugnisth (Turkana); Mugoiduet (Nandi)

A small tree, occasionally shrubby, growing to 5 m in height; widespread; often found in colonies on stony sites or on mountain slopes at altitudes ranging from 2 150–3 350 m.

Bark: Grey-brown.
Leaves: Lance-shaped; hard texture; 10–15 cm long and about 2 cm broad; apex obtuse; base slightly tapered.
Flowers: Heads up to 10 cm in diameter; perianth white; up to 2 cm long; densely hairy; stamens and style pinkish; bracts about 3– 4 cm long.
Fruit: Pale, golden brown; about 1 cm long.
Uses: The wood is used for fuel and the bark for medicinal purposes.

Tree

Flower

Bud

Prunus africana (Pygeum africanum)

ROSACEAE

Red stinkwood

Indigenous

Local names: Mkonde-konde (Chagga); Muiri (Kikuyu); Ntasesa (Luganda)

An evergreen tree, growing up to 25 m or more, that occurs in moist evergreen forest, in riverine areas (often in remnants) and on margins, at altitudes of 1 500–2 300 m. In forest, the high foliage is open, the branches often pendulous, but in grassland the tree is shorter and the crown is more rounded.

Bark: Rough; grey-black; scaling irregularly; branches corky and brown; branchlets dotted with lenticels.

Leaves: Glossy, dark-green above; oval; up to 20 cm long; base rounded; margin has shallow, rounded teeth; leaf stalk pink or red; up to 2 cm long; crushed leaves have a bitter-almond smell.

Flowers: Very small; scented; green-white in short sprays; many stamens.

Fruit: Rounded; about 1 cm across; dark red to purple when ripe; two-lobed; extremely bitter.

Uses: Excellent timber, used in house-building, for furniture and poles, and as fuel.

Traditional medicine: Bark infusion serves as a purgative, and features in treatment of prostate problems; the bark is also pounded, water added and the red liquid drunk as a remedy for stomachache; a leaf infusion is taken to improve appetite.

Tree

Fruit

Flowers

Prunus puddum (P. cerasoides) ROSACEAE

Flowering cherry, Himalayan bird cherry   Exotic, native to the Himalayas

Local name: None known

A quick-growing, well-shaped, deciduous ornamental tree that reaches a height of about 8 m but is usually smaller. It has a much-branched crown that becomes rounded in certain instances.

Bark: Shiny; copper-brown; easily recognized; peeling in horizontal strips.

Leaves: Glossy; green; up to 18 cm long; elongated apex; toothed margin; young leaves bronze in colour.

Flowers: Pink; abundant; each flower has 5 petals and 5 pink stamens; at the start of the rainy season the bare branches are covered with clusters of flowers.

Fruit: Small; oval; yellow berries on the ends of long stalks; eaten by birds.

Uses: An attractive ornamental tree.

Fruit

Flowering branch

Flowers

Psidium guajava

MYRTACEAE

Guava

Exotic, native to the tropical Americas

Local names: Mpera (Swahili); Mubera (Kikuyu); Mupeera (Luganda)

A small, evergreen tree growing up to 8 m in height; widely cultivated in the tropics for its fruit, almost naturalized in East Africa.

Bark: Smooth; light brown; peeling and flaking; young shoots four-sided.
Leaves: Opposite; oval; up to 15 cm long; side veins clear and parallel.
Flowers: White; 1–3 together; many stamens.
Fruit: Green when not ripe, yellowish when ripe; rounded; up to 6 cm long; calyx lobes persistent.
Uses: Highly edible. The delicious pink, white or yellowish flesh is used to make jam, jelly and a refreshing juice. The wood is used for fuel and tool handles. Birds, and especially bats, love this fruit, and distribute the seeds.

Fruit

Flowers

Tree

Ravenala madagascariensis

Traveller's palm   Exotic, native to Madagascar

Local name: None known

A fan-shaped tree with a 10 m high trunk, planted as an ornamental from the coast to the highlands. The species is not a palm but a giant woody herb, belonging to the Banana family. In its native forests of Madagascar the trunk may reach a height of up to 30 m.

Leaves: Very large; leathery; on long stalks; grow only in one plane; the bases overlap to form a fan up to 8 m across, flaring out at the tips. The leaf blades are often split into narrow strips like banana leaves.

Flowers: White; in groups arising from large boat-shaped bracts between the leaf stalks. The nectar attracts birds.

Fruit: Woody capsules.

Uses: An ornamental tree for gardens and, especially, the grounds of hotels and resorts.

Trees

153

Rothmannia urcelliformis (Gardenia urcelliformis) RUBIACEAE

Forest rothmannia   Indigenous

Local names: Mukombokombo (Kikuyu); Munyaburo (Rutoro)

An evergreen tree or shrub growing to 9 m in height with low, sweeping branches; widely distributed in highland forest at altitudes up to 1 800 m.

Bark: Grey-brown; smooth; rough with age.

Leaves: Opposite or in threes; broadly oval; light green when young; dark and glossy when older; apex tapering.

Flowers: Erect; solitary; trumpet-shaped; up to 10 cm across; 5 creamy white petals with maroon markings; stalk absent.

Fruit: Egg-shaped; up to 6 cm long; brown-black and hard when mature; persists on the tree; slightly ridged.

Uses: An ornamental species; the wood is used for poles, and as fuelwood and charcoal.

Traditional medicine: The bark features in the treatment of malaria, and is also said to confer strength.

Flowers

Fruit

Tree

Schinus molle

Pepper tree   Exotic, native to Andes (notably Peru); almost naturalized

Local names: Mpilipili (Swahili); Mugaita (Kikuyu)

An evergreen tree with weeping foliage, up to 15 m in height, with a short trunk and spreading crown, commonly planted in dry, warm climates, almost naturalized in places. Tolerant of most soils, including dry sands and black cotton. Extremely drought resistant once established.

Bark: Dark brown; peeling; very sticky resinous latex seeps out if cut.

Leaves: Compound; up to 30 cm long; many narrow leaflets, up to 7 cm long, with no stalk; peppery smell when crushed.

Flowers: Very small; creamy white.

Fruit: Hangs on female trees; small round berries; green to red, then black.

Uses: The wood is used as fuel, for posts, and serves as bee forage. Leaves and berries feature in the making of spice mixes and in traditional medicine.

Berries

Tree

Flowers

Schinus terebinthifolius (S. terebranthi)   ANACARDIACEAE

Brazilian pepper tree, Christmas berry tree   Exotic, native to Brazil

Local name: None known

A small, attractive tree, reaching 7 m in height: fast-growing in conditions that are not too harsh.

Bark: Dark grey; deeply fissured with age; stiff, angular and crowded branchlets.
Leaves: Dark shiny green; compound; 3–6 leaflets; one large terminal leaflet; oval; margin serrated; papery smell if crushed.
Flowers: White; very small; bell-shaped; in erect spikes.
Fruit: Deep pink to scarlet; in conspicuous clusters.
Uses: This species is grown as an ornamental shade tree. The wood is used as fuel, and to make posts. Leaves and berries are used as spices.

Flowers

Berries

Trees

156

Schizolobium parahybum

Guapiruvu

Exotic, native to Brazil, tropical America

Local name: None known

A handsome deciduous tree growing to 10 m or more in height, with an unusual branching system resembling the spokes of an umbrella.

Bark: Greyish green; clear horizontal scars from detached leaves.
Leaves: Bipinnate; very large and feathery.
Flowers: Bright yellow; in erect, dense heads covering the tree before the leaves appear.
Fruit: Thin and flat, like giant almond-shaped pods; split on the ground; each pod contains a wafer-thin winged seed.
Uses: The tree is grown as an ornamental (on golf courses and in gardens), especially in the highlands.

Fruit and seeds

Flowers

Tree

Schrebera alata

OLEACEAE

Schrebera, Wing-leafed wooden pear

Indigenous

Local names: Mutoma (Kikuyu); Ol-embenek-uni (Maasai); Lamaiyat (Kipsigis)

A widespread and graceful tree that grows 9–25 m in height, occurring in open woodland and drier forests at altitudes of 1 500–2 300 m.

Bark: Pale grey; smooth or longitudinally fissured.

Leaves: Leaflets in 2 pairs plus a larger terminal leaflet; up to 12 cm long; leaf stalk characteristically winged (alate); apex tapering; notched and rounded.

Flowers: In terminal heads on short branches; creamy white marked with purple centre; sweet-scented; 1.5 cm across; tubular corolla powdered with brown; 2 yellow stamens.

Fruit: Pear-shaped capsules; about 3–6 cm long; often in groups of 4–5; pale-brown; persist on the tree; split open when ripe, releasing papery winged seeds.

Uses: The wood is hard and heavy; pale brown in colour with dark markings; makes excellent firewood. Also used in house construction and for furniture.

Traditional medicine: The Maasai and Kipsigis chew bark or twigs for toothache. Chewed leaves are applied to cuts as a pain killer.

Tree

Fruit

Flowers

Senna brewsteri (Cassia brewsteri) CEASALPINIACEAE

Cigar cassia Exotic, native to Australia

Local name: None known

A deciduous tree, growing to 12 m in height; its long, hanging orange-red sprays look very attractive when it is in full flower.

Bark: Brownish black; longitudinally fissured when old.

Leaves: Compound; 5–7 pairs of leaflets; glossy and dark green; tip rounded, slightly notched.

Flowers: Double-coloured, orange and red; in long hanging sprays.

Fruit: Long, brown-black pods when dry; 30–50 cm long and 3 cm wide.

Uses: A spectacular ornamental tree for gardens.

Tree

Flowers

Fruit pods

Senna siamea (Cassia siamea)

CAESALPINOIDEAE

Black-wood cassia, Ironwood

Exotic, native to Southeast Asia

Local names: Mjohoro (Swahili); Nsongoma (Suku); Oyieko (Luo); Ikengeta (Kamba)

An evergreen tree, reaching up to 15 m in height, often shrub-like, cultivated in the lowland areas of East Africa. It prefers a high water table but will tolerate extended drought. Grows from sea level to 1 600 m; common at the coast and lower altitudes.

Bark: Smooth; pale grey-brown.

Leaves: Compound; stalk up to 30 cm long; oblong leaflets; round at the base and tips; dark shiny green above notched tip.

Flowers: Pale yellow; in dense heads; each flower about 3 cm in diameter.

Fruit: In dense clusters; flat; yellow-brown; slightly curved; 20–25 cm long.

Uses: The wood is termite-resistant and is used for general timber, poles and furniture, and as fuel. Leaves serve as fodder. A good ornamental shade tree. Also features in agroforestry.

Traditional medicine: Bark, leaves, pods and flowers are used to treat stomachache, ringworm and coughs.

Tree

Fruit

Flowers

Senna spectabilis (Cassia spectabilis)

Cassia   **Exotic, native to the tropical Americas**

Local names: Mhomba (Swahili); Mwenu (Kikuyu)

A rounded, deciduous tree growing 10–20 m in height, bearing showy clusters of yellow flowers, but bare for several months of the year. Planted at altitudes of up to 2 000 m.

Bark: Smooth; grey; with horizontal markings; becomes rougher with age.

Leaves: Compound; up to 40 cm; with many pointed leaflets; usually softly hairy below.

Flowers: Golden yellow; in erect pyramid clusters up to 30 cm or more in length.

Fruit: Cylindrical pods; up to 30 cm long; sometimes flattened; turning from green to black.

Uses: The Cassia is quick-growing, spectacular in flower and a very popular ornamental tree. The wood is used as fuel, for tool handles and poles, and flowers serve as bee forage.

Fruit pods

Flowers

Tree

Solanum macranthum

SOLANACEAE

Brazilian potato tree

Exotic, native to Brazil

Local name: None known

A small ornamental tree growing 10 m high; very fast-growing but short-lived. Branches and leaves may bear sharp, hooked prickles.

Leaves: Large; 25–30 cm long; in terminal clusters; rough above and a little hairy below; margin deeply and irregularly lobed; apex blunt; base unequal-sided.

Flowers: Star-shaped; with 5 joined petals; up to 5 cm across; in small terminal clusters; petals purple fading to white; yellow stamens.

Fruit: Large berries; soft; up to 3 cm across; green to yellow when ripe; calyx persistent.

Uses: Planted as an ornamental tree in East Africa.

Fruit

Tree

Flowers

Spathodea campanulata (S. nilotica)   BIGNONIACEAE

Nandi flame, African tulip tree   Indigenous

Local names: Kibobakasi (Swahili); Kifabakazi (Luganda); Sebetaiyet (Kipsigis)

A decorative tree with a rounded crown, usually growing 10–30 m high, widely planted throughout the tropics; does well in red or forest soil, but can also grow in black-cotton soil at altitudes of 1 500–2 000 m.

Bark: Pale; smooth; becomes rough with age.

Leaves: Compound; leaflets in 3 to 6 pairs with a terminal leaflet; each one oval; up to 12 cm long; tip pointed; wavy, yellow-brown hairs on shoots, buds, branchlets and underside of leaves.

Flowers: Bright orange-red clusters; frilly petals edged with yellow; spathe-like buds contain a watery liquid.

Fruit: Woody capsules; green when young, dark bown when mature; up to 25 cm long; single or in pairs; erect; splitting on the ground.

Uses: A yellow-flowered variety, propagated from trees that evolved naturally in the indigenous forests of Uganda; also occasionally found as an ornamental tree in the bigger cities of East Africa. An ideal tree for parks, gardens and avenues. The wood is soft and light, and can be used for fuel, and to make carvings.

Traditional medicine: Bark features as a cure for liver complaints and, when boiled, is used in the treatment of infant skin rash.

Yellow flowers

Tree

Fruit

Red flowers

Sterculia africana

STERCULIACEAE

African star chestnut, Tick tree

Indigenous

Local names: Ngoza (Swahili); Mluze (Gogo); Muusya (Kamba)

A small, deciduous tree with a thick, fluted trunk; usually grows 5–8 m in height, but may reach 12 m. The erect branches spread to a rounded crown. The species is commonly found in hot, dry areas, on rocky hills and on the fringes of woodlands at altitudes from sea level to 1 000 m.

Bark: Smooth; shiny grey or liver-red; flaking to show yellow-green underbark.

Leaves: Spaced on young shoots, or crowded at the tips in older branches; deeply divided with 3–5 lobes, over 10 cm across; lobes pointed; leaf stalk up to 10 cm long.

Flowers: Appear on the bare tree; green-yellow sepals (no petals); sepals joined together; clustered in terminal panicles; streaked with red inside; up to 2.5 cm across.

Fruit: 1–5 woody, beaked follicles; ellipsoid; each lobe 4–10 cm long; break open to free 3–10 flat, blue-grey seeds that hang like ticks around the open edge.

Uses: The bark yields a fibre used to make rope and for tying thatching materials. The soft, light wood provides material for local furniture, and for poles in house construction. It yields a good (and expensive) resin that serves as a varnish. Notable for its contribution to the acoustic quality of musical instruments such as violins.

Traditional medicine: Boiled bark and roots used as an inhalent for fever and influenza.

Tree

Fruit and flowers

Stereospermum kuntianum

No English name known

Indigenous

Local names: Mti-sumu, Mtafuna panya (Swahili); Nemera (Luganda)

A deciduous tree, 4–9 m high, with weak, drooping branches; commonly occurs in rocky bushland, wooded grassland and forest margins from the coast to an altitude of 2 100 m.

Bark: Grey; smooth; scaling with age.

Leaves: Opposite; with 7–9 leaflets; oval; rounded tip; base tapering with small petiole.

Flowers: Showy; pink; in panicles; 20–30 cm long; frilly and velvety; tubular petals; appear when tree is bare.

Fruit: Linear; twisted; 30–60 cm long; dark brown when dry; split open on the tree to release many winged seeds.

Uses: The wood is used for posts, poles, in light construction and as fuel.

Traditional medicine: The bark and roots are considered effective in the treatment of coughs; an infusion of the leaves is used for washing wounds and in the treatment of ulcers; a decoction of boiled roots features in the treatment of venereal diseases.

Fruit

Flowers

Tree

165

Strelitzia augusta (S. alba)

STRELITZIACEAE

Great white strelitzia

Exotic, native to South Africa

Local name: None known

A single or multi-trunk tree that reaches 10 m in height, with a spindly, woody trunk covered with old leaf bases.

Trunk: One vertical plane; forms a characteristic fan-like canopy; stem smooth with elevated rings of old leaf scars.
Leaves: Huge, like banana tree leaves; break up to resemble giant feathers; shiny, leathery, thick leaf stalks.
Flowers: Resemble the head of a bird, with a white crest and purple beak.
Fruit: 3-lobed woody capsules, containing many seeds.
Uses: In East Africa the tree is planted as an ornamental.

Flowers

Trees

166

Syzygium cuminii (Eugenia cuminii)   MYRTACEAE

Java plum, Jambolan   Exotic, native to India, tropical Asia; naturalized

Local names: Mzambarau (Swahili); Lushanaku (Haya)

An evergreen fruit tree, growing up to 15 m in height, with hanging leafy branches and dense foliage, occurring from sea level to an altitude of 1 800 m.

Bark: Brown and rough; cracking and flaking with age.
Leaves: Opposite; large; oval; 6–20 cm in length; smooth and shiny; distinct pointed tip; strongly aromatic if crushed; young leaves reddish.
Flowers: Small; white; cluster below leaves; scented; attract masses of insects.
Fruit: Oval; up to 3 cm long; deep purple.
Uses: The wood is used for general timber, poles, tool handles and as fuel. Fruit is edible when ripe.
Traditional medicine: Liquid from the pounded bark and roots, mixed with water, is taken as a purgative.

Flowers

Fruit

Tree

Syzygium guineense

MYRTACEAE

Waterberry

Indigenous

Local names: Mzuari (Swahili); Kalunginsavu (Luganda); Masdi (Chagga)

A densely leafy forest tree, usually growing 10 to 15 m in height, although it can reach 25 m or more along river banks. It occurs in riverine areas and wooded grassland at altitudes from sea level to 2 100 m.

Bark: Light-brown to grey; flaking in patches with age.

Leaves: Dark green; in opposite pairs; smooth on both surfaces; tip long but rounded; 6–16 cm in length; shape variable – some are rounded and some pointed.

Flowers: Small; white; in dense heads; sweet fragrance attracts many insects.

Fruit: Oval; purple-black and shiny when ripe, up to 3 cm long; in big bunches.

Uses: The ripe fruit is edible. The wood is red, hard and strong, used for poles, posts, tool handles, as fuelwood and charcoal. Leaves serve as fodder and bee forage, and bark features in the preparation of dyes and tannin.

Traditional medicine: Liquid from the pounded bark and roots, mixed with cold water, is taken as a treatment for stomachache and as a purgative.

Tree

Tabernaemontana stapfiana (T. johnstonii)   APOCYNACEAE

Wild magnolia   Indigenous

Local names: Mwerere (Kikuyu); Erendet, Terendet (Kipsigis); Omobondo (Kisii)

An evergreen tree, growing up to 10 m in height, occurring in wet upland forests. All parts produce a milky latex.

Bark: Grey-brown; rough.
Leaves: Large; glossy-green above; up to 30 cm long.
Flowers: Creamy white; fragrant; up to 6 cm across; very much like those of exotic Frangipani (see page 254).
Fruit: In large, rounded pairs; up to 20 cm across; dark green mottled with white; ripe fruit splits open, releasing sticky orange pulp around the seeds; rotten fruit on the ground has an unpleasant smell.
Uses: The tree is a striking ornamental when in full flower. The wood is used as fuel.

Flowers

Tree

Fruit

Tamarindus indica

CAESALPINIOIDEAE

Tamarind

Indigenous

Local names: Mkwaju (Swahili); Moya (Chagga); Mukoge (Luganda)

A large tree, growing up to 30 m high, with an extensive, dense crown and drooping branches. Widely distributed in wooded grassland and bushland near the coast, also in open forest and riverine areas at altitudes up to 1 500 m. It is either evergreen, or deciduous in dry areas.

Bark: Rough; grey-brown; flaking.

Leaves: Compound; on hairy stalks; up to 15 cm long; dull green leaflets in 9–21 pairs; opposite; round at the tip and base; veins prominent.

Flowers: Small, about 2.5 cm across; petals yellow with red veins; in small bunches.

Fruit: Pale brown pods; sausage-shaped; hairy; about 10 cm long; split when mature to reveal sticky brown pulp surrounding hard, dark brown seeds.

Uses: The pulp of the fruit is sour but edible, popular for flavouring curries. The dark brown heartwood is hard, tough and well grained; used in boat-building and for furniture, poles, posts, carts and walking sticks, and as fuel. The fruit pulp makes excellent chutney, and a pleasant cooling drink. Overripe fruit is used to clean copper and brass. Leaves serve as fodder for stock.

Traditional medicine: The fruit pulp is used as a laxative; a root decoction is taken for coughs and fevers; the bark is boiled and used as a gargle for sore throats. A few twigs of *Sterculia africana* (see page 164), boiled with the leaves of *Tamarindus indica*, produces a warming drink, and serves as a remedy for diarrhoea and dysentery.

Fruit

Tree

Flowers

Tabebuia serratifolia

BIGNONIACEAE

Yellow poui tree

Native to Caribbean region, Venezuela

Local name: None known

A showy flowering tree, reaching 8 m in height, sometimes more, with grey-brown, smooth bark that becomes corky with age.

Bark: Grey-brown.
Leaves: Palmately compound; 5–7 narrow leaflets; up to 15 cm long.
Flowers: Bright yellow; in trumpet-shaped clusters; petals frilly; each flower 5–8 cm long; flowers appear when tree is completely leafless.
Fruit: Oblong; woody; dark brown; up to 15 cm long.
Uses: The wood is the source of green ebony, a hard, heavy timber used in construction and to make furniture.

Flowering branches

Flowers

Tree

Teclea simplicifolia

RUTACEAE

Teclea

Indigenous

Local names: Munderendu (Kikuyu); Olgelai (Maasai); Kuriot (Kipsigis)

A small, much-branched, ever-green tree or small shrub, 4–10 m in height. Widespread in dry forest, riverine thicket or wooded grassland from 300–2 300 m

Bark: Smooth; dark grey.
Leaves: Simple; smooth, dark green above; oval; 3–15 cm long; tapering, blunt tip.
Flowers: Greenish yellow; very small; scented; male and female separate; in axillary clusters.
Fruit: Orange or red; round; up to 1 cm in diameter.
Uses: Wood is used for roof beams, walking sticks and bows, also for firewood, charcoal, poles and as timber.
Traditional medicine: The Maasai use a leaf or bark decoction against pleurisy. A bark decoction is also used in the treatment of malaria and hepatitis.

Tree

Fruit

Flowers

Terminalia brownii

COMBRETACEAE

Red pod terminalia

Indigenous

Local names: Mbarao (Swahili); Mpoke (Chagga); Epiyei (Ateso Tororo); Onera (Luo)

A leafy, deciduous tree that grows from 7–13 m in height, densely shady, somewhat layered with drooping foliage; widely distributed in deciduous bushland or woodland at altitudes of 700–2 000 m. It is often seen near rivers in very dry areas.

Bark: Fissured; greyish brown.

Leaves: Spirally arranged; oval; 7–10 cm; wider at the tip; apex pointed or notched; edge wavy; side veins clear; leaf turns red before falling. The leaf stalk and underside of the leaf bear white hairs.

Flowers: White to cream; unpleasant smell; in spikes of up to 12 cm long.

Fruit: Reddish purple; winged; oval; smooth; up to 5 cm long.

Uses: This tree is drought and termite-resistant. Its wood is used for fuel, general timber, poles, posts and tool handles; the leaves and bark for fodder and mulch. A good species for agroforestry.

Traditional medicine: The bark is used among certain groups, notably to treat fevers and colds, and as a remedy for yellow fever, particularly in children.

Flowers

Tree

Fruit

Terminalia catappa

COMBRETACEAE

Indian almond, Bastard almond

Exotic, native to Andaman Island,
India, Madagascar

Local name: Mkungu (Swahili)

A conspicuous, semi-deciduous shade tree growing up to 15 m in height, common in maritime areas throughout the tropics and widely planted at the coast, where it has become naturalized. The young trees have clear horizontal layered branches; mature trees have a broad spreading crown.

Bark: Grey-brown; rough with age.

Leaves: Very large, up to 30 x 15 cm; leathery and shiny; in clusters; green turning to bright red before falling; broadly elliptic, wider towards the apex; pointed apex on young trees, otherwise rounded; base tapering; veins prominent.

Flowers: Small; green-white; on spikes; with 5 sepals; spike 7 to 20 cm long.

Fruit: Hard; about 7 cm long; green at first then turning red; more or less rounded; tip blunt and slightly flattened with two ridges but no wings.

Uses: The fleshy shell is rich in tannin; the kernel is edible (it has an almond-like taste). An oil is extracted from the fruits, which are sometimes found floating in the sea. The leaves are used as wrappers; the wood is used in boat-making.

Flower

Fruit

Tree

Terminalia kilimandscharica

No English name known   Indigenous

Local names: Mbambaro (Swahili); Muhuku (Kamba); Biress (Boran)

A dense, rounded tree reaching 5–10 m in height; common in dry deciduous bushland and wooded grassland, often found on rocky outcrops. The species grows at altitudes of 400–1 500 m.

Bark: Grey and fissured.

Leaves: Spirally arranged; mid-green; large, up to 9 cm long; more hairy below than above; elliptic or obovate; base rounded; apex rounded with slightly pointed tip; lateral veins prominent below.

Flowers: White or cream; in spikes up to 8 cm long.

Fruit: Reddish brown or purple pods; very conspicuous; about 5–8 cm long.

Uses: The timber is hard, durable and used in carpentry, for building poles, and as fuelwood.

Traditional medicine: The bark is boiled or soaked in hot water and used to treat colds.

Fruit pods

Tree

Terminalia mantaly

COMBRETACEAE

Terminalia

Exotic, native to Madagascar

Local name: None known

A shapely evergreen tree growing up to 10 m in height at higher altitudes. It has an erect, smooth and neat stem, layered branches, and is widely planted on streets and in gardens as a shade tree.

Bark: Pale grey; smooth.

Leaves: Bright green; smooth; in terminal rosettes of 4–9 unequal leaves on short, thickened stems; up to 7 cm long; apex rounded; broad, tapered base; wavy margin.

Flowers: Small, greenish white; in erect spikes up to 5 cm long.

Fruit: Small; green turning brown when dry; oval seeds.

Uses: A very popular, fast-growing, spreading shade tree; drought-resistant once established.

Seeds

Tree

Flowers

Thevetia thevetioides

APOCYNACEAE

Yellow oleander, Thevetia

Exotic, native to Central and South America

Local name: None known

An evergreen ornamental tree growing up to 8 m, cultivated in warmer areas at altitudes from sea level to 2 000 m; planted as an attractive ornamental tree throughout East Africa.

Bark: Grey; smooth; becomes rough with age.
Leaves: Narrow; linear; up to 15 cm in length; shiny, glossy green; quilted above; in spirals around the stem.
Flowers: Bright yellow; trumpet-shaped; up to 12 cm across; twisted in bud; scented; in terminal clusters.
Fruit: Large; green; rounded; up to 6 cm across; on a long stalk; contains two large seeds.
Uses: Planted as an ornamental, a shade tree and to form hedges. Good for soil conservation.
Traditional medicine: Seeds of this species used in a powerful drug for the treatment of heart ailments (the tree is cultivated in Hawaii and exported for this purpose).

Fruit

Flowers

Tree

Tipuana tipu (Machaerium tipu) PAPILIONOIDEAE

Tipu Tree, Pride of Bolivia   Exotic, Native to Bolivia, Brazil

Local name: None known

A large tree, reaching 20 m in height, semi-deciduous with a spreading crown and attractive golden-yellow flowers. It is drought-resistant, tolerating a wide variety of soils, including black-cotton, and grows at altitudes of 1 300–2 200 m.

Bark: Red-brown trunk; fissured and flaking with age; branches grey and cracked; sap from cut branches red and sticky.

Leaves: Compound; alternate leaflets; light green; narrow; oblong; up to 5 cm long; tip round, often notched; base round; stalk short.

Flowers: Numerous; in long, loose sprays; each with 5 wavy yellow-orange petals.

Fruit: Unusual and distinctive; single-seeded; flat-winged; yellow-green when young; grey-brown; fibrous; stay on the tree for a long time.

Uses: The wood is used for fuel, general timber, poles and posts; leaves serve as fodder. This large tree is usually planted in big cities for shade and ornamental purposes.

Flowers

Fruit

Tree

Toona ciliata (Cedrela toona)

MELIACEAE

Toona tree, Indian mahogany

Exotic, native to tropical Asia, southern China, Himalaya region

Local name: None known

A large, spreading, deciduous tree, growing up to 15 m high, with a thick trunk; introduced to East Africa as a coffee shade-tree. Found at altitudes up to 1 850 m.

Bark: Dark grey; very rough; furrow and crack in squares.
Leaves: Compound; very large; up to 90 cm in length; 10–14 pairs of leaflets; leaflets narrow; up to 15 cm long; unequal-sided; tapering tip; wavy margin; midrib and veins contrasting light green.
Flowers: Very small; white; bell-shaped; in long sprays.
Fruit: Brown capsules; split open into dark brown star shapes, releasing small, winged seeds.
Uses: The wood is red and soft, and the tree does not live to a great age. Best suited to very large gardens, golf courses and so on.

Flowers

Fruit

Tree

Trema orientalis (T. guineensis)

ULMACEAE

Pigeonwood

Indigenous

Local names: Mpesi, Mgendagenda (Swahili); Kasisa (Luganda); Mwezi (Chagga)

A small, spreading tree that grows up to 12 m in height; evergreen with drooping branches; widely distributed in Africa from sea level to an altitude of 2 000 m. Occurs in riverine forest, and in forest margins in disturbed soils.

Bark: Light grey; thin; smooth; branchlets hairy.
Leaves: Alternate; along drooping branchlets; up to 14 cm long; rough and dull above; hairy below; edge finely dentate all round; blade unequal-sided.
Flowers: Small; yellow-green; in dense axillary clusters.
Fruit: Small; round; fleshy; black berries when ripe.
Uses: The ripe black fruit is much favoured by doves and pigeons. The host tree also attracts many butterflies. Wood is used for poles and as fuel; leaves for fodder and mulch. A black dye is obtained from the bark, brown dye from the leaves.
Traditional medicine: Crushed leaves are mixed with lemon and the juice strained and drunk as a cure for coughs; also given to children with pneumonia and bronchitis, and as an antidote to poisoning.

Green fruit and flowers

Ripe fruit

Tree

Trichilia emetica (T. roka) — MELIACEAE

Cape mahogany — Indigenous

Local names: Muwamaji (Swahili); Mururi (Kikuyu); Mchengo, Mtutu (Chagga)

A large, striking, evergreen tree with hanging foliage, growing 15–30 m in height, commonly occurring in riverine areas and in places with a high water table. Found throughout East Africa at altitudes from sea level to 1 835 m.

Bark: Red-brown; fairly smooth (specially in small branches); becomes corky and scales, revealing green underbark.

Leaves: Compound; large; alternate; crowded towards the ends of branches and twigs; 3–5 pairs of leaflets, with a single leaflet at the top; dark-green above and paler underneath.

Flowers: Small; greenish white; sweet-smelling; trumpet-shaped; in inconspicuous clusters.

Fruit: Grey-brown capsules; rounded; furry; in bunches; capsules burst open when mature to reveal striking red-and-black seeds wrapped in bright red pulp.

Uses: Oil from the seeds is used to make soap. The timber is light, used for indoor furniture, poles and posts, and as fuel. The seeds are poisonous to humans but are relished by baboons and monkeys.

Traditional medicine: The oil is used in the treatment of cuts and bruises; a decoction of roots and bark is taken for fever and as a purgative; leaf and fruit poultices are applied to bruises, cuts and eczema; the seed oil is applied to relieve rheumatism. Bark, roots and leaves are used in a popular remedy for intestinal complaints; other ailments treated (mainly in the form of an enema) include dysentery, kidney problems, and infestation by parasites.

Tree

Fruit

Flowers

Turraea robusta (T. volkensii)

MELIACEAE

Honeysuckle tree

Indigenous

Local names: Ol-burobinik (Maasai); Muringa (Kikuyu); Kivunambasa (Lusoga)

A small tree or a shrub, growing up to 9 m high, sometimes up to 15 m; widely distributed in wooded grassland and bushland, also in riverine forest. The species occurs from sea level to 2 000 m.

Bark: Rough, brown when old; branchlets densely hairy.
Leaves: Glossy, dark green; soft hairs below; broadly oval; up to 15 cm in length; apex rounded; stalk short.
Flowers: Creamy white; in dense clusters; yellowing with age; fragrant; 2.5 cm across; strap-like, narrow petals; prominent orange staminal tube.
Fruit: Round, flattened capsules; about 1.5 cm across; green to brown; vivid when split open; look like small woody stars on the ground under the tree.
Uses: Wood used to make poles and posts, and as fuel.
Traditional medicine: Leaves provide an antidote against general poisoning; a decoction of boiled roots is taken as a remedy for diarrhoea, stomachache and other stomach troubles.

Tree

Fruit

Flowers

Vitex keniensis

Meru oak

Indigenous

Local names: Mfuu (Swahili); Mhuru (Kikuyu); Muuru, Moru (Meru)

An attractive deciduous forest tree; usually grows up to 20 m high, but can reach 30 m on river banks. Clear, straight bole; found at altitudes of 1 300–2 100 m.

Bark: Pale brown with narrow, vertical grooves; becomes darker with age.

Leaves: Compound; five leaflets on a long, hairy stalk; light green; droop when young; pointed tip; young stems and underside of the leaflets covered in pale, velvety hairs.

Flowers: Small, about 1 cm long; cream with one mauve petal lobe; in large heads.

Fruits: Rounded; 1.5 cm across; shiny green turning black when ripe; edible.

Uses: The timber is hard and durable, much prized for high-quality furniture and panelling. The species is now endangered due to the high demand for its timber. The fruit is edible. Also used as fuel, for windbreaks and planted for ornamental purposes.

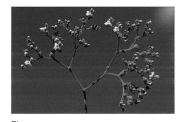

Flowers

Fruit

Tree

Leaves

Warburgia ugandensis (W. salutaris)

CANELLACEAE

Pepper-bark tree, East African green heart

Indigenous

Local names: Ol-msogoni (Maasai); Muthiga (Kikuyu); Mukuzanume (Luganda)

A large, evergreen tree growing up to 25 m in height, with a dense, leafy canopy; widely distributed in the lower rain forests and in the drier highland forest areas; occurs at altitudes ranging from 1 000–2 000 m.

Bark: Rough; black-brown; cracks in rectangular scales.
Leaves: Alternate; shiny, dark green above; midrib very clear and raised below; edge wavy; up to 10 cm long.
Flowers: Greenish cream; inconspicuous; axillary; less than 1 cm across.
Fruit: Hard; round to egg-shaped; 3–5 cm long on short stalks; green to purple with a waxy white surface; several edible seeds inside.
Uses: The leaves, which are very hot to taste, are sometimes used in curries as a chilli substitute. The resin serves as a glue. The wood makes good timber for building and furniture, but is not termite-resistant.
Traditional medicine: An infusion of bark and roots is taken as a cure for stomachache, toothache, fever, colds, malaria and general muscular pains. Dried bark is a popular and widely used remedy for coughs, colds and chest complaints. The bark may also be scraped off, dried, ground into a bitter, spicy powder and taken (in small quantities) as a remedy for toothache, stomachache, constipation, fever and muscular pains. The roots feature in the treatment of diarrhoea. A decoction of the bark or leaves is administered as a cure for malaria (though it causes violent vomiting).

Flowers

Fruit

Tree

Zanthoxylem gilletti (Fagara macrophylla)

RUTACEAE

African stainwood

Indigenous

Local names: Sagawoita (Kipsigis, Nandi); Munyenye (Luganda)

A large, deciduous forest species, growing 10–35 m in height, with a spreading crown, a straight trunk and clear bole up to 15 m. The bole has a diameter of 30–90 cm. This timber tree grows widely in tropical rain forests, especially at the lower and medium altitudes (from 1 500–2 300 m).

Bark: Smooth; grey; with thick spiny woody cones; branches have straight or slightly recurved spines.

Leaves: Compound; in terminal clusters; leaf stalks with straight prickles of up to 1 cm; 13–16 pairs of stiff leaflets plus one terminal leaflet, each one 14–30 cm long; pointed tip; base one-sided or rounded.

Flowers: Creamy white; small; in terminal pyramid clusters; 20–30 cm long.

Fruit: Rounded and red; in prominent clusters.

Uses: The wood is scented, hard, tough, and used in carpentry and boat-building. It is also used as fuel.

Traditional medicine: The bark is used in the treatment of coughs and colds.

Tree

Leaves and berries

Ziziphus mauritiana (Z. jujuba)

RHAMNACEAE

Indian jujube, Geb

Indigenous

Local names: Mkunazi (Swahili); Mtanula (Hehe); Tilomwo (Pokot); Olongo (Luo)

A thick-branched, spiny tree, quite short, can reach 7 m in height, with drooping angular branches and a rounded crown; widespread at the coast and inland up to an altitude of 1 400 m. The species is often found in disturbed or cultivated land, and is widely naturalized in the tropics.

Bark: Grey; branches have curved thorns.

Leaves: Alternate; thin; soft; shiny above and white below; 3 veins arise from the base; leaf base rounded and equal-sided.

Flowers: Small; greenish yellow; star-shaped; in axillary heads up to 2 cm long.

Fruit: Rounded to oval; up to 2 cm long; yellow then red-brown; pulp edible.

Uses: The fruit pulp can be made into both a thirst-quenching drink and a potent spirit. Leaves and fruit make good fodder. The tree is ideal as a live hedge. The wood is hard, heavy, used at the coast for making beds and dhow ribs; also for poles, bows and arrows, as carving material, and for firewood and charcoal. It also serves as a shade tree and windbreak, and is valuable as bee forage, for its role in soil conservation, and for the resin, gum, tannin and dyes it yields.

Traditional medicine: A root decoction is taken as a remedy for indigestion.

Tree

Fruit

Flowers

Vegetation zones such as bushland and bushed grassland consist mainly of shrubs. Bushland has two to three vegetation layers dominated by shrubs and bushes. The shrub stratum is open and continuous and between 2 m and 5 m high, with a few individual trees growing through the stratum. The bushes and shrubs are multi-stemmed, much branched, and have relatively large crowns. *Acacia-Commiphora* bushland is the most common type of semi-arid bushland.

In bushed grassland the dominant woody plants are less than 6 m high. A common example is the *Leleshwa,* which is found throughout the Rift Valley.

Acacia brevispica

MIMOSOIDEAE

Wait-a-bit acacia

Indigenous

Local names: Mwarare (Swahili); Ol-girigiri (Maasai); Ekurau (Turkana)

A low shrub or small tree growing from 1–5 m high, or a scandent shrub reaching up to 12 m, found in bushland, thickets, dry scrub, river valleys and upland forest edges at altitudes from sea level to 1 800 m. It is found throughout East Africa.

Bark: Grey; hairy; with minute reddish glands.
Spines: Scattered prickles, arising from longitudinal bands; recurved or spreading; 6 mm long.
Leaves: 6–18 pairs of pinnae; leaflets in 20–40 pairs; 6 x 1 mm in size.
Flowers: In round heads; creamy white; borne on branching stalks up to 10 cm long.
Fruit: Purple-brown pods; straight; up to 15 cm long; dotted with small reddish glands.
Uses: The pods and leaves are used for fodder; wood for live fences and as fuel.
Traditional medicine: An infusion of roots is taken as a remedy for intestinal worms; an extract from boiled roots features as part of an aphrodisiac, is believed to enhance fertility, and is also used in the treatment of rashes and snakebite.

Pods

Flowers

Shrub

Acacia drepanolobium

Whistling thorn, Ant-galled acacia

Indigenous

Local names: Eluai (Maasai); Muuga, Kiunga (Kamba); Eiyellel (Turkana)

This shrub or small tree, reaching up to 6 m in height, has either a flat or spreading crown and thrives in black-cotton and clay soils, on stony ground and is widespread in East Africa's wooded and bushed grasslands. It grows at altitudes of 700–2 500 m.

Bark: Grey or black; rough; finely fissured.
Spines: In pairs; long and narrow; up to 7 cm long. The bases are swollen into large 'galls', which are red when young, fading to black and grey-white when old. Galls are hollow and inhabited by ants.
Leaves: 3–13 pairs of pinnae; leaflets in 11–22 pairs; 6 x 2 mm in size.
Flowers: In heads; white or cream.
Fruit: Brown-red or black; falcate or spiral-shaped; 7 x 1 cm; split while on the tree.
Uses: The leaves and pods are eaten by game, especially giraffes. The hardy wood is used for fuel and charcoal.
Traditional medicine: The bark is chewed and the juice swallowed as a remedy for sore throats; roots are boiled, the liquid mixed with milk or tea and given to women after childbirth as a diuretic.

Flowers

Fruit pods

Shrub

Galls

Acacia hockii

MIMOSOIDEAE

White thorn acacia

Indigenous

Local names: Mgunga (Swahili); Ol-jarbolani, Iuaa (Maasai); Kasaana (Luganda)

This shrub or tree grows to 6 m in height, may reach 9 m, and has a flattened crown. It is widespread in Kenya, from the central lowlands in the west to wooded grassland. It is common in overgrazed grassland and in bushed grassland. It occurs at altitudes of 750–2 250 m.

Bark: Greenish brown; peels in red-brown papery strips exposing yellow bark; young twigs red-brown.

Spines: In pairs; straight and slender; usually less than 2 cm long; sometimes absent.

Flowers: In small round heads; yellow or orange.

Fruit: Red-brown when mature; narrow; falcate; up to 12 cm long.

Uses: The bark is used for making rope. The Maasai chew the white inner bark to slake thirst, and construct *bomas* (homes) from the branches.

Traditional medicine: A decoction of boiled roots is taken as a remedy for abdominal pain; pounded leaves and buds are mixed with ghee (clarified butter) and applied to abscesses.

Flowers

Shrub

Pods

Branches with flowers

Acacia mellifera

Hook-thorn acacia

Indigenous

Local names: Kikwata (Swahili); Panyirit (Pokot); Magokwe (Lugishu); Oiti (Maasai)

A low, shrubby acacia that grows to about 2 m, less frequently to a tree of up to 8 m in height. It is widespread, especially in dry bushland (but is also found in wooded grassland) at altitudes from sea level to 1 800 m.

Bark: Brown or light grey; smooth.

Thorns: Distinctive; small hooked prickles; in pairs; grey with black tip; 2–5 mm long.

Leaves: 2–3 pairs of pinnae; leaflets in 1–2 pairs; 22 x 16 mm in size.

Flowers: In spikes; up to 4 cm long; white or cream; often purplish in bud; attract bees and sunbirds.

Fruit: Pale brown or pale yellow; short and wide; straight; rarely up to 8 cm long; veined; 3 seeds within.

Uses: The shrub rapidly forms thickets, and is valuable as a live fence; its pods, leaves, flowers and twigs are much favoured by game and stock. The wood yields good timber and fuel (wood and charcoal).

Traditional medicine: Bark is boiled to make a liquid that is used as a remedy for stomach trouble, pneumonia, malaria and for clearing primary syphilis infections.

Flowers

Shrub

Pods

Acacia nubica

MIMOSOIDEAE

No English name known

Indigenous

Local names: Ol-depe (Maasai); Epetet (Turkana); Wanga (Boran)

A shrub or a small tree growing 1–5 m high, branching from the base, widespread in dry, deciduous and semi-desert scrub, at altitudes of 200–1 400 m.

Bark: Grey-green; green below; unpleasant odour when cut.

Spines: Short, almost conical stipular spines; in pairs at the nodes; 0.4–2 cm long.

Leaves: 2–8 pairs of pinnae; leaflets in 5–16 pairs; small; narrow; 7 x 2.5 mm.

Flowers: In round heads; axillary; white or cream.

Fruit: Pale yellow; straight; 4–13 cm x 1–2 cm; oval; tapering to both ends; dehiscent; seeds olive-grey.

Uses: Leaves and pods are browsed by goats and sheep.

Traditional medicine: A bark decoction is used as an emetic to treat malaria and rheumatism; ash from the burnt plant is used as protection against anthrax.

Flowers

Shrub

Flowers and pods

Acacia reficiens

False umbrella thorn

Indigenous

Local names: Anywa, Panyarit (Pokot); Eregae (Turkana); Khansa (Somali)

A shrub or a tree that grows 1–7 m in height, branching at or near base, with a flattened or rounded canopy. Common in dry lowland semi-desert scrub, at altitudes of 50–1 450 m.

Bark: Grey or reddish brown; rough; fissured when old.
Thorns: Hooks in axillary pairs; 2–6 mm long; grey-brown.
Leaves: 1–3 pairs of pinnae; leaflets in 5–11 pairs; elongated and narrow; 6 x 1.3 mm.
Flowers: In round heads; white or cream; in small axillary groups.
Fruit: Reddish brown pods; straight; papery, brittle; 2.6–8 cm x 0.6–1.2 cm; longitudinal veins; dehiscent.
Uses: The bark yields a strong fibre; foliage is eaten by game and livestock; the gum is edible.
Traditional medicine: An infusion of the roots is used to treat swelling of the scrotum; the infusion is also taken as a sexual stimulant.

Pods

Shrub

Flowers

Acacia senegal

MIMOSOIDEAE

Sudan gum arabic, Three-thorned acacia

Indigenous

Local names: Kikwata (Swahili); Mzasa (Gogo); Ekonoit (Ateso Tororo)

A shrub or tree that usually grows to less than 5 m, although it will occasionally reach twice that height. It is a slow-growing plant, very variable, usually low-branched and rounded when young, flattened when mature, often forming thickets. Widespread in dry grassland or woodland at altitudes from sea level to about 1 900 m.

Bark: Peeling; colour varies from yellow-brown to red-brown to grey-brown.

Spines: Three dark grey to blackish brown hooks below each node; outer two curve upward and the centre hook curves downward; set close together; 3–7 mm long.

Leaves: 3–6 pairs of pinnae; leaflets in 8–18 pairs; 7 x 2 mm.

Flowers: In spikes; 2–10 cm long; white or cream.

Fruit: Variable; grey-brown or dark brown with permanent veins; straight; flat; oblong; tapering to both ends.

Uses: A valuable component of dryland agroforestry, and a useful erosion control measure. The hard wood is used for fencing posts, poles and fuel; the root fibres are used to make fishnets. The tree produces edible, high-quality Arabic gum that features in beer, confectionery, pharmaceuticals and other industries in northern Kenya. The leaves and pods are protein-rich, eaten by rhino, camels, sheep and goats.

Traditional medicine: A decoction of the bark is taken as a remedy for diarrhoea and stomach disorders; a root decoction acts as a mild purgative, and also in the treatment of stomachache and gonorrhoea.

Shrub

Pods

Flowers

Adenium obesum

APOCYNACEAE

Desert rose, Elephant's foot

Indigenous

Local names: Madiga (Swahili); Oleteti (Maasai); Egales (Turkana)

A succulent shrub, occasionally a tree, that grows to 6 m in height; widespread in dry bushland, especially in rocky sites; occurs from sea level up to 1 500 m.

Bark: Grey; smooth; lower part of stem bulbous.
Leaves: Thick; flesh; bluish green; narrowly elliptic; up to 15 cm in length; crowded at the ends of branches.
Flowers: Vary from pink to deep rose or white; funnel-shaped; about 5 cm across.
Fruit: Grey or grey-brown capsules; tapering at both ends; in pairs of about 24 x 2 cm; dry capsules split to release narrow cylindrical seeds about 1 cm long.
Uses: A useful ornamental in dry and rocky areas; grows in pure sand or very well-drained soil. Seeds and roots yield arrow poison and fish poison. A bark infusion is used to remove ticks and lice on camels and cows.

Flowers

Fruit capsules

Shrub

195

Aloe ferox

LILIACEAE

Candelabra aloe, Bitter aloe

Exotic, native to South Africa

Local name: None known

A succulent, perennial, single-stemmed plant, usually growing up to 2 m in height but older specimens can reach up to 5 m. It occurs in a variety of habitats, including mountain slopes, rocky sites and flat, open areas.

Stems: Thick; single-stemmed; densely bearded with old dry leaves.

Leaves: Broad; dull green to greyish green; can turn reddish under drought stress; dark brown spines along the margins and sometimes also on upper and especially the lower surfaces of the leaves.

Flowers: Inflorescence branched; 5–12 erect, conical spikes; each flower tubular; bright orange to red; yellowish and even white forms are also found.

Uses: This plant is commonly grown in gardens, and especially in rock gardens. Cultivation is by offsets from the base of adult plants.

Traditional medicine: Leaves or roots, boiled in water, are taken as a laxative, for stress, arthritis, eczema, conjunctivitis and hypertension. Leaf sap is applied externally to treat skin irritations, bruises and burns.

Flowers

Plant

Arundinaria alpinia

Mountain bamboo

Indigenous

Local names: Murangi (Kikuyu); Mwodi (Luo); Banda (Luganda)

Mountain bamboo grows in irregular patches at altitudes of 2 300–3 300 m, has a taller but more slender stem (culm) than its Golden cousin and grows up to 25 m in height.

Stem: Smooth; woody; hollow; yellow-green; can reach 7–10 cm in diameter. Grows from swollen underground stems (rhizomes). Whorls of thin branches grow at the upper nodes between stem sections.

Leaves: Grow from branchlet nodes; pale green; up to 20 cm long and 1 cm wide; tips long and thin; rough to touch because of short hairs.

Flowers: Rarely seen; in heads 10–20 cm long. After flowering the plant dies down.

Uses: Alpinia is used for fences, tea-packing baskets, and to make poles and tool handles. In Tanzania, it has been extensively used to construct village water pipes.

Mountain bamboo

Culms

Bambusa vulgaris

GRAMINEAE

Golden bamboo

Exotic, native to Southeast Asia

Local names: Murangi (Kikiuyu)

All bamboos grow in clumps of various sizes, most of them in the humid forests. Golden bamboo is a common ornamental in towns and is seen in large clumps at altitudes above 1 800 m. The tall stems (culms) grow to 15 m and are yellow, streaked with green.

Stem: Large; thick; hollow; can be green, yellow, yellow streaked with green or green streaked with yellow.

Leaves: Grow from branchlet nodes; pale green; up to 25 cm long; tip long and pointed; rough to touch.

Uses: Used for making fences, poles, furniture, in building, basketry and as food and fodder. Planted as an ornamental in exotic gardens.

Stems (culms)

Golden bamboo

Bauhinia tomentosa

CAESALPINIOIDEAE

Bauhinia, Camel's foot

Indigenous

Local names: Musaponi (Swahili); Murema (Kikuyu); Mulema, Muandia (Kamba)

A low shrub or small tree, growing to 7 m in height, often with drooping branches. It occurs along dry forest edges, and in riverine forest and bushland, wooded grassland and deciduous bushland, at altitudes from sea level to 2 100 m. Found mainly in Tanzania and Kenya, not as yet recorded in Uganda.

Bark: Grey-brown; smooth.

Leaves: Bilobed to one third or less (rarely to half-way); light green; 7 cm across; three main veins in each lobe.

Flowers: Bright yellow; drooping; do not open fully; 5 petals up to 5 cm long; one petal sometimes has a dark maroon spot near the base.

Fruit: Flat pods; up to 10 cm in length; green turning to brown; split open explosively on the tree.

Uses: This is a beautiful shrub, widely grown as a hedge or ornamental.

Flowers and fruit pods

Flower

Shrub

Beaucarnea recurvata (Nolina tuberculata) AGAVACEAE

Pony tail, Elephant's foot

Exotic, native to Mexico

Local name: None known

This is a slow-growing species, but with time the trunk will reach a height of 2 m or more and the base will swell like a huge bulb. The bulb stores water, so the plant is well able to tolerate occasional dryness around the roots.

Bark: Long, slender stem; grey; smooth; lower part of stem bulbous.

Leaves: Long, strap-like; growing up to 2 m in length; edges sharp, pointed and brittle, which gives the plant its common name (Pony tail).

Uses: This showy plant is very popular in gardens throughout East Africa.

Shrub plant

Bougainvillea glabra

Bougainvillea, Paper flower

Exotic, native to Brazil

Local name: None known

The species was named after the 18th-century French navigator Louis Antoine de Bougainvillea, who found specimens in Rio de Janeiro. It is now cultivated throughout the tropics and sub-tropics. Bougainvillea are robust and showy scandent shrubs or climbers that grow best in warm, dry climates, at altitudes from sea level to 2 000 m.

Bark: Brown; smooth; rough with age; multi-stemmed.
Leaves: Opposite or alternate; thick; oval; bright green.
Flowers: Small, white flowers surrounded by bright purple bracts. Varieties with orange, light pink, red, white and lemon bracts are available; also a double and variegated leaf form.
Uses: These decorative plants can be grown as fences, or as smaller bushes. Some reach a very large size, and can be used to great visual effect over the branches and foliage of tall trees. *Bougainvillea glabra* is a basic species; its hybrids are more showy and popular.

Orange flowers

Light pink flowers

Red flowers

Pink shrub

White flowers

Cadaba farinosa

CAPPARACEAE

No English name known

Indigenous

Local names: Mvunja-vumo, Kibalazi-mwitu (Swahili); Ol-amalogi (Maasai)

A slender, tangled and rather densely twigged shrub with arching branches. It grows 1–4 m in height, rarely to a tree of 7.5 m, and is found mostly in wooded deciduous grassland and woodland, in riverine thickets, in coastal thickets and in coastal bushland, at altitudes from sea level to 1 700 m.

Bark: Pale or dark grey; strongly grooved; branches stiff and sharp.

Leaves: Oval; greyish green; apex rounded.

Flowers: Yellow-green; in flowered racemes; 4 petals; 10–13 mm long.

Fruit: Cylindrical, greyish pods; 4–5 cm long; orange on the inside.

Uses: A preferred source of browse for giraffes, elephants, goats and other cattle.

Traditional medicine: A root infusion is used for protection against sexually transmitted diseases. A decoction of leaves is taken as a cure for gonorrhoea. Ground leaf-powder is effective in the treatment of ulcers. Plant ash is rubbed onto the skin as a remedy for general body pains.

Flowers and fruit pods

Shrub

Caesalpinia decapetala

Mauritius thorn, Mysore thorn   Exotic, native to tropical Asia, Mauritius

Local names: Mubage (Kikuyu); Kitandambo (Kamba); Olmashinga (Arusha)

A climbing or scrambling woody shrub or tree growing 7–9 m in height, armed throughout with sharp, recurved prickles. The plant, naturalized in East Africa, is often found in scattered tree grassland, bushland and in disturbed ground, at altitudes of 400–2 040 m above sea level.

Bark: Multi-stemmed; armed with dangerous prickles.
Leaves: Bipinnate; with 8–10 pairs of leaflets; elliptic-oblong; apex rounded; up to 2 cm in length.
Flowers: On long terminal spikes; up to 30 cm long; yellow; each 2 cm across; with protruding orange stamens in hanging groups.
Fruit: Clusters of hard, pointed pods; green turning to brown when dry; standing stiffly erect.
Uses: The shrub makes an effective hedge. Foliage and pods are good forage for domestic stock. Leaves used as mulch and bee forage.

Flowers

Shrub

Fruit pods

Caesalpinia gillesii (Poinciana gillesii) CAESALPINIOIDEAE

Poinciana Exotic, native to the Argentine; naturalized

Local name: None known

A deciduous shrub or small tree, with graceful, slender, hairy shoots, that grows 4–5 m in height, in rare cases up to 8 m.

Bark: Grey; smooth; branched on top.
Leaves: Compound; bipinnate; up to 20 cm long with numerous fine leaflets.
Flowers: Terminal racemes; up to 30 cm or more in length; composed of 5 pale yellow petals and long red stamens, which resemble a bird's head.
Fruit: Green, turning to dry brown pods; prickly-beaked.
Uses: The poinciana is recommended for tropical and subtropical gardens.

Shrub

Fruit

Flowers

Caesalpinia pulcherrima

Pride of Barbados, Dwarf poinciana

Exotic, native to tropical America

Local name: Mnyonyore (Swahili)

An splendid ornamental shrub or a small tree growing to 6 m in height, planted throughout the tropics. It does best at the lower altitudes, especially at the coast.

Flowers and fruit

Bark: Grey; smooth; with or without spines.

Leaves: Compound; bipinnate; up to 12 pairs of leaflets; oblong; apex round or notched; up to 2 cm in length; stalks often armed with prickles.

Flowers: Erect, terminal racemens; orange/scarlet; butterfly-shaped; frilled; with yellow borders; 5 petals, one narrower than the others, 3 cm across; stalk long, up to 6 cm; stamens 10 or less, long and protruding, with scarlet filament.

Fruit: Flattened, hanging pods; green turning to dark brown; irregularly oblong; up to 12 cm in length; twist open on the tree.

Uses: A decorative tree at the coast as it is almost always in flower. It is also grown as a fence.

Shrub

Calliandra haematocephala

MIMOSOIDEAE

Powder-puff tree

Exotic, native to Bolivia, tropical America

Local name: None known

An outstanding ornamental shrub, much-branched, spreading out to about 2–4 m.

Bark: Grey-brown; smooth.

Leaves: Compound; bipinnate; leaflets in 4–7 pairs.

Flowers: Made up entirely of numerous long stamens; brilliant red blossoms; rarely creamy white.

Fruit: Long pods; 10–12 cm long; green turning to brown; tapering at the base.

Uses: The plant, with its exquisite round flower-heads, can give a distinctive and beautiful look to otherwise ordinary gardens.

Fruit pods

Flowers

Shrub

Calotropis procera

ASCLEPIDIACEAE

Dead Sea fruit

Indigenous

Local names: Muvuthu (Kamba); Etetheru (Turkana); Labechi (Samburu)

A shrub or small tree growing 1–4 m tall, with a soft, woody stem containing much latex. It is commonly found in dry areas, usually along seasonal rivers or along roadsides, at altitudes of 300–1 200 m above sea level.

Leaves: Oval; stalkless; markedly veined; pointed tip; hairy beneath.
Flowers: White and purple; closely massed; in long-stalked axillary umbel.
Fruit: Big; green; inflated; oblong.
Uses: The wood is used to make canoe paddles and fire sticks.
Traditional medicine: A root infusion is used as a remedy for coughs and snakebite; a decoction of roots plays a role in the treatment of hookworm, and also serves as an emetic.

Fruit and seeds

Shrub

Flower and fruit pod

Camellia sinensis

THEACEAE

China tea bush

Exotic, native to China

Local name: Mchai (Swahili)

A large evergreen shrub or tree that grows to 5 m or more; commonly cultivated at the higher altitudes in the wetter areas of the tropics.

Leaves: Long; oval; pointed; leathery; usually 5-10 cm long; shiny, dark green above; edge finely dentate.
Flowers: White and fragrant; usually solitary; 2–4 cm across; with 5 petals.
Fruit: A 3-angled capsule with 3 seeds; surrounded by persistent sepals.
Uses: A very important cash crop in East Africa. The wood is used as fuel.

Flower

Fruit capsules

Shrub

Seeds and ripe fruit

Carica papaya

Pawpaw, Papaya —— **Exotic, native to tropical America; naturalized**

Local name: Mpapai (Swahili); Papaali (Luganda)

A shrub or small tree, usually with only one trunk that grows up to 6 m high; the trunk is about 20 cm in diameter, narrowing to a crown of leaves. Widely cultivated as a tropical fruit.

Bark: Pale grey; smooth; well marked with leaf scars.
Leaves: Simple; deeply lobed, large blade; on a long stalk; clustered in a spiral at the end of the stem.
Flowers: Monoecious; creamy white; 5 sepals; joint; 5 petals; more or less free in female; male flowers have 10 stamens.
Fruit: A large, fleshy berry; numerous black seeds; green at first, turning yellow or orange when ripe.
Uses: The fruit is edible; also features in the preparation of preserves (pickles, jam) and juices. The leaves and fruit are used to tenderize meat.

Flowers

Fruit

Tree

Carissa edulis

APOCYNACEAE

Carissa

Indigenous

Local names: Mtanda-mboo (Swahili); Muyonza (Luganda); Manka (Chagga)

A scrambling bush, sometimes found as a spiny evergreen shrub, which grows to 5 m in height; widespread in bushland and dry forest edges at altitudes from sea level to 2 000 m. Very common throughout East Africa.

Bark: Grey; smooth; with straight woody spines up to 5 cm long; often in pairs; rarely branching; milky latex is present.
Leaves: Opposite; leathery; dark green; shiny; up to 5 cm long; tip pointed; base rounded; stalk very short.
Flowers: In pink-white, terminal clusters; each flower up to 2 cm across; highly scented.
Fruit: Red to black berries; about 1 cm across; can be either round or ellipsoid.
Uses: The purple-black berries are sweet and edible. The plant tolerates dry conditions and most soils; also grows as an attractive and impenetrable hedge.
Traditional medicine: A decoction of roots is used as a painkiller and to treat malaria. Taken warm and in small quantities it is also helpful for indigestion and for abdominal pains during pregnancy. The fruits help in the treatment of dysentery.

Shrub

Flowers

Fruit

Cassia abbreviata

Long-pod cassia

Indigenous

Local names: Mbaraka (Swahili); Malandesi (Kamba); Limulimuli, Mulimuli (Hehe)

A many-branched shrub or a small tree that grows 3–7.5 m in height, occasionally up to 10 m, with a rounded crown. It is found in coastal areas and in dry bushland, especially in *Acacia-Commiphora* bushland, at altitudes of 50–1 500 m.

Bark: Brown; cracked.

Leaves: Compound; with 5–12 pairs of leaflets, each up to 4 cm long; elliptic or oblong; apex rounded to sub-acute.

Flowers: Fragrant; golden yellow; in either terminal or axillary clusters.

Fruit: Cylindrical pods; grey-green turning to black when dry; 30–90 cm long and 1.5–2.5 cm wide; glabrous or velvety.

Uses: The bark is used in the process of tanning leather; the wood is used for poles and posts, and as fuel.

Traditional medicine: Root and bark are used in the treatment of stomach disorders; a decoction of the roots relieves gonorrhoea, pneumonia and other chest complaints, malaria and uterus troubles; roots are also taken orally as a remedy for syphilis.

Mature fruit

Flowers

Shrub

Chaetacme aristata (C. microcarpa)

ULMACEAE

Thorny elm

Indigenous

Local names: Muyuyu (Kikuyu); Olmorogi luwaso (Maasai); Chepkaket (Kipsigis)

A scrambling, thorny or bushy shrub, can grow into a much-branched tree of up to 10 m high, evergreen, with drooping, zigzag branches. Occurs in evergreen forest, forest edges and bushland throughout East Africa at altitudes of 900–2 100 m.

Bark: Smooth; grey; trunk and branches armed with sharp spines; often paired and axillary; up to 3.5 cm long.
Leaves: Glossy; leathery; elliptic; up to 9 cm long; with pointed tip; midrib prominent below; margin serrated only in very young leaves.
Flowers: Small; greenish; in dense axillary clusters.
Fruit: Ovoid; about 1.5 cm long; green first, then orange-yellow when ripe; with two persistent styles.
Uses: The wood is yellowish, very heavy and difficult to cut; used as fuel and to make clubs. Leaves and fruit browsed by game.

Young fruit

Flowers

Shrub

Citrus sinensis

RUTACEAE

Orange tree

Exotic, native to southern China, Vietnam

Local names: Mchungwa (Swahili); Muchungwa (Luganda)

A shrub or small tree, growing 4–6 m in height; it is widespread in regions with tropical and temperate climates.

Bark: Grey-brown; branches greenish brown, armed with spines.

Leaves: Simple; alternate; spicily aromatic when crushed.

Flowers: Small; regular; 5 white petals; free; scented; attract bees.

Fruit: A hesperidium (as in all citrus); green to orange when ripe.

Uses: The family Rutaceae includes the orange (*Citrus sinensis*) lemon (*Citrus limon*), tangerine (*Citrus reticulata*), grapefruit (*Citrus paradisi*) and lime (*Citrus aurantifolia*). All citrus fruits are juicy, full of vitamin C, and used to make jams, jellies, marmalades and fresh squash. Wood is used as firewood. Flowers, leaves and peel produce aromatic oil.

Shrub

Flowers

Ripe fruit

Green fruit

Coffea arabica

RUBIACEAE

Arabian coffee

Indigenous

Local names: Kahua (Kikuyu); Kaawa (Kamba)

An evergreen shrub or a small tree that reaches 3–7 m in height, but in cultivation it is usually pruned to about 2 m. It grows at altitudes of 1 350–1 500 m.

Leaves: Opposite; elliptic; dark, shiny green; up to 20 cm long.

Flowers: White; 2–20 per axil; scented.

Fruit: Cherries; green turning to red when ripe; 1–2 cm long; in dense clusters, each containing 2 grooved seeds in a silvery skin.

Uses: The seeds are the familiar coffee beans, which are washed, dried, roasted and ground into the beverage.

Traditional medicine: A leaf decoction is taken as a treatment for hepatic (liver) problems.

Fruit

Flowers

Shrub

Commiphora africana

Commiphora   **Indigenous**

Local names: Mturituri, Mbambara (Swahili); Ekadeli, Etopojo (Ateso Kramojong)

A deciduous, spiny shrub or a small tree that usually grows 5–10 m in height. The plant is widely distributed throughout the drier coastal regions, in bushed grassland, and in *Acacia-Commiphora* bushland at altitudes of 50–1 800 m.

Trunk: Cylindrical; usually beset, from near the base, with horizontal spiny branches; grey-green; peeling in shiny reddish brown or grey scrolls; exudes pale milky sap; slightly scented.

Leaves: Trifoliate; terminal leaflet much larger; up to 8 cm long; tapering to base; apex rounded; margin serrated.

Flowers: Small; up to 5 mm across; green turning red; in axillary clusters.

Fruit: Round; pointed; pinkish red; about 1 cm long; flesh contains one stony seed.

Uses: It is sometimes planted as a fence. Wood is used as fuelwood, and young shoots as fodder. Tea is made from the bark.

Traditional medicine: This species has many medicinal properties; especially its resin, bark and fruit. Leaves contain bitter tannins; steam from bark and roots helps with fever and colds; a decoction of boiled roots is taken for swollen testicles and stomach disorders. The bark is also chewed with tobacco and applied to the area of a snakebite. The resin is used as a sealant and disinfectant for wounds. Fruits feature in the treatment of typhoid fever.

Bark

Trees

Fruit

Branches and tiny flowers

Cotoneaster pannosa

ROSACEAE

China berry

Exotic, native to southwestern China

Local name: None known

A splendid, wide-spreading shrub growing to about 4 m high, with arching branches; commonly planted in the highlands.

Leaves: Small; oval; up to 3 cm long; dull green above; pale grey and softly hairy below.
Flowers: Small; white with rose tint; in dense, attractive clusters.
Fruit: Scarlet or red berries; in showy clusters.
Uses: A slow-growing and drought-resistant plant, suitable for most soils. Very attractive and showy in fruit; suitable for flower arrangements.

Berries

Flowers

Shrub

Crotolaria agatiflora

Lion's claw

Indigenous

Local names: Muchingiri, Mwethia (Kikuyu); Olontwalan (Maasai); Iviinzi (Kamba)

A handsome, soft-wood herb shrub that grows up to 6 m in height, found in bushed grassland in the uplands, along roadsides and on waste ground, at altitudes of 1 400–2 400 m.

Bark: Green; smooth; rough when older; multi-stemmed.
Leaves: Trifoliate leaflets; elliptic to ovate; apex acute; sometimes hairy; long petiole.
Flowers: Pale yellow; beak-like keel; keel sometimes reddish with black tip; in many flowered racemes.
Fruit: 7–10 cm long; glabrous, inflated pods.
Traditional medicine: A root decoction is used in the treatment of gonorrhoea.

Shrub

Flowers

Fruit pods

Crotolaria lebrunii

PAPILIONOIDEAE

Crotolaria

Indigenous

Local name: Muchingiri (Kikuyu)

A shrub that grows 2–5 m in height; confined to forest margins and clearings at altitudes of 1 800–2 400 m.

Bark: Light brown or grey-brown; branched.

Leaves: Elliptic; apex obtuse and base cuneate; densely hairy beneath.

Flowers: Yellow with purple markings; in loose, long racemes; keel 20 mm long.

Fruit: Purple-brown pods; elliptic; pointed; 5–7 cm long.

Uses: The wood is used for fuel, the leaves and twigs as fodder.

Flowers

Shrub

218

Crotolaria mauensis

PAPILIONOIDEAE

No English name known

Indigenous

Local names: Mwethia (Kikuyu); Mugumba (Meru)

A shrub or woody herb of the upland areas that grows up to 4 m in height; widely distributed in forest margins, grassland, secondary bushland; often on roadsides, at altitudes of 1 500–2 550 m above sea level.

Leaves: Trifoliate; leaflets elliptic; apex acute or rounded; soft, pale green.
Flowers: Yellow, fading to red; dense racemes.
Fruit: Oblong to club-shaped pods; 4–6 cm long.
Traditional medicine: A leaf decoction is used in the treatment of eye problems; a decoction of roots serves as a remedy for urinary infections.

Shrub

Pods

Flowers

Dalbergia melanoxyon

PAPILIONOIDEAE

African blackwood, African ebony

Indigenous

Local names: Mpingo (Swahili); Kidamo (Chagga); Motangu (Luganda)

A spiny shrub or small tree that grows to 7 m in height, often several-stemmed and much-branched, scattered on savannah and woodland at low altitudes (below 1 300 m).

Bark: Smooth; greyish yellow; fissured or flaking in older trees; branches short and twisted; spiny-tipped.
Leaves: Compound; up to 8 leaflets; obovate; dark green; small and variable; about 1.5 cm long.
Flowers: Small; white; sweet-scented; in short, branched sprays.
Fruit: Small, thin, flat pods; oblong; 3–7 cm long.
Uses: The plant has excellent heartwood, purplish black, very durable, making it a very valuable timber in East Africa. Due to over-exploitation, the species is becoming rare and it needs to be strictly conserved.
Traditional medicine: Leaves are boiled into a kind of soup and taken to relieve aching joints. A bark decoction serves to clean wounds; a root decoction is taken for abdominal pains, as an anthelmintic or vermifuge (for worms) and as a part of a compound prepared as a remedy for gonorrhoea.

Shrub

Flowers

Fruit

Datura suaveolens (Brugmansia suaveolens)   SOLANACEAE

Angel's trumpet, Moon flower   Exotic, native to Mexico

Local name: Maduudu (Luganda)

A shrub or small tree that reaches 3–5 m in height, with strong woody stems. It has large, pendent, trumpet-shaped flowers and makes an excellent ornamental.

Bark: Multi-stemmed; woody; light brown.

Leaves: Ovate-oblong; velvety; tapering tip; often white and downy underneath; 15–30 cm long.

Flowers: Huge; pendulous; musk-scented; about 25 cm in length; pure white at first but mellowing to cream with age; single or double forms.

Uses: Datura is available in a variety of colours, notably *Datura chlorantha* (yellow flowers) and *Datura sanguinea* (orange-red flowers). All these shrubby plants are highly poisonous. In Mexico, the foliage is smoked and the flowers are used in the treatment of asthma. In East Africa, it is popular for hedging and as an isolated lawn specimen.

Orange flowers

Yellow flowers

White flowers

Dichrostachys cinerea

MIMOSOIDEAE

Sickle bush

Indigenous

Local names: Mkingiri (Swahili); Muwanika (Luganda); Muvilisya (Kamba)

An acacia-like spiny shrub or small tree that reaches up to 6 m in height, found in a variety of habitats – bushed grassland, wooded grassland, rocky hillsides, coastal plains and in overgrazed and disturbed areas. Occurs at altitudes from sea level to 1 700 m.

Bark: Rough; spines terminating in lateral twigs.

Leaves: Feathery; with 2–19 pairs of pinnae; leaflets in 9–41 pairs; linear or oblong.

Flowers: Pendulous; two-coloured; the top half bearing long pink, mauve or white filaments and the lower half bearing short yellow stamens.

Fruit: Brown to black, flat pods; twisted or spiral; in strangely shaped clusters.

Uses: The timber of this plant is very hard, used for tool handles, poles, posts, and as fuel. Leaves and pods are good fodder. The bark fibres are used to make ropes. Also useful as a live fence, and for soil conservation and nitrogen fixation.

Traditional medicine: A decoction of the roots is used as an astringent for scorpion bite; leaves serve the same purpose (they are chewed and poulticed on the bite). Leaves are pounded to produce a local anaesthetic, which is also used in the treatment of ulcers and gonorrhoea. Roots may be crushed, mixed with food and eaten (or boiled and the solution drunk) as an aphrodisiac. An extract of the leaves mixed with a little salt serves as a remedy for stomachache.

Shrub

Flowers

Bare tree

Flowers and fruit pods

Dodonaea angustifolia (D. viscosa)   SAPINDACEAE

Sand olive   Indigenous

Local names: Mkengata (Swahili); Muwema-muthua (Kikuyu); Musambya (Rukiga)

A shrubby tree, usually reaching 3–8 m in height, with a light crown. It is widely distributed from sea level to 2 700 m, mostly in evergreen bushland, on rocky, stony or lava sites, and in forest margins. It can withstand fires to an amazing degree.

Bark: Dark grey; fissured and peeling; branchlets red and sticky.
Leaves: Thin; narrow; stiffly erect; up to 10 cm long; tapering to a stalk; apex pointed; young leaves light green, shiny and sticky.
Flowers: Small; yellow-green; sepals; no petals; in short, dense terminal panicles. Male flowers have pale brown stamens.
Fruit: Distinctive capsule; pinkish or reddish; 2–3 papery wings; sometimes inflated.
Uses: A good hedge species for dry areas. The wood is hard and heavy, used for tool handles and walking sticks, as fuelwood and for charcoal.
Traditional medicine: A decoction of leaves and twigs is used as a remedy for colds, influenza and other fevers, stomach troubles, measles, arthritis, and as a gargle for sore throats and oral thrush. Roots are boiled in water and the decoction taken by women to stimulate milk production after childbirth. Pounded leaves, steeped in cold water and then strained, serve as a remedy for diarrhoea.

Fruit

Flowers

Shrub

Dovyalis caffra

FLACOURTIACEAE

Kei apple

Exotic, native to South Africa

Local name: Kaiyaba (Kikuyu)

A thorny evergreen shrub, usually growing 3–5 m tall and found at altitudes well above 1 200 m. It prefers well-drained soils.

Bark: Grey; smooth; with strong spines up to 6 cm long.
Leaves: Thin; shiny; dark green; up to 5 cm long; rounded apex; occasionally notched.
Flowers: Small; creamy yellow; in dense clusters; with prominent stamens.
Fruit: Round; fleshy; up to 4 cm in diameter; orange-yellow when ripe.
Uses: The plant is extremely hardy, and is cultivated as a border, hedge or live fence. Regular trimming may be needed to maintain a good hedge. The leaves are used as fodder. The fruit is edible, and makes excellent jam.

Fruit

Flowers

Shrub

Dovyalis macrocalyx

FLACOURTIACEAE

No English name known

Indigenous

Local names: Olmorogo (Maasai); Cheptabirbiriet (Kipsigis); Mutunku (Luganda)

A shrub or a small tree growing 3–8 m in height, often in dense shade. It is multi-stemmed with drooping foliage, and occurs widely in moist, dry, and riverine forest at altitudes from sea level to 1 500 m.

Bark: Smooth; grey, branches with straight axillary slender spines, 1–6 cm long.

Leaves: Elliptic or ovate; glabrous.

Flowers: Yellow-green; small flowers.

Fruit: Red; plum-shaped; with an enlarged red calyx with many glandular hairs; fruit contains a single seed.

Uses: The fruit is sweet and edible.

Shrub

Berries

Flowers

Dracaena ellenbeckiana (D. kedongensis) LILIACEAE

Kedong dracaena Indigenous

Local names: Ol-ekidong (Maasai); Emisth (Turkana); Motiet (Kipsigis)

A palm-like shrub or small tree with thin branches, usually reaching about 4 m in height but occasionally growing to 10 m. Found on dry, steep, rocky hill slopes at altitudes from 1 050–2 000 m.

Bark: Grey; with leaf scars.

Leaves: Blue-green; tufted near tree top; lance-shaped; very narrow – about 50 cm in length with tapering tip.

Flowers: Small; yellow-green; in terminal panicles; up to 75 cm in length.

Fruit: Small berries; round or 2–3 lobed; orangey-red when ripe.

Uses: In East Africa, the hollowed-out stems of the plant are used for arrow quivers.

Traditional medicine: The plant features in ritual ceremonies among some local groups.

Fruit

Shrub

Ehretia cymosa (E. sylvatica)

No English name known

Indigenous

Local names: Murembu (Kikuyu); Endalati-ekolok (Maasai); Musuga (Luganda)

A shrub or many-branched tree growing to 12 m in height, found at forest margins or in secondary vegetation derived from forest, at altitudes of 1 100–2 300 m.

Bark: Smooth; grey; young branchlets covered in dense white hairs.

Leaves: Ovate or elliptic; base round; apex pointed; rough; dark green above; paler below; midrib and veins prominent beneath, and covered with fine hairs.

Flowers: White; small; 6 mm across; in dense terminal clusters; often covering the tree; stamens protrude.

Fruit: Orange or red berries; round; up to 1 cm across in terminal heads.

Uses: The wood is used for tool handles and yokes, the branches for fire-sticks. The fruit is edible but very acid.

Traditional medicine: Leaf juice is styptic and used in the treatment of wounds; roots and leaves are used as an aphrodisiac (but are also toxic).

Flowers

Flowers and fruit

Shrub

Erythrina crista-galli

PAPILIONOIDEAE

Cockscomb, Cockspur, Coral bean, Coral tree

Exotic, native to Brazil

Local name: None known

A large deciduous shrub or a small tree that reaches up to 2.5 m in height, with spiny green branches and stems. It grows at the higher altitudes.

Bark: Brown; fissured when old.

Leaves: Trifoliate; oval-shaped; each leaf has a pointed tip and a stalk of about 1 cm; midrib prominent; margin entire.

Flowers: Brilliant red in terminal racemes; each about 4 cm in length.

Fruit: Dry, brown, axillary pods; up to 20 cm long; split open on tree to release 4–6 black, bean-shaped seeds.

Uses: This shrub is a garden ornamental in East Africa. It is very showy when in bloom. It remains without leaves for most months.

Fruit pods

Flowers

Shrub

228

Euphorbia cotinifolia

Red euphorbia   Exotic, native to Mexico, South America, West Indies

Local name: None known

A very fast-growing deciduous shrub or small tree, widely planted as an ornamental, which grows to 6 m in height. It remains bare for months on end.

Bark: Greyish green; smooth.

Leaves: Coppery red in colour; narrowly oval; long red stalk; up to 2 cm long; leaves frequently secrete latex.

Flowers: Very small; cream-coloured; in terminal clusters.

Fruit: Very small; 3-lobed capsule.

Uses: The plant is easily grown from cuttings. The white sap is an irritant (and carcinogenic). A dye, extracted from the leaves, is used for woollen fabrics.

Flowers

Shrub

Euphorbia cuneata

EUPHORBIACEAE

No English name known

Indigenous

Local names: Mchongoma, Mlimbilimbi (Swahili); Echokokile, Lokilei (Turkana)

A much-branched shrub growing to 3 m in height, with alternate, spine-tipped branches. It occurs in *Acacia-Commiphora* bushland or semi-desert scrub, on the coast and in mixed bushland at altitudes from sea level to 1 350 m. At first sight the plant may be easily mistaken for a *Commiphora* species, but the copious white latex that emerges when a stem or leaf is cut or broken is the easiest way to recognize it as a Euphorbia.

Bark: Yellow or grey-brown; branches often reddish purple; peeling; woody; ending in spines.

Leaves: Glabrous; bunched on very short shoots; apex rounded; 2.5 cm long and 1.2 cm wide.

Flowers: Yellow or yellow-green; on very short shoot; usually on leafless branches; 2–3 in a cluster.

Fruit: Reddish purple capsule.

Uses: Common in northern and coastal districts, where it is sometimes used as a hedge plant.

Traditional medicine: Curative sap from the branches is applied to wounds and sores.

Flowers

Shrub

Euphorbia heterochroma

EUPHORBIACEAE

No English name known

Indigenous

Local name: Enleusanoi (Maasai); Harkeena (Gabbra)

A much-branched, thorny, leafless succulent bush or shrub that grows 1–3 m in height, found in Kenya and Tanzania (not recorded in Uganda) in bushland, in dry rocky areas and on lava flows, at altitudes of 450–2 050 m.

Bark: Ascending stem; branches 4–6-angled; light green; with margin slightly denate; spines very short; up to 3 mm long; in pairs; diverging.

Flowers: Red; in short cymes; stalkless.

Fruit: Purple-red; 3-lobed; about 4 mm across.

Uses: The plant makes a good live fence, especially in very dry areas.

Flowers

Shrub

Euphorbia leucocephala

EUPHORBIACEAE

White lace euphorbia, Snowball tree   Exotic, native to Mexico, Guatemala

Local name: None known

A very fast-growing, deciduous shrub that reaches 2–4 m in height. A very common garden plant, it makes a magnificent show with its clusters of sweet-scented white bracts. It grows well at the higher altitudes.

Bark: Multi-stemmed; greyish brown; smooth.
Leaves: Small; bright green; oval; in whorls; each with a pink stalk; soft-textured.
Flowers: Small; surrounded by 5 white star-like glands that resemble thin petals; white, leafy bracts, tinged with pink; up to 1.5 cm long; borne in large heads.
Fruit: Small, 3-lobed capsule.
Uses: Suitable as an ornamental garden shrub. It requires pruning after the flowering season.

Flowers

Shrub

Euphorbia pulcherrima

Poinsettia, Mexican flame leaf

Exotic, native to Mexico

Local name: None known

A small, striking shrub, growing up to 4 m high, with a woody brown trunk and angular branches, widely planted as an ornamental.

Leaves: Oval-lanceolate; with 12 teeth on either side; veins very clear; up to 20 cm long; apex tapering; margin often lobed.

Flowers: Inconspicuous; held in terminal groups; small; greenish yellow, with large, scarlet, petal-like bracts surrounding them. There are also white and yellow forms of bracts.

Fruit: Very small, 3-lobed capsule.

Uses: Poinsettias grow as single garden plants or in groups as a hedge, which makes a striking feature, and are popular as pot-plants. The species needs full sun and good soil, and is best cut back after flowering.

Shrub

Flowers

Euphorbia tirucalli

EUPHORBIACEAE

Finger euphorbia, Milk bush, Pencil euphorbia

Indigenous

Local names: Mnyara, Mtupa (Swahili); Ol-oile (Maasai); Nkoni (Luganda)

A succulent shrub or tree growing up to 6 m or more, commonly occurring in bushland, thickets and coastal bushland, at altitudes from sea level to 1 600 m.

Bark: Dense; straight-stemmed; the branches smooth, green and cylindrical in dense masses.

Leaves: Small; up to 6 mm long; only on young stems; soon dropping.

Flowers: Cream or yellow-green; occur in short, terminal clusters.

Fruit: 3-lobed capsule; 6 mm across; hard; purple-green.

Uses: This succulent shrub is frequently planted as a hedge, in dry areas, around cattle *bomas* (enclosures). The latex is highly poisonous (and especially harmful to the eyes), and is used for fish poison and as an insecticide. The young branches serve as fodder, the wood as fuel.

Traditional medicine: Young branches can be roasted and chewed, the juice acting as a remedy for sore throats and stomach complaints. Boiled root solution serves as an emetic in cases of snakebite, and also as a remedy for sterility in women. The plant is highly toxic, however, and is approached with extreme caution.

Shrub

Fruit

Branches

Gardenia ternifolia *var.* jovis-tonantis   RUBIACEAE

Large-leafed gardenia   Indigenous

Local names: Kimwemwe (Swahili), Geninyet (Maasai); Mukumuti (Kamba)

A savannah shrub or low-branched tree that grows to 6 m in height; usually stunted and twisted. It is found in wooded grassland and riverine woodland at altitudes from sea level to 2 100 m.

Bark: Pale; greenish grey; dotted with lenticels.
Leaves: Opposite or in whorls of 3; on short branchlets; spoon-shaped, wavy; up to 12 cm long; stipules brown, membranous, sheathed around the stems midway between the leaf pairs.
Flowers: White, turning yellow; solitary; funnel-shaped; very fragrant; up to 8 cm across; petals twisted in buds, later splaying out.
Fruit: Woody; egg-shaped; grey-brown; warty; up to 8 cm long; crowned with a persistent calyx.
Uses: The wood is very hard, fine-grained; used for spears, knife handles, as well as other tool handles.
Traditional medicine: A decoction of the fruit is used in the treatment of malaria, taken as a purgative, and as a remedy for eye complaints. A root infusion is administered for snakebite (this causes the subject to vomit heavily, which counteracts the toxic effects).

Flower

Fruit

Shrub

Grewia bicolor

TILIACEAE

No English name known

Indigenous

Local names: Mkone (Swahili); Olsitete (Maasai); Mulawa (Kamba)

A low, much-branched shrub or small tree that usually grows to 3 m, occasionally to 9 m, producing branches from the base of the main trunk. It is widespread in dry Acacia bushland, bushed grassland and woodland, often on rocky sites. It occurs at altitudes from sea level to 2 000 m.

Bark: Grey-brown; deeply fissured and peeling; branchlets speckled with pale lenticels.

Leaves: Oval to oblong; pointed; 1–8 cm long; edge finely dentate; shiny green above and silvery white or yellow below.

Flowers: Bright yellow; sweet-scented; small petals bent back over larger petals; often in profusion.

Fruit: Usually round, with one lobe about 6 mm in diameter; green and hairy, becoming glossy orange-brown.

Uses: The ripe fruit is sweet and edible. Leaves are browsed by domestic stock. The wood is used for poles, implement handles, walking sticks, bows and arrows, general timber, and as fuel.

Traditional medicine: Roots are used in the treatment of chest pains, snakebite and colds; bark is used to treat intestinal infestations and syphilis.

Flowers

Shrub

Fruit and flowers

Fruit

Grewia similis

No English name known

Indigenous

Local names: Mkole (Swahili); Mutuya (Kamba); Ol-neligwat (Maasai)

A shrub, occasionally a small tree, growing to 3 m, often a climber to 9 m or higher. The plant is common in bush and grassland but does not occur in dry areas; found at altitudes of 600–2 200 m.

Bark: Smooth, becoming rougher, grey to greyish brown.

Leaves: Broadly oval; almost rounded; about 5 cm long; glossy green above; apex rounded or notched; base rounded; margin serrated; 3 veins arise from base, very prominent beneath; young shoots hairy.

Flowers: Bright mauve or pink with yellow anthers, mauve filaments; 2 cm across; in 3–6 or more flowers in terminal or axillary groups.

Fruit: Fleshy berries; green at first, then turning orange to bright red when ripe; deeply 4-lobed, each lobe about 5 mm across.

Uses: The ripe fruit is edible, and much favoured by birds. The wood is used for bows, and for building-poles.

Traditional medicine: The sticky substance under the bark was used in the treatment of sores.

Flowers and fruit

Shrub

Flowers

Grewia tenax

TILIACEAE

Grewia

Indigenous

Local names: Toronwo (Pokot); Eng'omo (Turkana); Damak (Somali)

A shrub, growing up to 2 m in height, found in Acacia bushland or bushed grassland. Found at altitudes from sea level to 1 500 m.

Leaves: Round to oval; usually 5 cm long; apex and base rounded; margin finely dentate; 3 veins arising from the leaf base; slightly sandpapery in texture.

Flowers: White; solitary; 2 cm across; borne on long, slender branches.

Fruit: Green turning to orange-red when ripe; 3–4 lobes; glabrous.

Uses: The wood is used for making bows, arrows and *rungus* (local weapons); the fruit is edible.

Uses: Young shoots and leaves are browsed by domestic stock.

Traditional medicine: The bark yields a sticky gum that acts as an insect repellant.

Flowers

Fruit

Shrub

Hibiscus rosa-sinesis

MALVACEAE

Rose of China, Shoe flower

Exotic, native to China

Local name: None known

A magnificent evergreen shrub reaching 2 m in height, up to 5 m if unpruned.

Leaves: Pointed; oval; coarsely dentate; green.
Flowers: Either single or double; large, up to 13 cm in diameter; variety of colours from showy pink, red, yellow to orange, usually with prominent yellow stamens and long red stigmas.
Uses: Hibiscus makes a charming hedge (either low or high) and garden plant.

Pink-flowered shrub

Red-flowered shrub

Single pink flower

Double orange flower

Single red flower

Double pink flower

Hibiscus schizopetalus

MALVACEAE

Coral hibiscus, Fringed hibiscus

Indigenous

Local name: None known

A much-branched shrub or small tree reaching 5 m in height, though it is sometimes stunted. It occurs in coastal woodland, is common in many parts of the tropics, and is popular as a garden ornamental.

Bark: Multi-stemmed; brown; roughens with age.

Leaves: Oval; up to 10 cm long; pointed apex; base rounded; margin serrated.

Flowers: Red with white markings; hangs from long, jointed stalks; up to 10 cm long; 5 petals, deeply incised, twisted and curled back; staminal tube pink, very long, hangs a further 8 cm below the petals; short-lived.

Fruit: 5-celled, dry capsules; up to 2.5 cm long.

Uses: The bark yields a strong fibre, which is used for making rope.

Red flower

Hypericum kiboense

St. John's wort

Indigenous

Local name: Susimua (Kikuyu)

A small shrub, growing from 0.5–2 m in height, found in dry forest margins, and in the *Hagenia* bamboo and *Hypericum* mountain zones, at altitudes of 2 250–3 250 m.

Bark: Red-brown, smooth.

Leaves: Slightly ovate; base and apex rounded; 6–17 mm long; glabrous; with translucent dots.

Flowers: Bright yellow; solitary or in groups of a few flowers; terminal; petals 0.8–1.3 cm long; with black marginal dots.

Fruit: Round; 4 mm long; green at first, turning dark brown when ripe.

Uses: St. John's wort is a garden shrub. It has recognized curative properties and is widely used in homeopathy (notably as a remedy for depression).

Traditional medicine: Bark and leaves used in the treatment of backache, fevers and wounds.

Flowers

Shrub

Hypericum revolutum (H. lanceolatum) GUTTIFERAE

Giant St. John's wort Indigenous

Local names: Susimua (Kikuyu); Biriwarokiet (Kipsigis); Osasimwa (Maasai)

An attractive shrub or a small tree that grows 1–10 m in height, commonly found near forest margins in the Aberdare highlands and on Mount Kenya. It occurs at altitudes of 2 100–3 250 m.

Bark: Red-brown, scaly.

Leaves: Narrowly elliptic; base narrow and apex pointed; up to 1 cm long.

Flowers: Bright yellow; solitary and terminal; with numerous, bright yellow stamens.

Fruit: Ellipsoid; 11–15 mm long.

Uses: The species is valued both as a garden shrub and as a medicinal plant throughout the world.

Traditional medicine: Powdered, dried leaves and stems are used as an antidiarrhoeal and for rheumatism. Oily extract of the plant is used to treat wounds and burns.

Shrub

Flowers

Fruit

Lagerstroemia indica

LYTHRACEAE

Pride of India, Crepe myrtle

Exotic, native to China, Korea

Local name: None known

A large deciduous shrub or small tree growing up to 8 m in height, with stiff, erect branches. The stem is attractively mottled in grey, pink and cinnamon. The plant grows as an ornamental tree in the highlands.

Bark: Grey; smooth.

Leaves: Opposite; alternate or in whorls of 3 smooth leaves; broadly oval; thick and fleshy; up to 6 cm long; pointed tip.

Flowers: Showy; in terminal heads; 6 petals; pink to deep red; crinkly; with numerous golden-yellow stamens.

Fruit: Small, woody capsules; dark brown when ripe.

Uses: A decorative ornamental tree for gardens; suitable only for areas receiving plenty of sun.

Flowers

Shrub

Lantana camara

VERBINACEAE

Lantana, Curse of India

Exotic, native to tropical America

Local names: Mukigi (Kikuyu); Kitavisi (Kamba); Nyamrih (Luo)

An evergreen shrub growing 2–3 m in height, with prickly stems. The plant forms large and dense thickets, and is now a serious weed on roadsides, spreading throughout East Africa at altitudes up to 1 900 m.

Bark: Multi-stemmed; with many small, recurved prickles.
Leaves: Opposite; ovate; aromatic; apex acute; margin dentate; upper surface rough; up to 8 cm long.
Flowers: Pink, yellow or mauve; up to 1 cm long; 5-lobed; in flat rounded heads.
Fruit: Small green berries, turning black when ripe; occur in round heads.
Uses: The leaves are poisonous to livestock, the berries toxic to humans (although not to birds). There are several drought-resistant hybrids, with rounded heads of small, axillary, differently-hued flowers; colours range through white, yellow, red and orange. These cultivated hybrids are planted as ornamental hedges and borders.
Traditional medicine: Leaves can be chewed to alleviate toothache; the ash of burnt leaves, together with a little salt, acts as a remedy for coughs, sore throat and toothache. The leaves are also used as an inhalent for the relief of headaches and colds.

Red flowers

Pink-yellow flowers

White flowers

Yellow flowers

Fruit

Shrub

Lantana trifolia

Lantana   Indigenous

Local names: Mvepe (Swahili); Mukenia (Kikuyu); Muvisavisi (Kamba)

A scrambling herbaceous shrub, up to 3 m high, whose stem has hairs rather than prickles. The plant is widespread, found in open bushland, wooded grassland and dry forest margins, at altitudes from sea level to 1 900 m.

Bark: Multi-stemmed; hairy; very thin stems.

Leaves: In threes; ovate; apex tapering; base rounded; margin serrated; sandpapery above.

Flowers: Mauve, pink or purple; rarely white; in spikes; on long stalks; rounded head.

Fruit: Red or purple berries.

Traditional medicine: Leaf juice or a leaf decoction is used as a remedy for hepatic (liver) diseases. Leaves are also pounded, mixed with hot water and applied to sore eyes; also used in the treatment of glandular disorders. Roots are crushed, mixed with hot water and the extract is taken as a remedy for rheumatism.

Shrub

Flowers

Leucaena leucocephala (L. glauca)   MIMOSOIDEAE

Leucaena   **Exotic, native to Central America**

Local names: Mlusina, Lusina (Swahili); Lusia (Luo)

A semi-deciduous shrub or tree that grows from 5–20 m in height depending on the variety. The leucaena has a moderately leafy canopy and is planted widely in the tropics from sea level to an altitude of 1 600 m. It thrives in sun and in well-drained soil.

Bark: Thick; rough; green-brown; cracks with age.

Leaves: Compound; alternate; with many leaflets, each thin and pointed; up to 1.5 cm long. Leaves and leaflets fold up with heat, cold or lack of water. There is a conspicuous round mark on the leaf stalk just before the leaflets.

Flowers: White, round heads; about 2 cm across; on a long stalk from the leaf axil.

Fruit: Numerous bunches; thin, green pods turning dry and brown; 10–15 cm long; persist on the tree, releasing 12–25 hard, shiny brown seeds.

Uses: The leaves and shoots are valuable for fodder, mulch and green manure; wood from the big trees is used for poles, general timber and as fuel. The species is also a good shade tree, and helps to fix nitrogen.

Shrub

Flowers and fruit

Malus domestica

Domestic apple

Exotic, native to northern Europe

Local name: None known

A small shrub whose fruit, the familiar apple, is of major economic importance The species, which reaches 2.5 m in height, is grown mostly in the highlands. It needs plenty of sunshine and rich, well-drained soil.

Bark: Greyish brown, rough with age.

Leaves: Dark green; rough texture; lanceolate; margin serrated; tapering tip.

Flowers: Pale pink; 4–5 petals; numerous yellow stamens; grow in clusters.

Fruit: Big; round; green, red or yellow; in bunches.

Uses: The fruit is very sweet, though some varieties produce sour fruit; widely used to make fresh apple juices, jams and jellies.

Flowers

Fruit

Shrub

Maytenus senegalensis (Gymnosporia senegalensis) CELASTRACEAE

Confetti tree   Indigenous

Local names: Mdunga-ndewe (Swahili); Akwichanian (Pokot); Ekaburu (Turkana)

A shrub or small tree that reaches about 3 m in height, but occasionally grows to 8 m; widely distributed in wooded or bushed grassland and in semi-arid riverine areas, at altitudes from sea level to 2 100 m.

Bark: Grey-brown, fissured, spines often present; up to 5 cm long; axillary or on short side branches.

Leaves: Blue-green, alternate or in small groups, thick, semi-succulent, apex rounded, notched, base tapering, shape and size variable; from 2–12 cm in length.

Flowers: Small, greenish white or cream, in dense axillary clusters covering the tree.

Fruit: 3-lobed capsules, up to 6 mm across; yellow or red.

Uses: The wood is fine and hard, used to manufacture small implements and axe handles.

Traditional medicine: Roots, leaves and bark contain a reputed cure for snakebite, and have various other medicinal uses. A solution of crushed leaves soaked in water is applied as an eye-wash; an infusion from the roots is widely used as a remedy for diarrhoea, fever and rheumatism.

Flowers

Fruit

Shrub

Nerium oleander

Oleander — Exotic, native to Mediterranean region; Asia Minor

Local name: None known

One of the most popular evergreen shrubs, growing 2–4 m high, often multi-stemmed, with long slender, upright branches. It is cultivated throughout East Africa at altitudes up to 2 200 m, and thrives on plenty of sun, air and water.

Leaves: Opposite or in threes; narrow; lance-shaped; up to 20 x 3 cm; dull greyish green.

Flowers: Red, pink, peach, yellow or white; in terminal masses; funnel-shaped each up to 5 cm across; with 5 petals, turned somewhat to the right, single or double, variegated or non-variegated.

Fruit: Thin, long, double capsules; about 12 cm long; split to release seeds bearing tufts of hairs.

Uses: The plant is used as an ornamental along roadsides and in garden planting. It also makes an excellent flowering border. All parts of the oleander are highly poisonous; the leaves and flowers contain cardiac glycosides. The sap is so toxic that just 20 g of leaves will kill a horse or cow; 1–5 g can kill a sheep. Be warned: even smoke from an oleander barbecue fire can prove hazardous, if not fatal, when inhaled.

White shrub

Pink single flowers

Pink shrub, double flowers

Pink double flowers

White single flowers

Opuntia vulgaris (Platyopuntia)

CACTACEAE

Prickly pear

Exotic, native to Bolivia, the Argentine

Local name: None known

A medium-sized stem succulent. Shrubby to tree-like, the plant grows from 2–4 m in height and is found in open or bushy grasslands, at altitudes below 1 700 m, in Kenya and Tanzania. There is no record of its presence in Uganda. Species in the genus *Opuntia* have round, flattened, green, fleshy joints called pads.

Spines: Tufts of spines or bristly hairs; virtually no leaves.
Flowers: Yellow or orange; 22–30 mm across; often tipped with red; petals and stamens are numerous.
Fruit: Size of a large egg; soft; green; covered with spiny bristles; fleshy and edible.
Uses: This species was introduced to East Africa for use as a hedge plant in dry areas, and continues to serve the same purposes. Fruit is eaten by some local tribes.

Yellow flower and green spring fruit

Orange flower

Shrub

Pithecellobium dulce

Madras thorn

Exotic, native to South America; naturalized

Local names: Mkwaju wa kihindi, Maramata (Swahili)

A thin, shapeless shrub or tree growing 4–15 m in height, armed with short spines at the base of each leaf pair. The plant is widely cultivated in the tropics and naturalized in East Africa. It occurs at the lower altitudes (from sea level to 150 m).

Bark: Pale; smooth with horizontal marks; bole short; young branches thorny, drooping.

Leaves: Thin stalks bear 2 pairs of leaflets, each up to 5 cm long; oval; tip rounded or notched.

Flowers: Small; creamy yellow; on a short stalk; bunches of green-white stamens; 1 cm across.

Fruit: Heavy pods; about 12 cm long; spirally twisted; constructed between seeds; green turning red when mature; split to release glossy black seeds almost entirely covered with fleshy red-and-white, edible aril.

Uses: The plant is popular as a spiny hedge or live fence. The wood is used for poles and in construction work, and as fuel. Wood, leaves, pods and seeds serve as fodder. Tannin and oil can be extracted from the seeds.

Flowers

Fruit with arils

Shrubs

Podranea brycei

BIGNONIACEAE

No English name known

Exotic, native to tropical America

Local name: None known

A strong, woody and profusely flowering scandent shrub that grows to 6 m or more in height. It likes full sun and plenty of space. It is usually found at altitudes of 1 000–1 800 m.

Bark: Greyish brown; smooth; branched.

Leaves: Compound; bipinnate; leaflets in 5–8 pairs, one terminal leaflet; dark and shiny; lanceolate; tapering tip.

Flowers: Showy; fragrant; mauve/pink; tubular; netted crimson; with a hairy throat; 5 joined petals; 4 stamens.

Fruit: Long pods; green turning to dark brown when dry; 20–25 cm long; with pointed end; many of them hang upside down.

Uses: A very fast-growing shrub, excellent for fences and hedges. Looks extraordinary when in flower.

Pods

Flowers

Shrub

Prosopis juliflora

Mesquite, Algarroba

Exotic, native to Central America, Mexico

Local name: Eterai (Turkana)

A thorny shrub, which can become a tree growing to 15 m, with a short bole. The plant is cultivated throughout the tropics, growing well in arid regions, in rocky or otherwise poor or saline soils, at altitudes from sea level to 1 500 m.

Bark: Thick; rough; grey-green; scaly with age; young branches green.

Leaves: Compound; alternate; stalk up to 6 cm long; leaflets oblong, narrow; 1–5 cm long.

Flowers: Golden yellow; densely crowded in spikes 5–10 cm long; fragrant.

Fruit: Yellow pod; 10–20 cm long; sweet.

Uses: Very fast-growing; the plant can become a weed in the wetter areas. The wood is used for poles, posts, carvings, general timber and as fuel. Leaves and pods are eaten by livestock; roots are soil-friendly, helping in nitrogen fixation. Grow as live fences in dry areas.

Flowers

Fruit pods

Shrub

Pulmeria rubra

APOCYNACEAE

Frangipani

Exotic, native to Central America

Local name: None known

A large, commonly seen succulent shrub or small tree that reaches 5 m in height. It is much favoured in the tropics, growing at altitudes from sea level to 2 000 m.

White flowers

Pink flowers

Bark: Grey; smooth; with prominent leaf scars. Branches thick, forking, exuding a milky sap when wounded; sap very poisonous.

Leaves: Large; dark; leathery; lanceolate; in terminal bunches at the ends of branches; tapering to base and apex; 20–22 cm across; prominent veins; regular; usually shed during the dry season, when flowers appear.

Flowers: White, yellowish, pink or reddish purple; 5 petals, overlapping at the centre and curled at the edges; 6 cm across; scented; in terminal bunches.

Fruit: Paired capsules up to 25 cm in length.

Uses: According to legend a 12th-century Italian called Frangipani combined certain volatile oils, including the oil of these flowers, to create an exquisite perfume, which made his name and fortune. Today the plant, to which many names and stories are attached, is widely cultivated throughout the tropics. In Asia, it is often grown near Buddhist temples, where it is known as the 'pagoda tree', and the flowers are sometimes called 'temple flowers'. It is also frequently planted near graves, especially those of Muslims and Buddhists. The latex in the branches is poisonous, though apparently useful in the treatment of skin cuts and inflammation.

Pink shrub

White shrub

Punica granatum

Pomegranate

Exotic, native to western Asia,
Mediterranean region; naturalized

Local name: Nkomawawanga (Luganda)

A large shrub that grows 5–6 m high, cultivated and naturalized in East Africa. It is valued for its bright red and yellow fruit but is also planted as an ornamental garden tree. It requires well-drained soil and plenty of sunshine.

Bark: Light brown; smooth.

Leaves: Shiny green; oval; opposite; smooth; coppery red when young.

Flowers: Brilliant scarlet; with crinkly petals and a purple-red calyx; 5–8 sepals; 5–8 petals and many stamens.

Fruit: Big (orange-sized); with tough, leathery rind; enclosing many seeds, each with a juicy red aril.

Uses: The fruit is edible; also makes an excellent syrup and a refreshing juice.

Traditional medicine: An infusion or tincture of dried or fresh fruit rind is used as a remedy for diarrhoea and stomachache; a mixture of root bark, occasionally with stem bark and leaves, is a well-known and widely used treatment for tapeworm.

Flowers

Shrub

Branches heavy with fruit

Fruit

Punica granatum *var.* nana

PUNICACEAE

Miniature pomegranate

Exotic, native to the Mediterranean region

Local name: None known

A charming, dwarf pomegranate that reaches 1.5 m in height. It needs plenty of water and sunshine to grow.

Trunk: Thin; multi-stemmed; greenish brown; smooth.
Leaves: Narrow; pointed; almost sessile; smooth; shiny.
Flowers: Orange-scarlet; numerous.
Fruit: Small; orange-red; round yellow striations.
Uses: This species is cultivated as a pot-plant for terraces and patios. Also suitable for the garden (especially rock-gardens).

Shrub

Flowers and fruit

Quiabentia chacoensis

Thorn cactus

Exotic, native to Argentina

Local name: None known

A small, thorny, shrubby plant that grows up to 3 m tall; fiercely armed; found in open bushy grassland at altitudes below 1 700 m.

Stems: Many-branched; green and succulent; barbed spines 15–20 cm long; very dangerous.

Leaves: Glossy; fleshy; green in colour; pointed tip; only appear in the growing season.

Flowers: Bright pinkish red; petals and stamens are generally numerous.

Uses: This introduced species is used as a hedge plant in dry areas.

Shrub

Flower

Rhus natalensis

ANACARDIACEAE

No English name known

Indigenous

Local names: Mkono-chuma, Mkumba (Swahili); Ol-mesigie (Maasai)

A many-branched, bushy shrub, occasionally a tree, that reaches 2–8 m in height; widespread in wooded savannah, dry forest edges and evergreen bushland; found at altitudes from sea level to 3 000 m.

Bark: Grey-brown; branchlets pale, dotted with lenticels; branches angular.

Leaves: 3 leaflets; terminal leaflet larger; up to 9 cm long; leathery; hairless; apex rounded; margin smooth.

Flowers: Very small; greenish or yellowish white; in loose heads up to 15 cm in length.

Fruit: Oblong to kidney-shaped; smooth; red; with thin flesh; drying dull and papery; falling easily.

Uses: The fruit is edible (the thin flesh has a sweet taste) and much favoured by rural children. The wood is used for general timber and fuel; twigs serve as toothbrushes.

Traditional medicine: Leaves are pounded and steeped in hot water to produce a cough cure; the steam from the process relieves head-cold symptoms. A decoction of boiled leaves is used as a remedy for stomachache, especially in young children. A solution of pounded roots soaked in either hot or cold water is taken for influenza, abdominal pains and gonorrhoea.

Flowers

Shrub

Fruit

Rhus vulgaris

No English name known   Indigenous

Local names: Muthigiu (Kikuyu); Ol-munyushi (Maasai); Mutheu (Kamba)

A bush or shrub similar to *Rhus natalensis* (see page 258), 1–7 m high, widespread in wooded grassland, bushed grassland, rocky sites and dry forest margins at altitudes of 1 200–2 700 m.

Leaves: Trifoliate; softly hairy; dull green; often rounded with apex notched; stalks, branchlets and the undersides of the leaflets are densely hairy.
Flowers: Greenish yellow.
Fruit: Flat round discs; only 3–5 mm across; brownish red when dry.
Uses: The wood is used as general timber, for farm tools, and as fuel. The fruit is edible.
Traditional medicine: Fruit decoction taken for diarrhoea.

Fruit

Ricinus communis

EURPHORBIACEAE

Castor-oil plant

Indigenous

Local names: Mbarika, Mbono (Swahili); Ol-dule (Maasai); Nsogasoga (Luganda)

A woody herb, growing 1–5 m in height, with hollow stems. It thrives in a wide variety of habitats from bushed grassland to rain forest; and in disturbed ground, at altitudes of 600–2 000 m.

Bark: Multi-branched stems; often red; becoming hollow with age; well-marked leaf nodes and scars.
Leaves: Large; 5–9 leaflets; palmately and deeply lobed; margin serrated; long stalk.
Flowers: Male flowers have creamy yellow stamens; female flowers a showy red stigma borne on the upper part of the spike.
Fruit: Round, deep red capsules with soft spikes; in dense clusters; 3-valved, each valve containing one seed.
Uses: The leaves and residue from the pressed seeds are poisonous to stock.
Traditional medicine: A decoction from the boiled roots is taken as an appetite stimulant and for abdominal trouble. Stems and leaves are pounded, and the juice drunk as a remedy for ulcers, stomachaches and diarrhoea. The seeds are poisonous, but the oil extract is heated and used as a purgative. Pure oil extract is also applied to relieve ear problems.

Fruit

Flowers

Shrub

Rubus steudneri

No English name known   Indigenous

Local names: Mutare (Kikuyu), Engaiyagut (Maasai); Tagaimamiet (Kipsigis)

A stout, scrambling shrub that grows 1–3 m in height, with a reddish green, hairy stem and hooked prickles up to 3 mm long. The plant is found at the moist montane forest margins, and in bamboo margins, at altitudes of 1 500–3 200 m.

Stem: Spiny, often with arching shoots.

Leaves: Trifoliate; touching the ground; leaflets broadly ovate; serrated margins; hairy above and beneath.

Flowers: Pink; 5 sepals; numerous stamens.

Fruit: Red to black; up to 1.5 cm across.

Uses: The fruit is edible.

Traditional medicine: A decoction of roots is taken as a remedy for indigestion.

Flowers and fruit

Shrub

Salvadora persica

RUTACEAE

Toothbrush tree

Indigenous

Local names: Mswaki (Swahili), Ol-remit (Maasai), Esekon (Turkana)

An evergreen trailing shrub or small tree reaching 3–7 m in height, most often seen along rivers and lakes, also in dry bushland and wooded grassland.

Fruit

Bark: Grey-brown; older wood twisted, rough and cracked. Branches often hanging.

Leaves: Yellow green; slightly succulent; oblong to rounded; up to 5 cm long.

Flowers: Small; greenish cream; in loose heads up to 10 cm long.

Fruit: Translucent white, then pink to purple; pea-sized; one-seeded; juicy and strongly flavoured.

Uses: A very important emergency fodder species in dry areas (ie. valuable when nothing else is available). The fruit is edible. The wood is also used as fuel.

Traditional medicine: The stem is used as a toothbrush: it contains an antibiotic that keeps the mouth clean and prevents toothache. A decoction of the root is taken as a remedy for gonorrhoea, spleen pain and general stomachache. Roots also feature in the treatment of chest diseases; the latex is used in the treatment of skin sores.

Shrub

Schefflera actinophylla (Brassaia actinophylla) ARALIACEAE

Octopus tree, Queensland umbrella tree

Exotic, native to
Queensland, Australia

Local name: None known

An attractive evergreen tree with spectacular tentacle-like flower-heads, reaching up to 10 m in height and found at altitudes of 1 000–2 000 m.

Bark: Grey; smooth.

Leaves: Palmately compound; with 7–16 long, stalked leaflets; glossy green; narrowly elliptic; up to 25 cm long; tapering at the base and apex.

Flowers: Small; dark red; in clusters along the long spikes; a metre or more in length radiating from upper branches, like the tentacles of an octopus.

Fruit: Small; rounded; purplish red when ripe.

Uses: The species is very bushy when young, and highly recommended as an indoor pot-plant. Also an excellent ornamental tree.

Shrub

Flowers

Senna alata (Cassia alata)

CAESALPINOIDEAE

Candle bush

Exotic, native to California, tropical America

Local name: None known

A very attractive, short-lived, deciduous shrub that grows 1–4 m in height; commonly found on lake-shores, near riverine areas and as a weed on cultivated land, at altitudes up to 1 000 m.

Bark: Dark brown; woody; multi-stemmed.

Leaves: Compound; large; with pinnate foliage; each leaflet 6–12 cm long; obovate; base and apex rounded.

Flowers: Golden yellow; in erect, candle-like spikes.

Fruit: Long, boat-shaped pods; 6–16 cm long; green when young, blackish when dry; split open on the plant to release numerous brown, pointed seeds, up to 5 mm in size.

Uses: An ornamental garden shrub that also serves as an effective fence.

Traditional medicine: Leaves are used in the treatment of skin diseases (notably ringworm).

Fruit

Flowers

Shrub

Senna biflora (Cassia biflora)

Cassia

Exotic, native to Mexico, West Indies

Local name: None known

A woody tropical shrub that reaches 3 m in height, with erect branches. It develops into a small tree spreading from a short trunk. It grows as an ornamental shrub at altitudes from sea level to 1 700 m.

Leaves: Compound; pinnate; with narrow, oblong leaflets; 3–4 cm long.
Flowers: Showy; bright yellow; 2–3 cm across; in twos.
Fruit: Flat pods; 5–10 cm long; straight or curved.
Uses: Very showy garden shrub, especially in full bloom.

Flowers

Flowers and fruit

Shrub

Senna didymobotrya (Cassia didymobotrya) CAESALPINOIDEAE

Candle bush, Peanut-butter cassia

Indigenous

Local names: Mwenu (Kikuyu); Osenetoi (Maasai); Mukyula (Luganda)

A bushy, poisonous shrub, occasionally growing to a tree of up to 6 m in height; commonly found in riverine and lake-shore areas, and along forest edges, in damp and well-watered sites. Occurs at altitudes of 700–2 100 m.

Leaves: Compound; up to 45 cm long; leaflets in 10–18 pairs; leaflet apex rounded with stiff hair-like tip.
Flowers: Bright yellow; unopened dark brown buds crown the flower spike.
Fruit: Flattened pods; green turning dark brown; oblong; 12 x 2.5 cm.
Uses: The leaves, pods and roots are poisonous. The bark contains tannin; leaves are used as a fish poison.
Traditional medicine: A leaf infusion acts as an emetic in the treatment of malaria; stems and roots also feature in malaria treatment; a decoction of leaves, stems and roots serves as a purgative, as a remedy for gonorrhoea, and for backache in women. Roots are used as an antidote to general poisoning. A solution of boiled leaves is applied to the skin of someone suffering from measles, and is taken for stomach disorders. Decoctions of roots and leaves are taken as remedies for headache, fevers and excess bile – but with extreme caution (an overdose can prove fatal).

Shrub

Flowers

Fruit

Senna obtusifolia (Cassia obtusifolia) CEASALPINIACEAE

No English name known Indigenous

Local names: Cheporon (Pokot); Emang, Emany (Turkana)

A woody herb or shrub growing 0.5–2 m in height, commonly found in riverine areas, on lake shores and as a weed on cultivated land. Occurs from sea level to 1 700 m.

Leaves: Compound; with 3 pairs of leaflets; leaflets obovate; apex and base rounded; 1.5–5 cm by 1–3 cm.
Flowers: Orange-yellow.
Fruit: Linear, straight or slightly curved; tapering at the base; apex rounded; 11–23 cm long; contain many brown oval seeds.

Traditional medicine: A root decoction is used in the treatment of childhood ailments. Upper part of the plant is pounded, mixed with water and taken as a remedy for stomach disorders. Roots are chewed by pregnant women during labour.

Flowers

Fruit pods

Shrub

Senna septemtrionalis (Cassia floribunda) CAESALPINOIDEAE

No English name known   Exotic, native to Mexico; naturalized

Local names: Esenetoi (Maasai), Omochegechege (Kisii)

A shrub or small tree that usually grows 3–4 m high, occurring in grassland, wooded grassland, dry upland evergreen forest, as hedges and along roadsides, on disturbed ground and waste ground, at altitudes of 910–3 200 m. The branchlets are glabrous and green.

Leaves: Compound; leaf stalk 7–8 cm long; 3–4 pairs of leaflets, each leaflet lanceolate; tapering tip; soft; with very small petiole.

Flowers: In terminal racemes; often aggregated near the ends of branchlets; bright yellow; 4 sepals; 5 petals; many stamens.

Fruit: Cylindrical pods; indehiscent; brown; 6–10 cm long and 1–1.5 cm in diameter; many brown seeds.

Uses: Planted as an ornamental; also used for fuel.

Traditional medicine: Leaves are crushed, mixed with water, shaken and the solution taken immediately after childbirth to help remove the placenta. A solution of fruit and roots acts as a purgative.

Fruit pods

Flowers and fruit pods

Shrub

Senna singueana (Cassia singueana)

No English name known

Indigenous

Local names: Mbaraka (Swahili); Mukengeka (Kamba); Msua (Taita)

A shrub or small tree that reaches 6 m in height, with scaly and fissured grey or brown bark. The species is found throughout the warmer, medium-rainfall savannah areas and in tropical Africa from sea level to 2 000 m.

Leaves: Compound; 6–10 pairs; ovate; round apex; dull green in colour.

Flowers: Masses of flowers; glorious golden yellow; clustered at the ends of branches.

Fruit: Linear, straight or somewhat twisted; green turning dark brown when dry; indehiscent; with stiff and rather hard valves; rounded to acute tip.

Uses: The leaves and pods make good fodder; the wood is used as fuel.

Traditional medicine: Roots feature in remedies for wounds, gonorrhoea and general stomach problems. The young leaves are chewed and the sap sucked for stomachache, constipation and heartburn. The plant, however, is used with extreme caution: an overdose of the medicine can prove fatal.

Fruit pods

Shrub

Flowers

Sesbania sesban (S. aegyptiaca)

PAPILIONOIDEAE

Sesbania, River bean

Indigenous

Local names: Mwethia (Kikuyu); Mbondo (Haya); Muzimbandeya (Luganda)

A deciduous shrub or small tree, growing up to 6 m in height, that is usually found in or near water, and especially at the margins of freshwater lakes. The species can survive waterlogging, and tolerates acid and saline soil.

Bark: Red-brown; young shoots hairy.

Leaves: Compound; up to 12 cm long; leaflets narrow; blue-green; up to 2 cm long; in 10–25 pairs; apex rounded and notched; narrow.

Flowers: Pale yellow; speckled maroon; in isolated sprays up to 15 cm long.

Fruit: Abundant; green to pale brown; long, thin pods of up to 20 cm; hanging in clusters; with separated sections that cause seeds to rattle within.

Uses: The wood is light and soft but is an excellent source of fuel, and of material for poles and for light construction. The leaves produce a soap substitute, and are valuable fodder and fertilizer.

Traditional medicine: Ground leaves feature in the treatment of stomach disorders and swellings of various kinds; roots are crushed to a paste that is said to be an excellent remedy for scorpion stings.

Fruit and flowers

Fruit and flowers

Shrub

Solanum incanum

Sodom apple

Indigenous

Local names: Mutunguja-mwilu (Swahili); Mutongu (Kikuyu); Endulelei (Maasai)

An erect shrub, growing 0.5–2 m high, with thorns on its stem, branches and leaves. It is found throughout East Africa on waste ground, and along roadsides where soil has been scraped away or eroded, at altitudes from sea level to 2 300 m.

Bark: Multi-branched, thorny stems; greyish brown.
Leaves: Ovate to lanceolate.
Flowers: Mauve or purple; in isolated racemens.
Fruit: Yellow; round; 18–40 mm across.
Traditional medicine: The fruit pulp features in the treatment of warts, bleeding wounds and toothache; some local communities use the fruit juice to clot milk. Young leaves are chewed and rubbed into the area of a snakebite; an infusion of leaves is administered as a remedy for earache. Fruits feature in the treatment of skin diseases; a decoction of the roots is taken for abdominal pains, fever, stomachache and indigestion. Roots are also used to alleviate toothache.

Fruit and flowers

Fruit

Shrub

Solanum mauritianum

SOLANACEAE

Asian bug tree

Exotic, native to South America, Asia

Local name: None known

A shrub or small tree growing to 5 m in height, common on waste ground at altitudes of 1 500–2 800 m. It can sometimes be a troublesome weed.

Bark: Pale greenish brown; smooth; speckled.
Leaves: Large; grey-green; pointed tip; up to 30 cm long; leafy stipules clearly visible at the base of leaf stalks.
Flowers: Pale purple or mauve; small; star-shaped; in flat heads; about 12 cm across.
Fruit: Yellow, round clusters of berries on long stalks.
Uses: The fruit is very poisonous.

Fruit

Flowers

Shrub

Tarchonanthus camphoratus

Leleshwa bush

Indigenous

Local names: Mkalambati (Swahili); Mururicua (Kikuyu) Ol-leleshwa (Maasai)

A medium-sized bushy shrub or spreading tree, rarely growing to more than 6 m in height; occurs in evergreen or semi-deciduous bushland and bushed grassland, especially in stony soils, at altitudes of 1 500–2 300 m.

Bark: Grey or brown; rough; longitudinally fissured; peeling in long stripes.

Leaves: Camphor-scented when crushed; silvery white; lance-shaped; narrow; up to 10 cm long; with pointed apex; soft-textured. Young shoots and the underside of the leaves are densely covered with white hairs.

Flowers: Dioecious; flowers in large terminal panicles; male flower creamy brown; female flowers paler, developing into white, woolly fruiting heads.

Fruit: Tiny seeds, each bearing dense white hairs; heads resemble small balls of cotton wool.

Uses: The wood is hard and heavy, used in building of huts, as durable fence posts and as fuel. Splinters are poisonous, causing septic sores that are slow to heal. The aromatic leaves are used as a deodorant.

Traditional medicine: Smoke or fumes from the fresh or dried plant are inhaled for asthma, headaches, and rheumatism. Infusions and tinctures of the leaves and twigs are used to treat stomach disorders, abdominal pain, headaches, toothache, asthma, bronchitis and inflammation. A hot poultice on the chest is said to relieve headaches, asthma, bronchitis and inflammation.

Shrub

Flowers

Leaves

Tecoma stans

BIGNONIACEAE

Tecoma, Yellow elder, Yellow trumpet tree

Exotic, native to Mexico, tropical America

Local name: None known

A profusely flowering and branching shrub or small tree that grows up to 4 m in height, occasionally taller.

Bark: Grey-brown; rougher with age.

Leaves: Compound; 2–5 pairs plus a larger terminal leaflet; serrated margin; lanceolate; up to 10 cm long; with tapering apex and soft texture.

Flowers: Yellow; bunches of tubular flowers, each up to 6 cm long; with 5 rounded lobes marked with fine reddish lines.

Fruit: Narrow, green capsules up to 18 cm long; pale brown when dry; untidy clusters remain on the tree for quite long.

Uses: An ornamental tree for gardens, avenues and highways.

Flowers

Shrub

Fruit capsules

Tecomaria capensis

Tecomaria, Cape honeysuckle

Exotic, native to South Africa

Local name: None known

A multi-stemmed, bushy semi-deciduous shrub, climber or small tree that grows up to 5 m high.

Bark: Pale brown; heavily dotted with lenticels.
Leaves: Compound; opposite; about 10 cm long; leaflets in 2–5 pairs plus a larger terminal leaflet; shiny, dark green above; broadly oval; 1–3 cm long; apex pointed; margin serrated.
Flowers: Orange-scarlet, occasionally yellow; in terminal clusters; funnel-shaped; with protruding stamens.
Fruit: Greenish capsules turning brown when dry; up to 10 cm long; in upright clusters.
Uses: The species makes a good flowering shrub when planted in full sun; also serves as a flowering hedge.

Fruit

Shrub

Flowers

Thevetia peruviana

APOCYNACEAE

Thevetia

Exotic, native to Central and South America

Local name: None known

A multi-stemmed shrub, widely planted in the tropics as an attractive, ornamental bush.

Trunk: Smooth; grey.

Leaves: Shorter than those of other members of the genus (see *Thevetia thevetioides*, page 177); up to 10 cm in length; shiny; narrow.

Flowers: Yellow, white or salmon-orange; trumpet-shaped; slightly smaller than other members of the genus; with green base extending to the trumpet edge.

Fruit: Small; apple-shaped; about 3.5 cm across.

Uses: All parts of *Thevetia*, and especially the latex, are highly poisonous (a drop of latex on the skin will raise a fierce blister). The plant makes a tough, drought-resistant ornamental tree, useful as a hedge and for shade.

Fruit

Shrub

Yellow flowers

Orange flowers

Vernonia adoensis

Vernonia, Apple blossom

Indigenous

Local names: Ol-ekoru (Maasai); Kuom-tepengwet (Kipsigis); Nyang'ony-akuodi (Luo)

A woody herb or shrub that grows from 0.3–3.5 m, with attractive dense inflorescence; commonly found in disturbed bushland or grassland, at altitudes of 1 250–2 150 m.

Bark: Multi-stemmed; brown; smooth.

Leaves: Alternate, ovate or elliptic, apex acute, margin serrated; silvery green; slightly rough on top.

Flowers: White, in dense inflorescence; 1–3 flowers in every inflorescence.

Fruit: Tiny dry seeds with white hairs at one end.

Traditional medicine: The leaves are crushed in cold water and used in the treatment of tick-bite sores.

Shrub

Flowers

Vernonia auriculifera

COMPOSITAE

Vernonia

Indigenous

Local names: Muthakwa (Kikuyu); Ol-masakwa (Maasai); Kikokooma (Luganda)

A large, tall-growing, woody, spreading shrub that reaches 1.8–7.5 m in height, commonly found along forest edges, on clear land, in riverine areas and on lake-shores. It occurs at altitudes of 1 600–2 650 m.

Bark: Multi-stemmed; greyish brown; smooth.

Leaves: Narrowly elliptic or ovate; apex acute; margin serrated; densely hairy underneath; 6–50 x 1.5–22 cm.

Flowers: In large corymb of flower-heads; 3–4 mm across; flat or slightly rounded; varying in colour from deep purple to medium mauve and fading to pale violet.

Fruit: Tiny, dry seeds with stiff white hairs.

Uses: Leaves and stems used in the construction of huts.

Traditional medicine: Leaves are pounded, the juice extracted and taken as a treatment for fever.

Shrub

Flowers

Vernonia brachycalyx

Vernonia

Indigenous

Local names: Mutei (Kikuyu); Ol-ogomati (Maasai); Kuombereriet (Kipsigis)

A scandent shrub that grows 1–4 m in height, sometimes up to 6 m; very common in all dry forest edges, in riverine areas and along roadsides, at altitudes of 900–2 400 m.

Leaves: Ovate or elliptic; apex acute; margin dentate or entire; slightly sandpapery above.

Flowers: Purple or mauve; rather flat; solitary flower-heads; 3–5 mm across; in dense inflorescence; pappus (feathery hairs surrounding the fruit) violet at flowering stage, later brown.

Fruit: Tiny seeds with white hairs.

Uses: Twigs are used to make fire by friction.

Traditional medicine: An infusion of the leaves serves as protection against malaria.

Flowers

Shrub

Yucca gloriosa

AGAVACEAE

Adam's needle, Spanish bayonet

Exotic, native to Mexico, Texas (USA)

Local name: None known

An evergreen shrub or tree-like plant whose body form can vary from more or less stemless rosettes of long, thin leaves, usually 2–2.5 m long, to a tree-like specimen with a short, thick trunk up to 7 m tall. These plants have evolved a remarkable way to pollinate: at night they emit a scent that attracts Yucca moths, which ensures fertilization.

Bark: Single- or multi-stemmed; greyish brown; stems covered with dead leaves.

Leaves: Bold tufts of stiff, pointed leaves, green or bluish green in colour; up to 60 cm long; spined at tips; growing in rosettes.

Flowers: Very spectacular; creamy white in large panicles of 1–2 m or more; closely packed; tinged with red outside; hooded.

Uses: Yucca is a common plant for rock gardens and along roadsides, and is also cultivated as a hedge.

Flowers

Shrub

Ziziphus mucronata

Buffalo-thorn

Indigenous

Local names: Mkunazi (Swahili); Ol-oilale (Maasai); Oloilahi (Arusha)

A wickedly armed scrambler, shrub or small tree that grows to 7 m; with drooping, tangled branches and strong, sharp thorns; widely spread at the coast and along rivers, in bushland, woodland and wooded grassland at altitudes up to 2 000 m.

Thorns: Strong; sharp; in pairs; one straight, up to 2 cm long; the other smaller and recurved, with leaves arising between the pairs.

Leaves: Thin; hairless; same colour on both surfaces; 3–6 cm long; base rounded; tip pointed; margin with regular rounded teeth; 3 main veins from the base are prominent on the underside.

Flowers: Yellowish; very small; in heads of about 1.5 cm across.

Fruit: Rounded; dark reddish brown when ripe; edible.

Uses: The fruit is edible but sour. Wood is tough and elastic, used for house-building (poles), fuelwood and charcoal. Leaves and fruit serve as fodder. The plant makes a strong live fence.

Traditional medicine: Poultices from roots and leaves are applied to boils and skin infections. A decoction of the bark is used in the treatment of rheumatism and stomach disorders; a decoction of roots is taken as a remedy for snakebite.

Fruit

Shrub

PALMS

Palms, all of which form part of one ancient family, Palmae, are an integral and important part of the vegetation of the tropics and subtropics. Altogether, there are some 3 800 known species in various parts of the world and, contrary to popular perception, they are by no means confined to desert oases and the wide white beaches of tropical islands! The great majority grow in the gloomy depths of rain forests and perhaps never see the sun, especially when they are young and hidden beneath the canopy; a good number of species actually prefer cool climates, and will thrive outdoors in temperate areas.

A few palm species are economically important, among them those that yield sustaining fruit (dates, coconuts) and vegetable oil (the oil palm of Central Africa). Most palm species originate in tropical America and Asia. The principal groups are the fan palms, feather palms and fish-tail palms. These names reflect the respective leaf types. In comparison with the species richness of Asia and the Americas, there are very few (no more than half a dozen) indigenous African palms, but a large number of exotic species have been planted in East Africa as eye-catching ornamentals. All grow from seeds, and many make attractive indoor as well as outdoor plants.

Archontophoenix alexandrae

Alexander palm, King palm

Exotic, native to eastern Australia

Local name: None known

A beautiful, easily cultivated, popular palm that grows in the tropics and subtropics, reaching 18 m in height. Very common in East Africa. Planted outdoors; the seeds germinate within a few weeks. Fast-growing; requires high levels of light and humidity.

Trunk: Single; light grey; covered with old leaf scars; often swollen at the base; mid-green crown shaft.

Leaves: Pinnate; held flat; sometimes twisted and thus perpendicular to the ground; the underside of the leaflet is silvery – a key identification factor.

Flowers: Flower stalk situated below the crown shaft; cream-coloured.

Fruit: Round; 18 mm in diameter; red when ripe; borne in huge numbers.

Fruit

Palms

Borassus aethiopum

African fan palm, Borassus palm (indigenous)

Local names: Mvumo (Swahili); Katungo (Luganda); Muhama (Suku)

The tallest of the indigenous palms, reaching 25 m in height, very slow-growing. It occurs in the coastal belt.

Trunk: Grey; older trees develop swelling above the middle of the trunk; young stems are clad with persistent dead leaves.
Leaves: Fan-shaped; very large; up to 4 m long and 3 m across; divided into numerous deep segments.
Flowers: Dioecious; male trees produce very large pollen-bearing catkins.
Fruit: Large; orange; round; about 15 cm long; the pulp fibrous but edible; seeds brown and woody, each 8 cm long.
Uses: The leaves are used as material for weaving; the sap is fermented into an excellent palm wine.

Palms

Brahea edulis

Guadeloupe palm (exotic, native to the Caribbean islands of Guadeloupe)

Local name: None known

An attractive and fast-growing fan palm that reaches 15 m in height. The round seeds germinate easily. An outdoor palm that requires full sun; not suitable as a house plant.

Trunk: Stout; old leaves self-pruned, leaving leaf scars.
Leaves: Mid-green; palmate; stiffly held.
Flowers: Flower stalks among the leaves.
Fruit: Hang down in bunches; dark brown to black; with an edible, sweet pulp.
Uses: Planted as an ornamental.

Palm

Caryota mitis

Fish-tail palm

Exotic, native to Southeast Asia

Local name: None known

An interesting and easily cultivated palm, easily grown in the tropics, reaching 8 m in height. It is commonly planted as an outdoor tree in Kenya, especially in Mombasa and Nairobi.

Trunk: Multiple; slender.

Leaves: Bipinnate; leaflets triangular; with a ragged margin and a distinctive fish-tail shape.

Flowers: Cream-coloured; appear from the highest leaf axil first, then progressively downwards (when the last one has flowered and fruited that stem dies, to be replaced by others in the clump).

Fruit: Round; about 18 mm across; green at first and dull red when ripe; contain stinging crystals in the pulp, and should be handled with care.

Uses: The palm is usually grown as an indoor plant, and needs bright indirect light (outdoors it grows in full sun). Easily cultivated from fresh seeds.

Fruit

Palm

Caryota urens

Wine palm, Jaggery palm

Exotic, native to India, Burma
(Myanmar), Sri Lanka

Local name: None known

A tall, beautiful fish-tail palm that reaches up to 18 m in height. It grows in climates ranging from tropical to warm temperate. Seeds germinate within a few weeks, and without difficulty if they are fresh. It requires shade, humidity and warmth.

Trunk: Solitary; grey; with old leaf scars (one for each old leaf).

Leaves: Arching and pendulous; leaflets are the usual fish-tail shape, but generally a darker colour than *Caryota mitis* (see page 285).

Flowers: Greenish cream; growing from the highest leaf axil first, then progressively downward (see *Caryota mitis*, page 285). When the last one has flowered and fruited, the tree dies.

Fruit: About 18 mm across; round; dark red when ripe.

Uses: Fresh seeds germinate easily. The palm is grown as both an indoor and outdoor plant. An alcoholic liquor, and a sugar, are made from the sap.

Palm

Fruit

Chamaedorea klotzschiana

Feathers palm (exotic, native to Mexico, Central America)

Local name: None known

This is a small tree, unusual in its leaf arrangement, which is unique in the palm world. It grows to a maximum height of 2 m. Fresh seeds germinate quickly. Ideally planted in tropical and subtropical gardens, but the tree needs a lot of shade.

Trunk: Multiple; slim; rings left by old leaves.
Leaves: Bright green; pinnate; leaflets arranged in irregular groups along leaf stem.
Flowers: Flower stalk grows from the lowest leaf axils.
Fruit: Green-red to black when ripe; small, round, tightly bunched.

Palm with fruit

Chrysalidocarpus lutescens

Butterfly palm, Golden cane palm (exotic, native to Madagascar)

Local name: None known

This is probably the world's most widely planted palm, growing easily in warm, temperate and tropical climates, reaching up to 9 m in height. The seeds germinate easily and the tree grows quickly, thriving in either full sun or partial shade.

Trunk: Multiple; slim; ringed; sometimes branching above ground level.
Leaves: Pale green; feather-shaped; with glossy leaflets spaced along graceful, arching leaf stalks that arise from prominent cylindrical crown shafts; petiole yellow if sun-grown, otherwise green.
Flowers: Stalk arises from the crown shaft.
Fruit: Oval; 18 mm long; seeds red or brown.
Uses: A beautiful, clumping ornamental palm for indoor and outdoor gardens.

Palm

Cocos nucifera

Coconut palm (exotic, native to the tropics, probably originated in tropical America)

Local name: Mnazi (Swahili)

A familiar coastal palm that grows to 30 m in height; common in the humid tropics. Tolerates salty soil. The tree produces its best yields between 12 and 60 years of age and can live to over 100 years.

Trunk: Slim; solitary; grey-brown; often bent by the wind; swollen at the base, with stem roots often visible.
Leaves: 20 to 30; in large terminal tufts; heavy; up to 6 m long; leaflets numerous; narrow; sharply pointed; green-yellow in colour.
Flowers: Dense creamy yellow on branched stalks; up to 300 male flowers at the tip and 12–20 female flowers at the base.
Fruit: Heavy, large, oval, hard-shelled nuts; yellow or green, becoming dry and brown.
Uses: A very useful tree. The hollow centre of the fruit contains a clear, sugary milk that develops into the white flesh. Sap can be fermented to make an alcoholic brew; dried flesh or copra, which is exported, is used in the production of commercial oils. Copra can also be eaten raw. The fibrous husk, known as the coir, is used to make ropes and matting.

Fruit

Elaeis guineesis

Oil palm (exotic, native to West Africa)

Local names: Mchikichi, Mjenga (Swahili); Mubira, Munazi (Luganda)

An important palm, planted commercially by many farmers in East Africa and by the millions in other tropical countries. It grows 18–21 m in height. Not a very attractive palm; easily grown in the tropics, though the hard seeds germinate with some difficulty.

Trunk: Circumference of up to 45 cm; covered with untidy old leaf bases and often epiphytic plants and ferns.
Leaves: Feather-shaped; the leaflets in two planes, giving a slightly plumate appearance.
Flowers: Stalk arises from the leaf bases.
Fruit: In large, light bunches; yellow, then red, and finally glossy black at maturity.
Uses: It has the highest commercial value of all palms: its reddish fruit produces excellent oil (superior to coconut oil) that is used to produce soap, margarine, candles, lubricants and vitamin A. The waste serves as cattle feed. The roots, leaves, stem and oil are used medicinally.

Palms

Howea forsteriana

Kentia palm   Exotic, native to Lord Howe Island off Australia's east coast

Local name: None known

One of the most popular of East Africa's ornamental palms, growing up to 15 m in height. The seeds germinate with difficulty, and should be absolutely fresh for the best results. The tree requires a sunny position in temperate or warm areas, but needs shade when young.

Trunk: Slim; dark green with prominent rings when young; grey and less prominently ringed when older.
Leaves: Broad; dark green; feather-shaped; leathery texture; leaflets held in a flat plane; do not rise upwards.
Flowers: Flower stalk arises from beneath the lowest leaves.
Fruit: Size and shape of an olive; dark brown when ripe; can take two years to ripen.

Palm

Hyphaene compressa (H. multiformis, H. thebaica)

Doum palm   Indigenous

Local names: Mkoma, Mkoche (Swahili); Eng'oli (Turkana); Mlala (Giriama)

One of the few truly branching palms, with the stems dividing regularly. Unmistakable and beautiful, it reaches 18 m in height, and grows at sea level and inland along seasonal watercourses, often in thickets covering a wide area.

Trunk: Slender, but much-branched, each branch dividing again and again, and ending in a crown of leaves.

Leaves: Fan-shaped; hard; waxy and durable; dead leaves often persist around the higher stems.

Flowers: Flower stalk arises from the leaf bases.

Fruit: The shape and size of a pear; very hard; orange-brown in colour.

Uses: The large orange-coloured seeds of this plant sometimes germinate extremely quickly, sometimes over many weeks. They are eaten by baboons and elephants (the latter swallow the whole fruit) who distribute the seeds. The sap makes a very strong, coarse brew. Finely woven baskets, thatched roofs (*makuti*) and mats are made from the young leaves.

Fruit

Palm trees and huts

Palms

Latania loddigessii

Blue latin palm (exotic, native to Mauritius)

Local name: None known

An interesting, beautiful fan palm that grows up to 12 m in height. These plants are easily cultivated from seed, both indoors and outdoors. They need a bright, sunny area for good growth.

Trunk: Grey; ringed with scars of old leaves.
Leaves: Stiff; fan-shaped; blue-green in colour; leaf stalk extends well into the leaf.
Flowers: Stalk arises from the leaf bases.
Fruit: Large and plum-like; dark brown when ripe; each fruit usually contains 3 seeds.

Palm

Licuala grandis

Ruffled fan palm (exotic, native to northern coastal Australia)

Local name: None known

This is quite a striking plant, immediately recognizable for its beautiful leaves. It is essentially a tropical palm and grows up to 3 m in height. The seeds germinate within a few weeks, and without difficulty if they are fresh. Grown as both an indoor and an outdoor plant, it requires shade, humidity and warmth.

Trunk: Slim; solitary.
Leaves: Unmistakable; beautiful; circular; dark green; undivided and regularly pleated leaves; with a notched edge.
Flowers: Flower stalk arises from among the leaf bases.
Fruit: Bright red when ripe; small and round.

Leaves

Neodypsis decaryi

Triangle palm (exotic, native to Madagascar)

Local name: None known

An instantly recognizable palm, extremely drought-resistant, growing up to 6 m in height. Its triangular shape allows it to be planted against a wall. The tree is rapidly gaining in popularity as an ornamental in most parts of the world.

Trunk: The leaf bases form a unique triangular shape at the top of the trunk; below this, the trunk is conventionally round.
Leaves: Long and elegant; silvery green in colour; feather-shaped; drooping at the tips.
Flowers: Stalk arises from the leaf bases.
Fruit: About 18 mm long; oval.
Uses: Easily grows from seed; a wonderful palm for both indoor and outdoor use. In the latter instance it is best grown in full sun. It tolerates low to medium light; prefers a brighter spot as an indoor plant.

Palm

Phoenix canariensis

Canary Islands date palm (exotic, native to the Canary Islands)

Local name: None known

One of the most widespread of the ornamental palms, growing up to 18 m in height in warm to temperate areas, although it is tolerant of the cold. Seeds germinate easily and quickly in hot conditions, but the tree needs a lot of space to develop fully.

Trunk: Solitary; stout; up to 1 m in diameter; rough; covered with distinctive old leaf scars, which form diamond-shaped patterns.
Leaves: Feather-shaped; 5–6 m long; in an arching crown; leaflets glossy, numerous, stiff and regular. The leaflets are smaller at the tip of the leaf stalk, and are reduced to spines at the base.
Flowers: Flower stalk arises from among the leaf bases.
Fruit: Small; green-yellow when ripe; inedible.

Palm

Phoenix reclinata

African wild date palm   Indigenous

Local names: Mkindu (Swahili); Makindu (Kamba); Olpiroo (Arusha)

This is a beautiful, clump-forming date palm, growing up to 8 m in height. It dislikes the cold (and of course frost). The seeds germinate easily. It is found beside swamps and rivers at altitudes from sea level to 3 000 m.

Trunk: Multiple; slim; 25 cm in diameter; sometimes bent over (reclinate); covered with old leaf scars.

Leaves: Mid-green; feathery; up to 2.5 m long; crown prominently downturned; leaflets narrow; up to 30 cm in length; stiff and sharp.

Flowers: Dioecious; arising from among the leaf bases.

Fruit: Oval in shape; about 2.5 cm long; edible; green when unripe, brown when ripe.

Uses: This tropical palm is grown as an ornamental in East African gardens.

Palm

Fruit

Phoenix roebelenii

Pygmy date palm (exotic, native to Southeast Asia)

Local name: None known

A comparatively small date palm, reaching a height of 1–3 m, that grows in tropical, subtropical and warm to temperate zones. It can tolerate low light but prefers bright, indirect light. The seeds readily germinate.

Trunk: Slim; solitary; sometimes old leaf bases project in a distinctive fashion, like pegs.
Leaves: 40 cm in length; feather-shaped; leaflets a soft, shiny dark green.
Flowers: Creamy yellow; flower stalk arises from among the leaf bases.
Fruit: Small; about 12 mm long; green-brown when ripe.
Uses: This is a very popular indoor and outdoor plant, forming a perfect miniature palm tree.

Palm

Raphia farinifera

Raffia palm (exotic, native to Madagascar)

Local names: Mwaale (Swahili); Kibo (Luganda); Mavale (Taveta)

This genus has the largest leaves of all palms. The tree reaches up to 21 m in height when mature.

Trunk: Multiple; each trunk growing to just 3 m; about 30 cm in diameter. The trunk dies after fruiting, and is replaced by others.
Leaves: Among the longest in the plant kingdom; up to 18 m in length; massive; feather-shaped; held erect; leaves grow on comparatively short trunks; leaflets roughly 100 x 8 cm, with spines of up to 3 mm along the margins.
Flowers: Massive structures that hang down from the leaves; greenish cream.
Fruit: Large; up to 7.5 cm long; covered with scales; shiny orange-brown; cone-shaped.
Uses: In the past the leaves were used in the production of raffia string and matting, but man-made materials have now largely replaced them.

Palm

Roystonea regia

Cuban royal palm (exotic, native to Cuba)

Local name: None known

One of the most beautiful of the palms, tall, striking-looking, reaching up to 21 m in height, with a prominent, glossy green crown shaft up to 2 m in length. Frequently planted as an ornamental in tropical countries.

Trunk: Massive; pale grey or whitish; ringed; often bulging at the base and in the middle.
Leaves: Feather-shaped; 6 m long; arching downwards; leaflets soft, narrow, growing at different angles.
Flowers: Flower stalk below the crown shaft; erect, pale yellow flowers in clusters.
Fruit: Brown and black; rounded; edible.
Uses: The seeds, which germinate easily and quickly, are rich in oil and carbohydrates, and are used for stock feed.

Palms

Syagrus romanzoffiana

Queen palm (exotic, native to Brazil)

Local name: None known

A very common exotic palm in East Africa, especially in Nairobi, Kenya. It can grow in a wide range of climates. The tree grows quickly, reaching 12–15 m in height, and shows some tolerance to cold. Germinates easily from the seeds.

Trunk: Solitary and ringed with old leaf bases; no crown shaft.
Leaves: Plumate; with leaflets that radiate outwards at different angles.
Flowers: Flower stalk arises from leaf bases.
Fruit: Small; green-yellow when ripe.

Palm

Thrinax floridana

Florida thatch palm　　　**Exotic, native to Florida, USA; Central America**

Local name: None known

This palm is not very common in East Africa, but the few that grace local gardens grow to a height of about 9 m. The small seeds germinate easily. These palms are drought tolerant, and are happy in full sunshine. They are not cultivated as indoor plants.

Trunk: Slim; solitary; lacking a crown shaft.
Leaves: Fan-shaped or sometimes forming an almost complete circle; the leaf segments are cut to about half the depth of the leaf.
Flowers: Flower stalk arises from among the leaf bases.
Fruit: Small; round; about 12 mm in diameter.

Young palm

Veitchia merrillii

Christmas palm (exotic, native to the Philippines)

Local name: None known

Often thought to be a miniature royal palm. A very popular exotic palm, planted both in gardens and indoors as an ornamental. It is easily grown from seed and can reach a height of 10–15 m..

Trunk: Solitary; pale; smooth; with indistinct rings; green crown shaft; usually swollen at the base.
Leaves: Feather-shaped and recurved; leaflets point upwards, forming a valley shape; each leaflet is usually twisted in on itself.
Flowers: Arise from below the crown shaft.
Fruit: About 2.5 cm across; bright red when ripe, resembling Christmas decorations.

Young palm

Washingtonia filifera

Desert fan palm (exotic, native to California, Arizona, USA)

Local name: None known

A fast-growing, striking fan palm that reaches 10–15 m in height, commonly planted in many parts of East Africa and especially along the highways. The small seeds germinate quickly and easily. It is drought-resistant and can adapt to any kind of climate. Grows in full sun.

Trunk: Solitary; up to 1 m thick; dark grey; straight; often swollen at the base; sometimes covered with a thick layer of old leaves.
Leaves: Fan-shaped; grey-green; deeply divided into 6 or more segments that bear thread-like fibres between the leaflets.
Flowers: White; on long stalks.
Fruit: Round; 1.5 cm across; black when mature.
Uses: A popular ornamental palm.

Palm

MANGROVES

The term 'mangrove' is a convenient group name for trees that thrive in the salt or brackish tidal fringes of river estuaries and bays. The 60 or so known mangrove species belong to a number of mostly unrelated families, many of whose other members cannot tolerate life in a mangrove swamp.

Mangroves form a coastal fringe of vegetation zones between land and sea. These zones are among the most prominent of the ecosystems along some tropical (and to a lesser extent subtropical) coastal stretches – complex wetland ecosystems which, under optimal conditions, attain the stature of forests, accommodating trees that reach heights ranging from a few meters to a lofty 25 m.

The swamps are extremely valuable both to the environment and to local communities. Among other things they concentrate and recycle nutrients, serve as nursery areas for commercially important fish and as habitats for animals and birds. They are a source of food, fuel, building materials and traditional medicines. Most importantly, they act as self-renewing barriers against tropical storms that would otherwise erode and destroy fragile estuarine ecosystems.

Mangroves are found in all the states in the region; Kenya, Tanzania, Madagascar and Mozambique having the largest stands. The mangroves of Madagascar have been estimated to cover 3 200 km^2, and those of Kenya, 587 km^2. Somalia has a few mangroves in the south. On the Tanzanian mainland there are extensive stands of mangroves near river mouths covering approximately 115 475 ha. Mangroves cover about 1 200 ha of Zanzibar's Pemba Island and more than 62 000 ha of Kenya's seaboard. Mangrove habitats in the East African region are diverse and are best developed in riverine estuaries where there is sufficient rainfall, such as the Rufiji delta, which has 53 250 ha of forest.

Nine species of mangrove tree have been recorded in the East African region, each belonging to a different plant family. They usually occupy specific portions, or zones, of the coastal forest, their presence depending on both the nature of the species and the particular ecological conditions present.

Unfortunately, East Africa's mangrove ecosystems are under threat. Their status as a resource remains unclear, and they continue to suffer from human exploitation, faulty policies and inadequate control measures.

Avicennia marina

White mangrove

Indigenous

Local names: Mchu, Mtu (Swahili)

This tree, which has an irregular canopy and grows to 12 m and more in height, is the region's most widely distributed mangrove, able to tolerate a high range of salinity, varied flooding regimes, sand-flats and newly deposited sediments. It is found on the margins, the seaward side and in the mid-portions of the forest. Unlike other mangroves, it is a sun-lover and often occurs on the fringes of other mangrove stands. It has horizontal roots that radiate far from the base of the trunk; small pencil-like aerial roots develop from these, extending above the mud and helping the tree to 'breathe'.

Bark: Yellow-green to pink with raised dots; flaky in older trees.

Leaves: Simple; opposite; thick; leathery; bicoloured – shiny olive green above, dense grey hair on the undersurface; pointed tip and base; up to 8.5 x 2.5 cm.

Flowers: Small; creamy white; fragrant; occur in dense round clusters.

Fruit: Pale green, velvety capsules, each containing a single seed; about 2.5–3 cm long.

Uses: The wood is used in the boiling of brine, in fish-smoking, in the production of lime, and in the construction of dhow ribs, drums, carts, beds and beehives. Leaves serve as goat and cattle fodder; twigs are used as toothbrushes. The bark and roots produce a brown dye, and feature in the tanning process. Flowers make a very sweet-scented local perfume. They also attract bees, which make an especially sweet honey.

Traditional medicine: Crushed leaves are used in the treatment of stomachache and stomach upsets; the wood yields a resin that was once applied to snakebites, and also used as a contraceptive; unripe fruit featured in the treatment of sores and skin lesions caused by smallpox.

Trees

Trunk and roots

Flowers

Fruit

Bruguiera gymnorrhiza

RHIZOPHORACEAE

Black mangrove

Indigenous

Local names: Muia, Mshinzi, Mchofi, Mkifu (Swahili)

A small, sturdy tree with a straight trunk, growing 3–10 m in height, stem base often buttressed by short prop roots and knee-like pneumatophores. The plant is mostly found in well-developed coastal mangrove forests, frequently in the deeper reaches of the muddy flats.

Bark: Dark red-brown and coarse; knobbly on older trees.
Leaves: Simple; elliptic; opposite; leathery; glossy; lime green in colour; crowded towards the ends of branchlets and twigs, forming rosettes of about 5 x 12 cm.
Flowers: Creamy white; with many hard, thick, rubbery petals; calyx of flower is red outside and green inside.
Fruit: Long; cigar-shaped; hanging down from the remains of the flower; up to 16 cm long.
Uses: The wood is red, very hard, termite-resistant; used for fish-smoking, fishing stakes, building and telephone poles. The bark, rich in tannin, features in the tanning process, yielding a reddish yellow leather. Leaves are eaten by large mangrove crabs; flowers by vervet monkeys and bats.

Flowers

Fruit

Tree

Roots

Ceriops tagal

Yellow mangrove

Indigenous

Local name: Mkandaa (Swahili)

An evergreen tree with a single trunk, up to 8 m in height. This is one of the mangrove trees that can survive in marginal habitats near bare, saline areas; mainly confined to coastal mud flats. The stilt roots, resembling five fingers closed together and rising from the mud, anchor the tree and extend visibly over a large area surrounding it.

Bark: Light brown.
Leaves: Green; shiny; leathery; oval-shaped; tip rounded; tapering below; 7 x 3.5 cm.
Flowers: Creamy white; star-shaped; with many maroon stamens.
Fruit: Long, up to 20 cm; cone-shaped; greenish brown.
Uses: The wood, hard and termite-resistant, is used for building-poles, fishing stakes, fence posts and local furniture, and as fuel. Bark and roots yield a light-resistant reddish dye that does not fade in the sun.

Tree

Flowers

Fruit

Roots

Heritiera littoralis

STERCULIACEAE

No English name known

Indigenous

Local names: Mkungu, Msikundazi, Mkokoshi (Swahili)

A slow-growing riverine mangrove species, reaching 10 m in height, sometimes up to 20 m; grows only in habitats of low salinity; restricted to areas in the vicinity of river mouths. The plant has strong, shallow roots that arise horizontally from the base of the main trunk.

Bark: Brown and rough in older trees.

Leaves: Simple; alternate; elliptic; tip pointed; 15 x 6 cm; characteristically shiny and silvery beneath; dark green above; with prominent midrib and side veins; brown and crispy when dried up.

Flowers: Very small; white; scented.

Fruit: Green turning to brown when mature; boat-shaped; up to 10 cm long; hard shell.

Uses: Stem and roots provide good-quality firewood, and timber for boat building, furniture and dhow masts; the bark has a high tannin content; fruit is eaten by large mangrove crabs, monkeys and wild pigs.

Fruit

Leaves and fruit

Tree

Bark and horizontal roots

Lumnitzera racemosa

No English name known

Indigenous

Local names: Kikandaa, Mkandaa-mwitu, Mkandaa-dume (Swahili)

An evergreen, dome-shaped, small tree that reaches up to 5 m in height; grows in habitats with low salinity and on sandy soils; bushy with thin, brittle branches. The branches are red when young.

Bark: Reddish brown.

Leaves: Simple; alternate; leathery; oval to elliptic; approximately 8 x 2.5 cm; midrib prominent underneath; tip oval; tapering end.

Flowers: White; very small; star-shaped.

Fruit: Very small; greenish yellow, turning black when mature; up to 1 cm long.

Uses: The fruit is eaten by birds, especially by the Golden Pipit. Wood is used for building-poles and as fuel.

Flowers

Tree

Fruit

Rhizophora mucronata

RHIZOPHORACEAE

Red mangrove

Indigenous

Local names: Mkoko, Mkaka (Swahili)

A very common mangrove, with a straight trunk, growing up to 10 m in height, dominant on muddy soils and often forming extensive stands occupied exclusively by Red mangroves. On sandy soils, however, the species fails to compete with other trees. It develops characteristic aerial prop roots, called stilt roots, up to 2 m in length, which arch over and anchor it in the mud. When the tide is high, the plant appears to be floating on the water.

Bark: Reddish brown to black; branches soft and brittle.
Leaves: Dark green; opposite; leathery; thick; up to 15 x 8 cm; distinctive hair-like tip.
Flowers: Creamy white; fleshy.
Fruit: Cone-shaped; up to 7 cm long; green; smooth. The seeds germinate while the fruit is still on the tree. The small green seedling emerges, growing downwards to 45 cm, and finally the whole torpedo-shaped structure drops and may float away to lodge in the mud, within hours of which it starts to produce true roots and leaves.
Uses: This mangrove is useful for firewood and fence posts, and produces excellent building and scaffolding poles, which are used both locally and exported, by dhow, to the Middle East, particularly from Lamu in Kenya. The bark is rich in tannin; roots are used for fishing-trap baskets (especially to catch prawns); split branches feature in basketry.

Trees

Fruit

Flowers

Stilt roots

Sonneratia alba

No English name known

Indigenous

Local names: Mlilana, Mpia, Mpira (Swahili)

A most attractive mangrove species, with a single trunk, growing 10–12 m in height. The plant occurs in areas exposed daily to tidal water, with a salinity close to that of sea water. The mature trees have a round canopy; numerous peg roots stand out above the mud and are visible over a large area around the tree. These roots help stabilize the sediment (and make walking in the forest extremely difficult).

Bark: Brown and fissured.
Leaves: Simple; opposite; light green; oval-shaped; with rounded tip.
Flowers: Double-coloured; 6–7 calyxes; green outside, red inside; with numerous white stamens.
Fruit: Green; calyx joined to the fruit, causing it to resemble a flower.
Uses: The wood is commonly used in boat-building, especially in the construction of dhows, and in general carpentry; also utilised as firewood (but of inferior quality). The pneumatophores are used to make fish-net floats; crushed leaves feature in the treatment of stomach upsets, and as camel fodder. The bark yields tannin; the fruit is said to be edible.

Peg roots

Flower and buds

Fruit

Tree

Xylocarpus granatum

MELIACEAE

No English name known

Indigenous

Local names: Mkomafi, Mtonga (Swahili)

A tall, evergreen tree that reaches 15 m in height, with a single trunk. It grows on raised areas where flooding occurs for a few days every month, and where there is an influx of fresh water. The shallow, ribbon-like horizontal root system originates from the lower part of the trunk.

Bark: Characteristic yellowish green.
Leaves: Dark green; oval-shaped; leathery; tip rounded; base tapering; 6 x 3 cm.
Flowers: Very small; white to creamy.
Fruit: Very large; brown; round (watermelon-shaped); solitary; on long stalk; up to 18 cm in diameter.
Uses: The wood is termite resistant; is used in fish-smoking, in building boats, carts, dhow masts, furniture, doors, window frames and as fuel. The seeds are edible; much favoured by baboons.
Traditional medicine: Seeds feature in the treatment of intensive stomach cramps and upsets, and of malaria; the fruit pulp is applied to skin rashes.
The fruit of *Xylocarpus moluccensis*, a species very similar to *X. granatum*, is known as 'Mkomafi'. It is blackish brown and smaller than that of *X. granatum*. Its wood is used to make dhow masts and in joinery, and as fuel.

Tree

Branches, leaves and fruit

Fruit

306

Classificaton of plants

Taxonomy is a broad field of science that deals with the description, identification and naming of living organisms (in this case, plants), and their classification into groups according to their resemblance and differences, mainly in their morphology (form and structure). It contributes greatly to the orderly study and systematization of our knowledge about the subject. The word 'taxonomy' comes from two Greek words: *taxis*, meaning arrangement (or classification) and *nomo*, indicating law or custom. So taxonomy deals with the laws governing the arrangement or classification of plants.

As far as angiosperms or higher flowering plants are concerned, it has been estimated that over 199 000 species (159 000 dicotyledons and 40 000 monocotyledons) are already known to us, and many more have yet to be discovered and recorded. Thus plants are not only numerous but also occur in a large number of different types, and it is not possible to study them unless they are arranged according to some orderly system.

Binomial nomenclature

This is a scientific method of naming species of plants or animals in two parts (for example *Mangifera indica*), the first indicating the genus and the second the species.

Units of classification

Species. A species is a group of individuals (plants or animals) of the same kind resembling one another so closely in almost all important morphological characteristics (both vegetative and reproductive) that they may be regarded as having been derived from the same parents. Occasionally, owing to variations in climatic or edaphic (soil) conditions, individuals of a species may show a certain amount of variation in form, size, colour, and other minor characteristics. Such plants are said to form varieties. A species may consist of one or more varieties, or none at all.

Genus. A genus is a collection of species that bear a close resemblance to one another in terms of the morphological characteristics of their floral or reproductive parts. For example, the various species of fig differ from one another in terms of their vegetative characteristics, such as shape, size and leaf surface, but they are related in terms of their reproductive characteristics, namely inflorescence, floral parts, fruit and seed. Thus all figs belong to the genus *Ficus*.

Family. A family is a group of genera whose members share a general structural resemblance, mainly in respect of their floral organs.

Glossary of botanical terms

Note: An asterisk* indicates that the word is defined elsewhere on the list.

achene small, dry, single-seeded fruit developing from one carpel*; indehiscent*.

acute sharply pointed.

alate having wings or wing-like extensions.

alternate leaves or flowers arranged singly at different heights on either side of the stem.

annuals plants that do not live longer than a year.

anther part of the flower that produces pollen.

anthocarp achene* surrounded by persistent perianth* lobes.

aril an appendage on certain seeds, often brightly coloured and fleshy.

aromatic having a pleasant and distinctive smell.

axil the upper angle between the leaf and the stem on which it is borne.

axillary rising from the axil*.

axis the real or imaginary line that divides a regular shape into two equal parts (vertical and horizontal axis).

berry many-seeded fleshy fruit, no hard layer, developing from syncarpus* pistil*.

biennial attaining full vegetative growth in the first year; producing flowers and fruits in the second year, after which plant dies off.

bifoliate consisting of two leaflets.

bilobed two-lobed.

bipinnate when the compound* leaf is further divided (twice pinnate*).

bisexual when both the male and female parts (stamens* and carpels*) of a flower are present.

bract a small, leaf-like organ or modified leaf with a single flower or inflorescence growing in its axil*.

bracteole when a small leafy or scaly structure (bract*) is present on any part of the flower stalk.

branchlet a small branch.

calyx lowermost whorl of the flower, consisting of a number of green leafy sepals*.

capitulum see head*.

capsule the dry fruit, dehiscent*, one to many-chambered, developing from a syncarpus* pistil*.

carpel female reproductive organ consisting of ovary*, style* and stigma*.

caryopsis small, dry, indehiscent*, one-seeded fruit that develops from a simple pistil*.

catkin spike* with a long and pendulous axis* that bears unisexual* flowers only.

climbers plants that climb neighbouring objects by means of special attachment organs.

complete when all four whorls of a flower are present.

compound descriptive of a leaf that is broken up into a number of segments, called 'leaflets'*, that are free from one another.

corolla second whorl of the flower, consisting of a number of usually brightly coloured petals.

corona a crown-like circle of living appendages between the corolla* and stamens*.

corymb an inflorescence* or flower form in which branches or pedicels* start from different points, reaching the same level to give a more or less flat top.

culm the hollow, jointed stem of a grass (eg bamboo).

cuneate wedge-shaped.

cymose an arrangement in which the main axis* ends in a flower and the lateral axis* also ends in a flower; the terminal flower is always older and opens earlier than the lateral one.

deciduous plant whose leaves last for only one season.

dehiscent refers to fruit that bursts open to liberate the seeds when mature.

dentate with a toothed edge.

dicotyledonous descriptive of plants that have two embryonic seed leaves and leaves with net-like veins; flowers have five or a multiple of five petals.

digitate leaflets* (generally five or more) radiating from a common point in the form of a spread hand.

dioecious descriptive of unisexual* flowers whose male and female organs are on different plants.

disc florets central, tubular florets*.

drupe a fleshy, permanently enclosed (indehiscent*) fruit whose seeds are contained by a hard, stony coating.

elliptic oval-shaped.

entire even and smooth margin* or edge, without teeth or lobes*.

epicalyx ring of sepal-like bracts* below true sepals*.

epiphytic when a plant grows on another plant, but is not parasitic on it.

evergreen a plant whose leaves persist for more than one season.

exstipulate without stipules*.

falcate sickle-shaped.

filament stalk of a stamen*.

floret small flower.

foliate bearing leaves.

follicle a dry fruit, one-chambered, which splits on one side.

glabrous hairless, free from outgrowths of any kind.

head descriptive of a form in which the main axis* is suppressed, becoming almost flat, bearing a mass of small sessile* flowers (florets*) on its surface.

herb plant whose aerial parts do not show above ground after the end of the growing season; a soft, non-woody plant.

herbaceous see herb*.

hesperidium a fleshy, many-celled fruit (notably of citrus plants), protected by separable skin or rind.

imparipinnate an odd number of leaflets* on a compound* leaf.

incomplete the absence of any whorl.

indehiscent fruit that remain closed when ripe.

inflorescence the flowering part of a plant and the arrangement of the flowers upon it.

internode the space between two successive nodes*.

involucral resembling a ring of bracts*, belonging to an involucre*.

involucre whorl of bracts* surrounding the base of a flower or a flower cluster.

irregular describing a flower that cannot be divided into two similar halves.

keel characteristic of legumes: the two smallest innermost petals apparently united to form a boat-shaped cavity.

lanceolate lance-shaped.

latex milky juice secreted by certain plants.

leaf base the part of a leaf attached to the stem.

leaf blade green, flat, expanded portion of leaf.

leaflet a single division of a compound* leaf.

legume dry, one-chambered fruit, developing from a simple pistil* and dehiscing to both the margins*.

lenticel breathing pore in plant stem.

liane a woody climbing plant, capable of climbing to the top of a large tree.

linear long, narrow and flat.

lobe division of a leaf, perianth* or anther*. Lobed margins* usually have large, rounded teeth and shallow notches.

margin the edge of the leaf, which may be smooth, or teeth-like, or spiny.

-merous part of a set (a five-merous corolla, for example, has five petals).

midrib a strong vein that runs centrally through the leaf blade• from its base to the apex.

monocarp plant that produces fruit only once before dying.

monocotyledonous descriptive of a plant with only one embryonic seed leaf, parallel-veined leaves, fibrous root system and flowers with parts in threes or multiples of three.

monoecious male and female reproductive organs in separate flowers on same plant.

multifoliate when leaflets are more than five in number.

naturalized descriptive of a plant so successfully introduced into a foreign region/country that it reproduces naturally.

node joint; point on a stem or branch at which a leaf or another branch is produced or borne.

oblique when the two halves of a leaf are unequal (asymmetrical).

oblong descriptive of a wide and long leaf blade•, with the two margins• running straight up.

obovate egg-shaped but inversely so, with the broader end towards the tip.

obtuse blunt or rounded at the tip.

opposite arranged in pairs on either side of the stem, or when one organ arises at the base of another (eg stamen• opposite petal).

ovary the swollen basal part (a kind of closed chamber) of the female reproductive organ that contains egg-like bodies called ovules•.

ovate shaped like the outline of an egg, with the broader end at the base.

ovule small body that contains the plant's egg cell and, after fertilization, develops into the seed.

palmate divided into lobes•, like the outspread fingers of a hand (as in palms).

panicle descriptive of the branched main axis• of a raceme•, where the lateral branches bear the flowers.

pappus tuft or ring of hairs or scales around the fruits of the plants of the family Compositae, features which help dispersal by wind.

paripinnate an even number of leaflets•.

pedicel stalk of a flower.

perennials plants that live for more than two years.

perianth the outer part of a flower, comprising the calyx• and the corolla•

pericarp the layers of ovary tissue in a fruit.

persistent when a plant part remains attached after normal withering.

petiolate when stalk is present on leaf.

petiole stalk of the leaf.

pinna (pl pinnae) the primary division of a pinnate• or bipinnate• leaf.

pinnate having leaflets growing on each side of a common stem or rachis•.

pistil the female reproductive whorl of flowers.

pneumatophore a special kind of respiratory root developed by plants growing in estuaries and salt lakes, areas occasionally inundated by tides.

pod see legume•.

pollen granular mass of small, male reproductive bodies, also called 'spores'•; contained in pollen sacs.

pollination transfer of pollen• grains from the anthers• of a flower to the stigma• of the same or another flower.

pollinium (pl pollinia) pollens• that are not free, but united into a mass.

pome fleshy, two- or more-celled, syncarpous• fruit.

raceme elongated• main axis• laterally bearing a number of flowers; lower flowers are older than the upper, with long stalks.

racemose when the main axis• of the inflorescence• does not end in a flower but continues to grow and give off flowers laterally.

rachis the axis* of an inflorescence* or of a compound* leaf.

ray florets marginal strap-shaped floret*.

recurved or reclinate, bent backward or downward.

regular symmetrical; flower can be divided into two exactly equal halves by any vertical section passing through the centre.

resins a group of substances found mainly in the stems of conifers; when present in the wood, resin adds to its strength and durability. The substance is the main ingredient of wood varnish.

rhizome thickened, prostrate, underground stem with distinct nodes* and internodes*.

scandent climbing.

sepal any of the separate parts of a calyx*.

serrate margin* cut like the teeth of a saw, the teeth directed upwards.

sessile without a stalk.

sheathed descriptive of a protectively expanded leaf-base, partially or wholly enclosing the stem.

simple descriptive of a leaf consisting of a single blade, unbranched or undivided.

solitary bearing a single flower.

spadix a spike* with a fleshy axis* enclosed by one or more large, brightly coloured bracts* called 'spathes'.

spathe see spadix*.

spike elongated main axis*, with older flowers below, younger ones above, all sessile*.

spines modifications of leaves or parts of leaves, for defensive purposes, into sharp, pointed structures.

spores see pollen*.

stalked see petiolate*.

stamen male organ of a flower, consisting of pollen* sacs (anthers*), and usually a stalk (filament).

stellate star-shaped.

stem main axis* of plant.

stigma the small rounded or lobed* head of the pistil*.

stipulate equipped with stipules*.

stipules two lateral outgrowths from leaf base*.

striations linear band of colour, ridge or groove, usually in parallel series.

style the slender stalk supporting the stigma*.

syncarpous fruit originating from many flowers but arranged close together.

tannins a group of compounds abundant in the bark, heartwood, leaves or unripe fruits of certain trees. Tannins are bitter, aseptic; their presence makes the wood hard and durable; extensively used in tanning.

tap root root that normally grows vertically downwards; the main root.

tapering pointed.

terminal borne at the end of a branch or stalk.

thorns modification of branches, for defensive purposes, into straight, hard, pointed structures.

throat mouth of corolla* tube.

trifoliate when pinnate* leaf consists of three leaflets.

tripinnate when compound* leaf is thrice pinnate*.

umbel umbrella-shaped inflorescence, in which main axis* is shortened, with a group of flowers at the tip; pedicels* more or less of equal length.

unifoliate when pinnate* leaf consists of only one leaflet.

unipinnate when midrib* of pinnately compound* leaf bears the leaflets.

unisexual descriptive of a plant that has either male or female reproductive organs, but not both.

whorled more than two leaves at each node*, arranged in a circle.

winged seeds, fruits that have developed one or more thin, membranous 'wings' for ease of dispersal by the wind.

xerophytic adapted to arid conditions.

zygomorphic can be cut in one plane, so that the two halves are mirror images.

Illustrated glossary

LEAF SHAPE

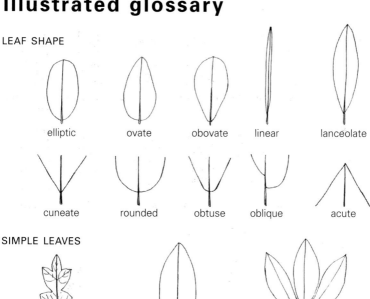

elliptic   ovate   obovate   linear   lanceolate

cuneate   rounded   obtuse   oblique   acute

SIMPLE LEAVES

pinnately lobed   simple, entire   simple, palmately lobed

COMPOUND LEAVES

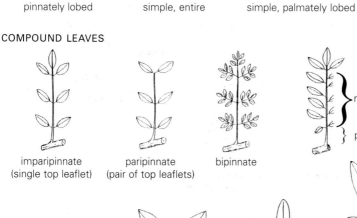

imparipinnate
(single top leaflet)   paripinnate
(pair of top leaflets)   bipinnate   rachis

petiole

bifoliate   trifoliate   digitately divided

TRUNK/BARK

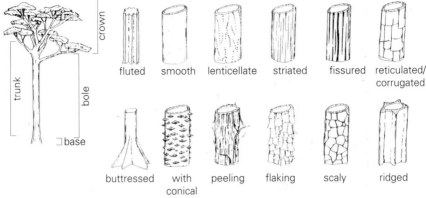

fluted smooth lenticellate striated fissured reticulated/corrugated

buttressed with conical bosses peeling flaking scaly ridged

LEAF ARRANGEMENT

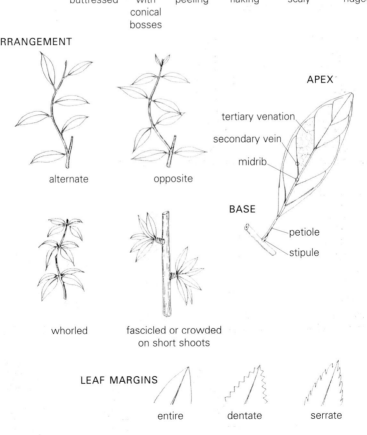

alternate

opposite

APEX

tertiary venation

secondary vein

midrib

BASE

petiole

stipule

whorled

fascicled or crowded on short shoots

LEAF MARGINS

entire dentate serrate

FLOWER PARTS

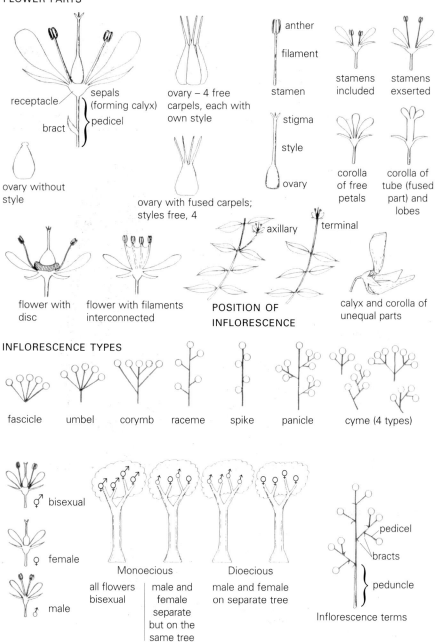

receptacle

sepals
(forming calyx)

bract

pedicel

ovary without
style

ovary – 4 free
carpels, each with
own style

ovary with fused carpels;
styles free, 4

anther

filament

stamen

stigma

style

ovary

stamens
included

stamens
exserted

corolla
of free
petals

corolla of
tube (fused
part) and
lobes

flower with
disc

flower with filaments
interconnected

axillary

terminal

**POSITION OF
INFLORESCENCE**

calyx and corolla of
unequal parts

INFLORESCENCE TYPES

fascicle

umbel

corymb

raceme

spike

panicle

cyme (4 types)

♂ bisexual

♀ female

♂ male

Monoecious

all flowers
bisexual

male and
female
separate
but on the
same tree

Dioecious

male and female
on separate tree

pedicel

bracts

peduncle

Inflorescence terms

FLESHY FRUITS

Berry
no hard layer, one- to many-seeded

Drupe
One to several seeds, each
surrounded by a stony layer

DRY FRUITS, INDEHISCENT

Achene   Winged achene
Small, single-
seeded

Nut
Single-seeded
with woody
outer layer

DEHISCENT FRUITS

Follicle
Splits on one side

Legume
Splits into 2 valves

Capsule
Splits into several valves; dry

GENERAL TERMS

Fruit with many
monocarps

Fruit syncarpous

Fruit with 2 mericarps

Glossary of medical terms

abscess a swollen part of the body in which a thick yellowish liquid (pus) has collected.

anthelmintic an agent that destroys or causes the expulsion of parasitic intestinal worms.

anthrax splenic fever, an infectious disease of animals affecting sheep, cattle and sometimes people.

antidote an agent that neutralizes a poison or counteracts its effect.

asthma a chest illness that causes difficulty in breathing.

astringent a substance that causes contraction of body tissue and blood vessels.

bilharzia a disease caused by worms.

bronchitis an inflammation of the bronchial mucous membrane.

carcinogenic producing cancer.

concoction a mixture of ingredients.

decoction preparation made by boiling crude vegetable drugs, then straining the resulting liquid; in exact work the proportions are 50 mg of the drug to 1 000 ml of water.

diarrhoea frequent, copious discharge of abnormally liquid faeces.

diuretic an agent that increases the flow of urine.

dysentery diarrhoea associated with blood, pus or mucus in the stool, indicating a bacterial or parasitic infection.

eczema a skin inflammation marked by redness, itching and lesions.

emetic a drug that causes vomiting.

enema liquid injected into rectum for the purpose of clearing out the bowel.

epilepsy a chronic nervous disorder, characterized by attacks of unconciousness or convulsions, or both.

glycoside any of a group of substances derived from simple sugars, such as fructose or glucose. Many are important medicinal drugs.

gonorrhoea a disease of the sexual organs, spread by sexual contact.

haemorrhoids commonly known as piles, an ailment of the blood vessels around the anus.

hepatic relating to the liver.

impotence (of men) inability to perform sexual intercourse.

infusion the process of steeping a substance (drug) in cold water in order to extract its soluble principles.

inhalent a substance that is taken into the body by inhaling it through the nose or trachea.

lactation the production of milk by women after childbirth.

leprosy an infectious disease causing painful white patches to appear on the skin and destroying the nerves.

poultice a moist dressing applied to an inflamed body part.

purgative a substance that causes evacuation of the bowels.

rheumatism an acute disease characterized by painful inflammation and swelling of the joints, muscles or connective tissue.

steep placing a substance (root, bark, leaves) in a liquid and leaving it there for some time to soften it.

styptic an agent that stops bleeding by contracting the blood vessels; haemostatic.

syphilis an infectious disease generally spread through sexual intercourse.

tincture drug that is dissolved in alcohol for use as a medicine.

tonsillitis inflammation of the tonsils, usually due to viral or bacterial infection.

venereal disease a disease spread by sexual contact, for example gonorrhoea and syphilis.

whooping cough an infectious disease, especially in children, characterized by a series of coughs followed by gasping for breath.

Further reading

Beentje, H.J. *Kenya Trees, Shrubs and Lianas*. 1994. National Museums of Kenya, Nairobi.

Blundell, M. *Guide to the Wild Flowers of East Africa*. 1987. Collins, London.

Brenan, J.P.M. *Flora of Tropical East Africa, Leguminosae subfamily Mimosoideae*. 1967. Crown Agents for Overseas Governments and Administrations.

Brenan, J.P.M. *Flora of Tropical East Africa, Leguminosae subfamily Caesalpiniodeae*. 1967. Crown Agents for Overseas Governments and Administrations.

Coe, M. & Beentje, H. *A Field Guide to the Acacias of Kenya*. 1991. Oxford University Press, New York.

Gibbons, M. *Palms*. 1993. Apple Identifier, London.

Grant, G. & Thomas, V. *Sappi Tree Spotting*. 1998. Jacana Education, Johannesburg.

Hessayon, D.G. *The Tree and Shrub Expert*. 1994. Expert Books, London.

International Centre For Research In Agroforestry. *A Selection of Useful Trees and Shrubs for Kenya*. 1992. Nairobi.

Jaccarani, V & Martens, E. *The Ecology of Mangroves and Related Ecosystems*. 1992. Kluwer Academic Publishers.

Kokwaro, J.O. *Flowering Plant Families of East Africa*. 1994. East African Education Publishers, Nairobi.

Kokwaro, J.O. *Medicinal Plants of East Africa*. 1993. Kenya Literature Bureau, Nairobi.

National Academy Press. *Neem, A Tree for Solving Global Problems*. 1992. Washington, D.C.

Noad, T. & Birnie, A. *Trees of Kenya*. 1994. Nairobi.

Perry, F. *Flowers of the World*. 1982. Optimum Books, Italy.

Perry, F. *Plants and Flowers*. 1981. Macdonald Encyclopeadia, London.

Regional Soil Conservation Unit/Swedish International Development Authority. *Useful Trees and Shrubs for Uganda*. 1995. Nairobi.

Regional Soil Conservation Unit/Swedish International Development Authority. *Useful Trees and Shrubs for Tanzania*. 1994. Nairobi.

Semesi, A.K. & Howell, K. *The Mangroves of the Eastern African Region*. 1992. United Nations Environment Programme.

United Nations Environment Programme. *Assessment and monitoring of climatic change impacts on mangrove ecosystems*. 1994.

Van Wyk, B-E., Van Oudtshoorn, B. & Gericke, N. *Medicinal Plants of South Africa*. 1997. Briza Publications, Pretoria.

Van Wyk, B. & Van Wyk, P. *Field Guide to Trees of Southern Africa*. 1998. Struik Publishers, Cape Town.

Index

320